Editing Documents and Texts

Sir   Philadelphia Feb. 18. 1791.

I return you the two volumes of records, with thanks for the opportunity of looking into them. they are curious monuments of the infancy of our country. I learn with great satisfaction that you are about committing to the press the valuable historical and state-papers you have been so long collecting. ~~xxxxxx~~ time & accident are committing daily havoc on the originals deposited in our public offices. the late war has done the work of centuries in this business. the lost cannot be recovered; but let us save what remains: not by vaults and locks which fence them from the public eye and use, in consigning them to the waste of time, but by such a multiplication of copies, as shall place them beyond the reach of accident. this being the tendency of your undertaking be assured there is no one who wishes it a more complete success than Sir

Your most obedient

& most humble servt.

Th: Jefferson

Mr. Hazard.

Letter from Thomas Jefferson to Ebenezer Hazard, Philadelphia, 18 February 1791. ALS, Historical Society of Pennsylvania. Printed in Julian P. Boyd, ed., *The Papers of Thomas Jefferson* (Princeton, 1950—), Vol. 19, pp. 287–89. Ebenezer Hazard, former postmaster general of the United States under the Confederation, had written Secretary of State Jefferson on 17 February 1791 seeking an endorsement of his proposed collection of state papers. Jefferson's quick and eloquent response is indicative of the importance he gave to the preservation of historical documents through publication.

Editing Documents and Texts

An Annotated Bibliography

Compiled for The Association for
Documentary Editing

by Beth Luey
with the assistance of Kathleen Gorman

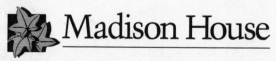 Madison House

MADISON 1990

Beth Luey, Editor
Editing Documents and Texts:
An Annotated Bibliography

LIBRARY OF CONGRESS CATALOGING IN PUBLICATION DATA

Luey, Beth
  Editing documents and texts : an annotated bibliography /
compiled by Beth Luey with the assistance of Kathleen Gorman. —
1st ed.
    p.   cm.
  "For the Association for Documentary Editing."
  ISBN 0-945612-13-3
    1. Editing—Bibliography.   2. Manuscript preparation (Authorship)-
I. Gorman, Kathleen.   II. Association for Documentary Editing.
III. Title.
  Z5165.L83   1990
  [PN162]
  016.808'027—dc20   89-14552
                                              CIP

Designed by William Kasdorf

Typeset in Trump Medieval by Impressions, Inc.
Produced for Madison House by
Impressions, Inc., P.O. Box 3304, Madison, WI 53704

Printed on acid free paper

FIRST EDITION

For Louis B. Sohn

Contents

Acknowledgments

IN 1985, Jo Ann Boydston, president of The Association for Documentary Editing, asked me to compile a bibliography that would include material on the editing of all sorts of texts—historical documents, literary texts, and the writings of people in all fields. Her idea derived, I believe, both from her intellectual commitments and from her political instincts. That is, such a bibliography would be useful to editors in many fields but would also demonstrate to them the values, interests, and concerns that they share. It would also suggest that there is more to be gained from listening to and learning from one another than from arguing about who is right. To Jo Ann and to the other editors who have recognized the importance of these shared concerns we owe the idea for this bibliography.

A number of editors contributed to the work in various ways. The starting point for this bibliography was the one compiled by Ross W. Beales, Jr. Anyone who knows the difficulty of starting such a project from scratch will recognize the debt I owe him for giving me an accurate, well-researched point of departure. C. James Taylor surveyed several journals and wrote the abstracts for articles found in them. Richard N. Sheldon read an early draft of the bibliography and made a number of useful suggestions, including the idea of cross-referencing articles in ongoing debates. He also read the penultimate draft with commendable thought and care. Joel Myerson read the penultimate draft, made valuable suggestions, and supplied several hard-to-find items. G. Thomas Tanselle permitted me to consult the bibliography he has compiled as the basis of part of his forthcoming MLA pamphlet intended to serve as an introduction to textual criticism and its literature. John P. Kaminski has offered moral support and has worked to find the best publisher for the volume.

Kathleen Gorman, my research assistant at Arizona State University for two years, did a tremendous amount of work in tracking down and abstracting the articles in the Beales bibliography and in helping me to get the computer program to work productively. She generously gave up vacation days to locate items in California libraries, and I appreciate her sacrifice of beach time.

I also appreciate the contribution of the Arizona State History Department in giving me Kathy Gorman's time, a computer, and the assistance of the computer laboratory staff. Gilbert Gonzales and Rodney Ito, both members of that staff, skillfully reconstructed files that I had mangled badly.

Finally, I want to thank Professor Louis B. Sohn, to whom this book is dedicated. In 1969 I worked for six months as Professor Sohn's research assistant. He was on sabbatical from the Harvard Law School, and among his many projects was a planned one-volume collection of documents on African and Asian regional organizations. I worked with him to locate the African documents and to compile and check the accompanying bibliography. By the time it was finished, the African part of the project alone occupied four volumes. Despite the proliferation of material, the difficulty of finding much of it, and its existence in a multiplicity of languages (only some of which Professor Sohn and I knew), he maintained an extraordinarily high standard of accuracy and scholarship. No item went into the bibliography that at least one of us had not seen, checked, and rechecked. And, in those precomputer days, no error went uncorrected, no matter how many trips to the library and the typewriter it took. Since then, as an editor and researcher, I have often had cause to wish that all scholars were as careful as

Louis Sohn. In compiling this bibliography, I have tried to maintain his standards.

I hope that whatever errors have slipped through will be few enough that the dedication will not embarrass him.

Editing Documents and Texts

Introduction

THE RATIONALE FOR COMPILING a bibliography on editing historical documents, literary texts, and materials in other fields is based on the belief that editors in all subject areas share certain concerns, commitments, goals, and techniques. Reading the books and articles in this bibliography has confirmed the truth of that belief—as well as the fact that they have many differences.

Many of the issues raised in the editorial literature are clearly of concern to all, regardless of field. These are problems that arise in dealing with the world outside the text, problems of politics, economics, and law. All editors must raise money, generate support from the academic community and the public, and work to enhance professional status and abilities. All must help to train future editors. All must deal with publishers and with institutions such as universities, foundations, and federal agencies. All must come to grips with the opportunities and problems raised by computer technology. Legal issues such as copyright and the right of privacy affect editors of modern materials in all subject areas. Editors in many fields have discussed these issues, and their ideas can be found through this bibliography.

Similarly, although emphases and conclusions may vary from field to field, the issues confronted in dealing with textual problems are for the most part the same. All editors must find and collect material, select what to edit, transcribe and annotate it, and provide appropriate accompanying material and apparatus. Whether one is trying to collect all of Benjamin Franklin's correspondence or all the known printings of Virginia Woolf's novels in her lifetime, the search process must be efficient and thorough. An appropriate annotation policy is vital whether the material to be annotated is a treaty or an epic poem. Editors in all fields have written extensively on these matters, and their experience and advice are invaluable.

The value of reading about the goals and techniques we share is obvious: although no editor can follow precisely in another's cart tracks, no one need reinvent the wheel. An editor facing for the first time the tasks of compiling and editing a mass of correspondence can learn from those who have edited the letters of diplomats, novelists, poets, inventors, explorers, and clergy. The writer of the letters is important, but so is the genre. Similarly, the editor of a diary can benefit from the experience of those who have edited journals of statesmen, soldiers, pioneers, miners, scientists, and essayists.

Editors can also benefit from the fact that those in other fields do, indeed, have different concerns. The choice of copy-text is of great importance to textual editors, and the theory of copy-text has occupied a great deal of their thought and writing. For historians, who most often edit material that exists in only one text, the issue is less crucial. But the historian faced with a copy-text question can be spared much agony and error by reading the debates in the literary journals and applying their lessons. Literary editors, dealing for perhaps the first time with material that the author did not prepare for publication (or even intend to publish), can use the work of historical editors to anticipate the problems they will face and experiment with some readymade solutions.

There is also value in learning from those who wrote on editorial issues some decades ago. Editorial theory and practice have changed far more than the problems that editors face. Some of the concerns that were raised nearly a half-century ago have been ignored, but they have not gone away. For example, during and after World War II, many European documents and records were microfilmed by historians and archivists concerned about their possible destruction in wartime. Since then, the threat of wartime destruction has certainly not disappeared, but the effort to disperse, copy, and preserve records seems to have lost its urgency. Although the NHPRC works diligently at these tasks, the financial resources provided by federal, state, and local governments remain inadequate. Reading about this work, now nearly half a century in the past, reminds us that we have not solved all our problems.

Nor have we faced all the new problems that are sneaking up on us. Although editors in all fields have greeted the dawn of the computer age and, with varying degrees of enthusiasm, embraced its ability to help with the routine tasks of the field, there is virtually no discussion of what current computer use will mean to future editors. What becomes of the theory of copy-text and authorial intention when the "document" or "text" last touched by the author is a computer disk used, erased, reused, edited, copy-edited, and coded by some combination of author, manuscript editor, proofreader, and compositor? How long will that disk last? Can it be "read" without altering it? Can it be studied the way a manuscript or typescript is studied? Historical and literary editors alike will soon be facing problems introduced by technological change, and solutions are most likely to come from a combined effort. For historical reasons, I have retained articles on the use of computers even when the specific technology discussed is now obsolete.

I must note three regrettable classes of omission. First, I have excluded material in languages other than English. Presumably editors who write in French, German, Spanish, Russian, Italian, Hindi, Chinese, and other languages have written on the same topics as those of us who work in English. Owing to limitations of time and linguistic ability, I have included only material published in English. Nevertheless, some of the articles in this bibliography discuss editorial work on documents and literature in other languages. It is clear from this limited glimpse that much would be gained by surveying the non-English-language literature and, when appropriate, translating it.

Second, I have omitted introductions and statements of editorial method that are included within editions. These are extremely useful when formulating editorial policy and, as I note in the next chapter, for teaching. However, to list all documentary, critical, and facsimile editions is a task well beyond the scope of this work. Nor do I feel qualified to assemble a selected list of exemplary editions. As those who read reviews know, even an NHPRC or NEH grant or a CEAA seal does not always exempt an edition from severe criticism. And excellent editions have been published without any imprimatur. Nor have I attempted to include all reviews of documentary editions and critical or facsimile texts. Only reviews that discuss editorial issues more broadly and at some length are included. Material in peripheral fields, such as archives and bibliography, is included only when it is clearly relevant to editorial concerns. I have also been more selective about material on Shakespeare, for which adequate bibliographies exist.

Finally, I have not included the enormous body of literature on editing classical and biblical texts. The roots of contemporary editing lie in the work of the editors of centuries-old Greek, Hebrew, and Latin texts. Editors today continue to work on these texts and, as G. Thomas Tanselle has noted (in "Classical, Biblical, and Medieval Textual Criticism and Modern Editing" [T3]), communication between editors of these materials and those working on modern European and American texts would be worthwhile. Again, considerations of time, space, and linguistic ability made it impossible to incorporate the relevant bibliography, which in any case is available elsewhere. However, I have listed here some basic histories of the field and published bibliographies, so that interested readers will know where to start.

Bibliographies

Halton, Thomas P. *Classical Scholarship: An Annotated Bibliography.* White Plains, N.Y.: Kraus International, 1986. Items DE 1–65 cover bibliographies, introductions to the field, manuals, and history of Greek and Latin textual criticism.

Metzger, Bruce M. *Annotated Bibliography of the Textual Criticism of the New Testament, 1914–1939.* Copenhagen, 1955.

Histories and Introductions

Cross, Frank Moore. "Problems of Method in the Textual Criticism of the Hebrew Bible." In *The Critical Study of Sacred Texts*, edited by Wendy Doniger O'Flaherty. Berkeley: University of California Press, 1979, 31–54.

Kenney, E. J. *The Classical Text: Aspects of Editing in the Age of the Printed Book.* Berkeley: University of California Press, 1974.

Metzger, Bruce M. *The Text of the New Testament: Its Transmission, Corruption, and Restoration.* 2d ed. New York: Oxford University Press, 1968.

Pfeiffer, Rudolf. *History of Classical Scholarship from the Beginnings to the End of the Hellenistic Age; History of Classical Scholarship from 1300 to 1850.* Oxford: Clarendon, 1968, 1976.

Reynolds, L. D., and N. G. Wilson. *Scribes and Scholars: A Guide to the Transmission of Greek and Latin Literature.* London: Oxford University Press, 1968.

Sandys, John E. *A History of Classical Scholarship.* 3 vols. Reprint ed. New York: Hafner, 1958.

West, Martin L. *Textual Criticism and Editorial Technique Applicable to Greek and Latin Texts.* Stuttgart: B. G. Teubner, 1973.

Willis, James. *Latin Textual Criticism.* Urbana: University of Illinois Press, 1972.

USING THE BIBLIOGRAPHY

This bibliography is arranged in alphabetical order, by author (or by title, when no author is listed), and each entry is numbered. Within each entry the user will find the standard bibliographical information, a list of key words, and a brief annotation. In the case of multiauthor works, complete publication information is given for the volume as a whole; listings of individual essays exclude place, publisher, and date. If the volume itself is not listed, individual article listings provide complete information. The key words provide a summary of all topics covered to any significant extent in the book or article, and they form the basis of the index. The annotation tells what a reader may expect to find in the article but makes no attempt to offer a complete summary or evaluation. It will help users decide whether or not to seek out the item, but it will not spare them the effort (or deny them the rewards) of reading it.

The presence of an item in the bibliography indicates that I considered it relevant and valuable to at least some of my anticipated readers. It does not mean that I agree with it or that I think it is the best thought on its topic. Because I hope that this bibliography will be of value to undergraduate and graduate students, beginning editors, and experienced editors, I have made it as inclusive as possible. By consulting the key words and annotations, users should be able to select readings that are relevant to their questions and appropriate to their level of knowledge. The suggestions for teaching that appear in the next chapter offer some ideas about which readings might be best for students at various levels.

I suggest that users of the bibliography begin with the index. It would be worthwhile to look through the headings, because they contain some unexpected topics. Under each topic, relevant items are listed by number. By combining the index entries for two or more topics, it is possible to narrow a search significantly. For example, one can see which items are indexed under both "history of science" and "notebooks" to find what has been written about editing the notes of scientists. Using one of the more general index entries facilitates browsing. For example, "editing, types of" lists the entries discussing the differences between "literary" and "historical" editing.

I have limited cross-references to one or two instances where related items might not be located by using the index and, more frequently, to cases where articles or letters to the editor are written in direct response to others. Some of these debates are quite lengthy and far-flung—so much so that even cross-references are not practicable. Thus, in the case of the debates over the Center for Editions of American Authors, I refer readers to the articles most closely related to the item in question and then to the index entry "CEAA."

Finally, a separate bibliography lists mystery novels in which documents or manuscripts provide clues or motivation, or in which an editor is either sleuth or victim. In this section I have been very selective. I would appreciate suggestions for additions to this and the basic bibliography. Like all bibliographies, they will need to be updated.

Suggestions for Teaching

EDITING CAN BE TAUGHT usefully and practically in college courses at all levels. In this section I have first suggested readings and methods for incorporating editing into traditional history and literature courses, both surveys and upper-level courses. I have then suggested readings for courses devoted exclusively to editing. Throughout, I have assumed that the instructor will want to expose students to a variety of opinions and approaches rather than urge a given point of view upon them.

EDITING FOR NON-EDITORS

The purpose of introducing editing to beginning students is to make them aware that editors exist and to help them understand something of the work editors do. For juniors and seniors, the minimal goal is to teach them to use documentary and critical editions intelligently in their research. In some classes, an instructor can teach editorial skills to enhance students' critical abilities and research skills (see, for example, the articles by Randall K. Burkett [B135] and Barbara Oberg [O4]). For a few students, an introduction to editing can inspire future research or even an editorial career.

Survey Courses

Undergraduate survey courses offer an opportunity to introduce the discipline of history or literature, teach some basic material, and inspire further study. Some information on editing can be included to enhance all three of these goals.

In a U.S. history survey, documentary material from any period can enhance students' understanding of the subject. In a course that focuses on political history, for example, the instructor can begin with the text of the Constitution, which is generally appended to textbooks. An easy next step is to raise questions about how the document came to take the form it did. Introducing letters to and from delegates to the convention or other relevant documents can lead to a discussion of how such materials have been gathered, edited, and published—as well as how they can be used in research. This, in turn, offers an opportunity to explain something of the nature of historical research and materials. Classes concentrating on later periods might study the development of a single amendment.

In a course that focuses on social history, unofficial materials such as diaries and letters of ordinary citizens can be used, with an explanation of how such materials are located, selected, and edited. Some textbooks incorporate family history materials that can be used as a starting point. Similarly, military history courses, often taken by students who will not major in history or even take further courses, can use editions of official documents and soldiers' diaries.

The entries in this bibliography best suited to a history survey would be general descriptions of documentary editing or descriptions of specific projects accessible to a popular audience:

Paul H. Bergeron, "True Valor Seen" (B38)

Donald Greene, "No Dull Duty" (G37)

Leonard W. Labaree, "In Search of 'B Franklin' " (L1)

Haskell M. Monroe, Jr., "Some Thoughts for an Aspiring Historical Editor" (M61)

Harold C. Syrett and Jacob E. Cooke, "The Papers of Alexander Hamilton" (S80)

Walter M. Whitehill, ed., "Publishing the Papers of Great Men" (W13).

Because most such articles relate to traditional Founding Fathers projects, it is worthwhile to add more recent writings on less traditional projects:

Ira Berlin et al., "Writing *Freedom*'s History" (B40)

Roy E. Finkenbine, "Garveyism and the 'New Documentary Editing' " (F10)

Patricia Galloway, "Dearth and Bias" (G7)

Patricia G. Holland, "The Papers of Elizabeth Cady Stanton and Susan B. Anthony" (H50)

Alton Hornsby, Jr., "The Hope Papers Project" (H58).

Another possible reading would be an article that shows the differences in interpretation that result from editorial decisions, such as Richard N. Sheldon's "Editing a Historical Manuscript" (S24), or an article such as George C. Rogers Jr.'s "The Laurens Papers—Half-Way" (R32), which lists the sorts of research that the project made possible. These readings introduce students to the purpose of documentary editing, some of its procedures, and its variety.

One might also wish to introduce students to the careers open to historians outside teaching, including documentary editing. For this purpose I would suggest Nathan Reingold's article about the daily activities of a federal historian (R22) or some of the informal discussions of the rewards and importance of editing:

Lester J. Cappon, "The Historian as Editor" (C6)

Stanley J. Idzerda, "The Editor's Training and Status in the Historical Profession" (I1)

Donald Jackson, "What I Did for Love—of Editing" (J6)

Haskell M. Monroe, Jr., "Some Thoughts for an Aspiring Historical Editor" (M61)

Robert J. Taylor, "One Historian's Education" (T25).

A literature survey offers similar opportunities. An explanation of why one edition of a Shakespeare play or Twain novel was chosen over another can introduce basic editorial issues. The discussion can be enhanced by reading a general discussion:

R. C. Bald, "Editorial Problems: A Preliminary Survey" (B9)
Fredson Bowers, "The Ecology of American Literary Texts" (B64)
J. E. Cross, "The Poem in Transmitted Text" (C47)
G. Blakemore Evans, "Shakespeare Restored—Once Again" (E12)
E. L. McAdam, Jr. "The Textual Approach to Meaning" (M13).

An article such as Donald Hall's "Robert Frost Corrupted" (H9), which demonstrates in accessible prose the effect of repunctuation, would be interesting to students and demonstrate the importance of a seemingly minor issue. Bowers's "The Walt Whitman Manuscripts of 'Leaves of Grass' (1860)" (B90) offers a fairly straightforward summary of the discovery, editing, and significance of a manuscript.

A selection of letters or diary entries by an author being studied can demonstrate the value of manuscript sources in literary research, as well as introduce the existence and activities of another variety of editorial work. Such reading could be supplemented with articles such as the following:

Kathleen Coburn, "Editing the Coleridge Notebooks" (C30)
William H. Gilman, "How Should Journals Be Edited?" (G20)
Robert Halsband, "Editing the Letters of Letter-Writers" (H15)
Robert N. Hudspeth, "Hawthorne's Letters and the 'Darksome Veil
     of Mystery' " (H69)
Charles Richard Sanders, "Editing the Carlyle Letters" (S3).

Advanced Undergraduate Courses

In upper-level courses in history or literature, in which students are expected to undertake original research, material on editing can improve research skills and broaden students' understanding of research materials. One of the easiest ways to do this is to make sure that students know what a documentary or critical edition is and how to use it. In specialized courses such as black studies or women's studies, material relevant to the field can be selected.

A useful assignment is to have each student select an edition of interest and present, either orally or in writing, a brief explanation of the editorial approach, followed by a reading of a document demonstrating the student's understanding of the editorial method and apparatus. This may sound rather elementary, but even when students are aware of the existence of documentary and critical editions, they tend to go straight for the text, without bothering to find out how it got there or what all the strange symbols mean. They may also be asked to seek out and evaluate reviews of the edition they chose, or to compare two editions of the same text.

An introduction to finding aids for manuscript materials will also be useful. To make sure students understand how to use such aids, they can be assigned a fairly simple, limited search for manuscripts in which they are to use the published finding aids and (if possible) the catalogue of your own library's manuscript collection.

At this level, students can benefit from reading articles on the process of searching for and collecting documents, some of which are quite entertaining:

Roy P. Basler, "Collecting the 'Collected Works' " (B12)
Theodore Besterman, "Twenty Thousand Voltaire Letters" (B41)
C. N. Fifer, "Editing Boswell: A Search for Letters" (F9)
John Matthews, "The Hunt for Disraeli Letters" (M11)
Thomas C. Reeves, "The Search for the Chester Alan Arthur Papers" (R8)
Howard C. Rice, Jr., "Jefferson in Europe a Century and a Half Later" (R23).

Another appropriate topic is annotation. Students inevitably find fault with notes, which never seem to answer precisely the question they have in mind. They will be enlightened by articles such as these:

Martin C. Battestin, "A Rationale of Literary Annotation" (B16)
John Carroll, "On Annotating *Clarissa*" (C15)
Charles T. Cullen, "Principles of Annotation in Editing Historical Documents" (C50)

Arthur Friedman, "Principles of Historical Annotation in Critical
Editions of Modern Texts" (F28)
A. C. Hamilton, "The Philosophy of the Footnote" (H20)
W. J. B. Owen, "Annotating Wordsworth" (O13).

Graduate Courses

At the graduate level, students genuinely interested in editing
should have available semester- or year-long courses on the subject.
All students, however, should be introduced to the subject in the
standard research methods courses, whether with a selection of
readings such as those suggested for undergraduates, an abbreviated
version of the reading list for a full-scale course, or the relevant
chapters in methods texts. James Thorpe's *The Use of Manuscripts
in Literary Research* (T37) would be especially useful in such a
course.

In short, it is possible to introduce editing into courses where
actual editing projects are neither appropriate nor practical. Readings and activities related to editing can reinforce and enrich the
content of history and literature courses and can enhance students'
research skills. With any luck, a few students in such courses will
become interested in more advanced work and provide an audience
for a course devoted exclusively to the theory and practice of
editing.

COURSES ON EDITING

Some of those who have taught editing to undergraduate and
graduate students have reported on their experiences in pamphlets,
articles, and surveys. Before embarking on an editing course, an
instructor would do well to consult such works:

Ross W. Beales, Jr., and Randall K. Burkett, *Historical Editing for
Undergraduates* (B19)
Randall K. Burkett, "Historical Editing and Researching Local His-
tory in an Undergraduate Black Studies Seminar" (B135)
Pete Daniel and Stuart B. Kaufman, "The Booker T. Washington
Papers and Historical Editing at Maryland" (D2)

Thomas E. Jeffrey, "The Education of Editors" (J13)

Stuart Bruce Kaufman, "The Samuel Gompers Papers as Literature" (K10)

Barbara Oberg, "Editing and the Teaching of History" (O4)

M. Palmer, "Archive Packs for Schools" (P2)

Walter Rundell, Jr., "Documentary Editing" (R40)

S. Schoenbaum, "Editing English Dramatic Texts" (S9).

No textbook is available for courses in editing. The closest approximation is the array of handbooks for practicing editors. Of these, the most thorough and recent is Mary-Jo Kline's *A Guide to Documentary Editing* (K23). Briefer, and more specialized, are:

Paul Baender and William B. Todd, *Rules and Procedures for the Mark Twain Edition* (B5)

James Franklin Beard and James P. Elliott, *The Cooper Edition: Editorial Principles and Procedures* (B20)

Larry I. Bland, *Publishing the Papers of George Catlett Marshall* (B57)

Clarence E. Carter, *Historical Editing* (C16)

Center for Editions of American Authors, *Statement of Editorial Principles* (C22)

Philip Gaskell, *From Writer to Reader* (G9)

R. F. Hunnisett, *Editing Records for Publication* (H71)

Charles Moorman, *Editing the Middle English Manuscript* (M66).

None of these can be used as the sole textbook for a course, but selections of readings can be added to supplement them.

Because a course in editing might be taught in a history or literature department, open to undergraduates or graduate students, and of various lengths, I have not attempted to suggest a syllabus. (Course syllabi are, however, available from The Association for Documentary Editing.) Instead, I have listed the topics that an instructor might wish to cover and suggested which of the items in the bibliography would be best suited to teaching a general course. The selection and weighting of topics, and the choice of readings, would depend largely on the subject emphasis of the course (colonial U.S. history versus twentieth-century British literature, for example). The list would also have to be supplemented, depending on the sort of practical editorial work the course involved. For example, if a series of letters is edited as a group project, the class would benefit from reading the literature devoted to editing correspondence.

Early in any course on editing, students should be sent to the library to browse through several published editions relevant to their interests. A handful of these should be the subject of closer scrutiny and written evaluation. Students can learn a great deal by reading introductions and statements of editorial method. They can learn still more by studying the texts that follow, to see how the method works in practice. Good editions provide models; failed editions provide object lessons. Both should be assigned.

My own teaching preference would be to offer a general introduction to editing for students in all disciplines, with a group project in the first semester. This would be followed by an optional second-semester course in which students would pursue individual editing projects. Manuscripts from the university's state history collection, its collection of literary papers, the state historical society, the state archives, or other special collections could be used in the second semester, as well as any appropriate family papers students might have uncovered. I prefer this approach because it combines background reading, practical work, a group assignment that would to some extent duplicate the actual workings of an editorial project, and an individual project long enough to tax a student's inventiveness, independence, vision, perseverance, organization, and attention to detail. An internship on an editorial project would complete the editor's preparation.

Here, then, are the topics that a course might cover, along with some suggested readings.

General Background

It is important for students to understand the general purpose of editing and the history of the discipline. The readings for general background can be selected from the following:

R. C. Bald, "Editorial Problems" (B9)

Paul H. Bergeron, "True Valor Seen" (B38)

Julian P. Boyd, "Some Animadversions on Being Struck by Lightning" (B97)

O M Brack, Jr., "Introduction" to *Bibliography and Textual Criticism* (B108)

Frank G. Burke, "The Historian as Editor" (B133)

O. Lawrence Burnette, Jr., "Preservation and Dissemination of Historical Evidence" (B139)

Lester J. Cappon, "The Historian as Editor" (C6) and "A Rationale for Historical Editing Past and Present" (C10)

Vinton A. Dearing, "Methods of Textual Editing" (D9) or "Textual Criticism Today" (D13)

A. E. Housman, "The Application of Thought to Textual Criticism" (H59)

Dan H. Lawrence, "A Bibliographical Novitiate" (L15)

Jerome J. McGann, *A Critique of Modern Textual Criticism* (M23)

John Y. Simon, "Editors and Critics" (S46)

G. Thomas Tanselle, "Textual Scholarship" (T19)

George L. Vogt, "Introduction: The Historical Editor's View" (V6).

On the history of editing, readings can be chosen from:

Whitfield J. Bell, Jr., "Editors and Great Men" (B27)

Fredson Bowers, "Principle and Practice in the Editing of Early Dramatic Texts" (B79)

Julian P. Boyd, " 'God's Altar Needs Not Our Pollishings' " (B94)

Lyman H. Butterfield, "Archival and Editorial Enterprise in 1850 and 1950" (B146) or "Editing American Historical Documents" (B149)

Worthington Chauncey Ford, "The Editorial Function in United States History" (F15)

Philip M. Hamer, " '. . . authentic Documents tending to elucidate our History' " (H18)

Oliver W. Holmes, "Documentary Publication in the Western Hemisphere" (H52)

Ian Lancashire, "Medieval Drama" (L8)

Brian Merrilees, "Anglo-Norman" (M42)

Haskell M. Monroe, Jr., "Some Thoughts for an Aspiring Historical Editor" (M61)

Arnold G. Reichenberger, "Editing Spanish *Comedias* of the XVIIth Century" (R9)

Donald H. Reiman, "The Four Ages of Editing and the English Romantics" (R13)

George C. Rogers, Jr., "The Sacred Text" (R33)

Robert A. Rutland, "Recycling Early National History Through the Papers of the Founding Fathers" (R43)

Willard Thorp, "Exodus: Four Decades of American Literary Scholarship" (T28).

I have excluded from these lists the debates over federal funding, the differences between historical and literary editing, and the CEAA editions. These debates (all well summarized in Mary-Jo Kline's *Guide*) are best left until later in the course, when students are sufficiently aware of the terms and issues involved to read more critically; I have listed them later on.

Audience

Although editors universally emphasize the importance of identifying and understanding the audience for an edition, they write very little on the subject. Because this decision affects every subsequent decision—including the extent of collection, selection, transcription, annotation, apparatus, and indexing—it needs to be raised repeatedly in any course. It is useful at least to introduce the topic early on. Some helpful readings are:

R. C. Bald, "Editorial Problems: A Preliminary Survey" (B9)

Fredson Bowers, "Editing a Philosopher" (B65) or "Practical Texts and Definitive Editions" (B78)

Ralph Hanna III, "A New Edition of Chaucer" (H24)

Hilary Jenkinson, "The Representation of Manuscripts in Print" (J18)

Sylvère Monod, " 'Between Two Worlds': Editing Dickens" (M58)

Lewis Mumford, "Emerson Behind Barbed Wire" (M74)

John Passmore, "A Philosopher of the Particulars" (P21)

G. Thomas Tanselle, "Recent Editorial Discussion and the Central Questions of Editing" (T15)

Edmund Wilson, "The Fruits of the MLA" (W22).

Search

Because students are unlikely to have the opportunity to do a real search for documents, it is especially important for them to undertake the job vicariously. The editors who will allow them to look over their shoulders include:

Roy P. Basler, "Collecting the 'Collected Works' " (B12)

G. E. Bentley, Jr., "William Blake's Protean Text" (B36)

Theodore Besterman, "Twenty Thousand Voltaire Letters" (B41)

Jo Ann Boydston, "Editing the Poems of John Dewey" (B102)

James C. Bradford, "The Papers of John Paul Jones" (B112)

Lyman H. Butterfield, "The Adams Papers" (B144)

Douglas E. Clanin, "A Phoenix Rising from the Ashes" (C28)

C. N. Fifer, "Editing Boswell: A Search for Letters" (F9)

Victor E. Graham, "Editing French Lyric Poetry of the Sixteenth Century" (G34)

Patricia G. Holland, "The Papers of Elizabeth Cady Stanton and Susan B. Anthony" (H50)

James F. Hopkins, "Editing the Henry Clay Papers" (H56)

Donald Jackson, "The Papers of George Washington" (J3)

Ralph L. Ketcham, "The Madison Family Papers" (K16)

Leonard W. Labaree, "In Search of 'B Franklin' " (L1)

Wilmarth S. Lewis, "Editing Familiar Letters" (L35)

John Matthews, "The Hunt for Disraeli Letters" (M11)

Harriet Chappell Owsley, "Discoveries Made in Editing the Papers of Andrew Jackson" (O14)

Thomas C. Reeves, "The Search for the Chester Alan Arthur Papers" (R8)

Howard C. Rice, Jr., "Jefferson in Europe a Century and a Half Later" (R23)

John Y. Simon, "The Collected Writings of Ulysses S. Grant" (S44)

Harold C. Syrett and Jacob E. Cooke, "The Papers of Alexander Hamilton" (S80)

Albert E. Van Dusen, "In Quest of that 'Arch Rebel' Jonathan Trumbull, Sr." (V3).

Selection

In class work, students are rarely faced with the same sorts of selection decisions that confront a working editor, but they may have to select a manuscript to work on or choose from a collection of letters. Whether or not they must actually make such decisions, however, they need to know how editors select what to include in an edition and the consequences of their choices. Some useful readings are:

John Brooke, "The Prime Ministers' Papers" (B118)

John L. Bullion, Review of *The Adams Papers* (B130)

Lyman H. Butterfield, "The Adams Papers" (B144)

G. C. F. Forster, "Record Publishing in the North-West in Retrospect and Prospect" (F17)

Patricia Galloway, "Dearth and Bias" (G7)

John A. Garraty, Review of *The Letters of Theodore Roosevelt* (G8)

Robert Halsband, "Editing the Letters of Letter-Writers" (H15)

James F. Hopkins, "Editing the Henry Clay Papers" (H56)

Nathan Irvin Huggins, Review of *The Correspondence of W. E. B. DuBois* (H70)

Aileen S. Kraditor, "Editing the Abolitionists" (K31) and James Stewart, "Garrison Again . . ." (S72)

David F. Nordloh, "Supplying What's Missing in Editions of Selected Letters" (N12)

Barbara Oberg, "Interpretation in Editing" (O5)

Ralph H. Orth, "An Edition of Emerson's Poetry Notebooks" (O10)

Jack N. Rakove, Review of *The Papers of Benjamin Franklin* (R2)

John M. Robson, "Principles and Methods in the Collected Edition of John Stuart Mill" (R30)

Peter Shaw and Robert J. Taylor, "A Dialogue" (S23)

John Y. Simon, "The Canons of Selection" (S43)
Gordon S. Wood, "Historians and Documentary Editing" (W27).

Choice of a Copy-Text

One could easily devote an entire semester to copy-text theory. As introductions to the subject, I suggest a few basic readings that would be useful in all courses. A course on American literature could then move into the literature on the application of copy-text theory to nineteenth-century texts. In more specialized courses, other relevant readings could be added; these can be located by using "copy-text" and another relevant key word, such as "drama," when consulting the index. For the basics, I suggest:

Fredson Bowers, "Current Theories of the Copy-text with an Illustration from Dryden" (B63), "Established Texts and Definitive Editions" (B69), "Greg's 'Rationale of Copy-text' Revisited" (B70)
Vinton A. Dearing, "Concepts of Copy-text Old and New" (D8)
W. W. Greg, "The Rationale of Copy-text" (G39)
Jerome J. McGann, *A Critique of Modern Textual Criticism* (M23)
James Thorpe, "The Aesthetics of Textual Criticism" (T29) and "The Establishment of the Text" (T30).

On applications of copy-text theory to more recent work, the following are helpful:

Fredson Bowers, "Some Principles for Scholarly Editions of Nineteenth-Century American Authors" (B83)
Tom Davis, "The CEAA and Modern Textual Editing" (D4)
Hershel Parker, "Melville and the Concept of 'Author's Final Intentions'" (P9)
G. Thomas Tanselle, "Greg's Theory of Copy-text and the Editing of American Literature" (T8).

Should one want to go into further detail, the following debates might be used:

Paul Baender, "The Meaning of Copy-Text" (B3), paired with G. Thomas Tanselle, "The Meaning of Copy-Text: A Further Note" (T11)

John Freehafer, "Greg's Theory of Copy-Text and the Textual Criticism in the CEAA Editions" (F23) and the discussion that followed

Donald Pizer, "On the Editing of Modern American Texts" (P30) and the discussion that followed.

Transcription and the Accidental/Substantive Distinction

Most of the handbooks listed earlier deal with practical matters of transcription. In addition, students would benefit from reading any of the following pieces:

Robert Stephen Becker, "Challenges in Editing Modern Literary Correspondence: Transcription" (B23)

Ralph H. Orth, "An Edition of Emerson's Poetry Notebooks" (O10)

Hershel Parker, "Regularizing Accidentals: The Latest Form of Infidelity" (P13)

Curt A. Zimansky, "Editing Restoration Comedy" (Z3).

Because transcription is a subject more often criticized than reflected upon, it is also worthwhile to assign a variety of reviews that discuss the topic. These can be located by pairing the key word "transcription" with the subject of a relevant review, e.g., "Jefferson, Thomas."

On theory, in addition to the readings suggested for the study of copy-text, students might look at:

Philip Gaskell, "Textual Bibliography" (G11)

Roger Laufer, "From Publishing to Editing *Gil Blas de Santillane*" (L14)

G. Thomas Tanselle, "The Editing of Historical Documents" (T4)

James Thorpe, "The Treatment of Accidentals" (T36) or *Watching the Ps & Qs* (T38).

Annotation

Annotation is a broad, controversial topic that has been written about extensively by editors in all fields. The most appropriate articles for students are the following:

Martin C. Battestin, "A Rationale of Literary Annotation" (B16)

Kenneth R. Bowling, Review of *The Papers of James Madison* and *The Papers of Thomas Jefferson* (B93)

Robert C. Bray, "Tom Sawyer Once and for All" (B115)

John C. Burnham, Review of *The Papers of Joseph Henry* (B141) and Saul Benison's response (B33)

John Carroll, "On Annotating *Clarissa*" (C15)

Charles T. Cullen, "Principles of Annotation in Editing Historical Documents" (C50)

Arthur Friedman, "Principles of Historical Annotation in Critical Editions of Modern Texts" (F28)

A. C. Hamilton, "The Philosophy of the Footnote" (H20)

Robert Latham, "Publishing Pepys" (L13)

W. J. B. Owen, "Annotating Wordsworth" (O13).

Students might also enjoy the debate between Juliette L. George, Michael F. Marmor, and Alexander L. George, on the one hand, and Arthur S. Link, David W. Hirst, John Wells Davidson, and John E. Little, on the other, over the annotation of the papers of Woodrow Wilson (G13–15, L39).

Apparatus

Students need to learn about the variety of apparatus that can be part of any edition and its practical use. They should also be exposed to the "barbed-wire" debate. For discussions of the varieties and uses of editorial apparatus, they can read:

Fredson Bowers, "Scholarship and Editing" (B82), "Some Principles for Scholarly Editions of Nineteenth-Century American Authors" (B83), and "Transcription of Manuscripts: The Record of Variants" (B89)

Charlton Hinman, "Basic Shakespeare" (H45)

Thomas L. McHaney, "The Textual Editions of Hawthorne and Melville" (M30)

James B. Meriwether, "A Proposal for a CEAA Edition of William Faulkner" (M40)

Joel Myerson, Review of *The Autobiography of Benjamin Franklin* (M78)

Hershel Parker, Review of the Centenary Edition of the *Works of Nathaniel Hawthorne* (P14)

Peter L. Shillingsburg, *Scholarly Editing in the Computer Age* (S38)

G. Thomas Tanselle, "Editorial Apparatus for Radiating Texts" (T5) and "Some Principles for Editorial Apparatus" (T17).

On the barbed-wire question, students might enjoy the following reviews and responses:

Robert C. Bray, "Tom Sawyer Once and for All" (B115)

John Freehafer, "*The Marble Faun* and the Editing of Nineteenth-Century Texts" (F25)

Eleanor D. Kewer, "Case Histories in the Craft of the Publisher's Editor" (K17)

Stephen E. Meats, "The Editing of Harold Frederic's Correspondence" (M35)

Lewis Mumford, "Emerson Behind Barbed Wire" (M74) and the subsequent discussion

Edmund Wilson, "The Fruits of the MLA" (W22) and the subsequent discussions.

Proofreading

If students are to complete a real editing project, they must learn that proofreading involves more than simply reading through one's manuscript or running it through a spelling checker. (Indeed, a speedy way to learn the limitations of spelling checkers is to try them on the literal transcription of, say, a seventeenth-century manuscript.) Students can learn standard proofreading signs from any good dictionary or from the *Chicago Manual of Style.* Most of the handbooks on editing also contain proofreading instructions. For further hints on proofreading students can consult:

Eleanor Harman, "Hints on Proofreading" (H29)
Beth Luey, *Handbook for Academic Authors* (L45).

Indexing

A group editing project may be lengthy enough to require an index, so that students can gain some practice in compiling one. All students, however, should be sufficiently familiar with the purpose of an index to evaluate one, and it is a good idea for them to be introduced to the procedure. Students who wish to learn how to index should consult:

Beth Luey, *Handbook for Academic Authors* (L45)
Sina Spiker, *Indexing Your Book* (S66).

David R. Chesnutt describes the use of computers in indexing in "Comprehensive Text Processing and the Papers of Henry Laurens" (C24, C25), as does Charles T. Cullen in "Twentieth-Century Technology and the Jefferson Papers" (C54).

Funding

In addition to learning that the money for projects does not fall from the skies and that there are funding sources in the federal and state governments as well as the private sector, students will be enlightened by debates within the profession over funding. These include:

Thomas H. Etzold, "The Great Documents Deluge" (E8), along with Frank G. Burke, "Rebuttal to 'Great Documents Deluge' " (B134) and Joseph Siracusa, "Reply" (S53)
Charles T. Cullen, "Some Reflections on the Soft Money Generation" (C53) and Helen C. Aguera, "In Response" (A6)
Simone Reagor, "Historical Editing: The Federal Role" (R6) and John Y. Simon, "In Response" (S47).

Students might also be asked to read Warren M. Billings and Raymond W. Smock, "A Proposal" (B52), Charlene N. Bickford,

"An Agenda for Professional Survival" (B45), and Raymond W. Smock, "A Bicentennial Legacy" (S59), so that they know the battle is still being fought. The furor raised by Edmund Wilson ("The Fruits of the MLA") and continued by countless others is in part over funding. The readings on this subject are listed shortly.

Them and Us

No matter what stand one takes on the debate over historical versus literary editing, or documentary versus textual editing, students should be exposed to some of the literature of the debate. One might begin with the unifying essay of Jo Ann Boydston, "The Language of Scholarly Editing" (B103) and then move on to any of the following:

Don L. Cook, "The Short Happy Thesis of G. Thomas Tanselle" (C37)
Wayne Cutler, "The 'Authentic' Witness" (C57) and David J. Nordloh, "The 'Perfect' Text" (N9)
Peter Shaw, "The American Heritage and Its Guardians" (S22)
John Y. Simon, "Editors and Critics" (S46)
G. Thomas Tanselle, "The Editing of Historical Documents" (T4) and "Literary Editing" (T10)
Robert J. Taylor, "Editorial Practices" (T24)
James Thorpe, "Literary and Historical Editing" (T32)
Gordon S. Wood, "Historians and Documentary Editing" (W27).

The CEAA and CSE Debate

In addition to the discussions of the applicability of copy-text theory to editions of nineteenth-century American authors and the barbed-wire debate (both listed earlier) students can be introduced to the polemics centering around the Center for Editions of American Authors and its successors, the Center for Scholarly Editions and the Committee on Scholarly Editions. These include:

Paul Baender, "Reflections upon the CEAA by a Departing Editor" (B4)

Wayne Franklin, "The 'Library of America' and the Welter of
American Books" (F22)

Peter L. Shillingsburg, "Critical Editing and the Center for Scholarly
Editions" (S35)

Edmund Wilson, "The Fruits of the MLA" (W22) and the official
MLA response, *Professional Standards and American Editions: A Response to Edmund Wilson* (M54).

Fraud and Other Criminal Activity

Although not central to the issues of editing, the exposure of
fraudulent documents is always of interest to students. It is especially of value to undergraduates, who tend to be overly credulous.
I recommend the following:

Paul M. Angle, "The Minor Collection: A Criticism" (A12)

James C. Bradford, "The Papers of John Paul Jones" (B112)

Arthur Pierce Middleton and Douglass Adair, "The Mystery of the
Horn Papers" (M46).

An extensive and entertaining description of the posthumous
exposure of a major documentary fraud is Hugh Trevor-Roper's
Hermit of Peking: The Hidden Life of Sir Edmund Backhouse
(New York: Knopf, 1977).

Although it relates to theft rather than fraud, Thomas E. Jeffrey's "Raiders of the Lost Archives" (J15) may be of interest.

I hope that these suggestions will encourage teachers of history
and literature to incorporate editing into their courses and to introduce new courses devoted to the discipline. Any student can
benefit from an understanding of what documentary and critical
editions are for, how they are compiled, and how to use and evaluate them. The professions of history and literature can benefit
from better understanding of editorial work as well. And certainly
editorial work will be appreciated better, used more extensively,
and supported more ardently if its audience is expanded.

Bibliography

A

A1. ABBOTT, CRAIG S. "A Response to Nordloh's 'Socialization, Authority, and Evidence.'" *Analytical & Enumerative Bibliography*, n.s. 1 (1987): 13–16.

authorial intention

In this response to David J. Nordloh's review of McGann's *Critique of Modern Textual Criticism*, in the same issue, Abbott agrees with much of Nordloh's criticism but argues that McGann's book contributes to the ongoing discussion of textual theory.

A2. ABERCROMBIE, JOHN R. *Computer Programs for Literary Analysis*. Philadelphia: University of Pennsylvania Press, 1984.

computers

Abercrombie provides programming instructions for entering text, collation, indexing, creating a concordance, and finding and listing variants.

A3. ADAMS, CHARLES FRANCIS, JR. "The Printing of Old Manuscripts." *Proceedings of the Massachusetts Historical Society* 20 (1882–83): 175–82.

history of editing; transcription

Adams outlines his principles for "antiquarian editing," with particular attention to transcription.

A4. ADAMS, ELEANOR. *Old English Scholarship in England from 1566–1800.* Yale Studies in English 55. New Haven: Yale University Press, 1917.

eighteenth century; history of editing; Old English; seventeenth century; sixteenth century

A history of Old English scholarship, with examples of work done in each of the centuries studied.

A5. ADAMS, THOMAS BOYLSTON, ET AL. "Proceedings of a Ceremony Held at the Massachusetts Historical Society, September 22, 1961, Commemorating the Publication of the Diary and Autobiography of John Adams." *Proceedings of the Massachusetts Historical Society* 73 (1961): 119–50.

Adams papers

A celebration of the publication of the first four volumes of the Adams Papers. Samuel Flagg Bemis, Lyman Butterfield, Thomas James Wilson, Paul Herman Buck, Julian Boyd, and Adams discuss the importance of the work.

A6. AGUERA, HELEN C. "In Response." *Documentary Editing* 6 (March 1984): 12.

NEH

A response to Charles Cullen's "Some Reflections on the Soft Money Generation," explaining the NEH role in influencing editorial policy.

A7. ALLEN, ROBERT R. "The First Six Volumes of the Northwestern-Newberry Melville: A Review Article." *Proof* 3 (1973): 441–53.

apparatus; Melville, Herman

Allen reviews the history of the project and discusses in detail the historical notes and textual principles and practices.

A8. AMERICAN HISTORICAL ASSOCIATION. Historical Manuscripts Commission. "Suggestions for the Printing of Documents Relating to American History." *Annual Report of the AHA for the Year 1905*, 1: 45–48. Washington D.C.: Government Printing Office, 1906.

format

The commission of the AHA lists its technical suggestions for the physical appearance of published historical documents.

A9. AMMERMAN, DAVID. Review of *Province in Rebellion: A Documentary History of the Founding of the Commonwealth of Massachusetts. William and Mary Quarterly* 33 (July 1976): 536–38.

audience; Massachusetts; microforms

Ammerman describes the volume as "an unsuccessful experiment in microform publication" that is suitable for neither general nor scholarly use.

A10. ANDERSON, FREDERICK. "Hazards of Photographic Sources." *CEAA Newsletter* 1 (March 1968): 5.

microfilm; photocopying; transcription

In this brief note, Anderson points out the problems raised by exclusive use of photographic copies, including omitted material, inability to compare papers and inks, and misleading marks introduced during the photographic process.

A11. ANDERSON, FREDERICK. "Normalization and Silent Emendation." *CEAA Newsletter* 3 (June 1970): 19–21.

apparatus; emendation; transcription

Anderson explains the purpose of silent emendation and limits on its permissibility. He lists the appropriate uses of normalization and silent emendation and explains the need to disclose editorial procedure.

A12. ANGLE, PAUL M. "The Minor Collection: A Criticism." *Atlantic Monthly* 143 (1929): 516–25.

authenticity; Lincoln, Abraham

Angle offers a point-by-point attack on the authenticity of Lincoln documents published earlier in the *Atlantic Monthly*.

A13. ANGLO-AMERICAN HISTORICAL COMMITTEE. "Report on Editing Historical Documents." *Bulletin of the Institute of Historical Research* 1 (1923): 6–25.

editing, general; England; transcription

This article contains the revised edition of the committee's report on editorial procedures.

A14. ANGLO-AMERICAN HISTORICAL COMMITTEE. "Report on Editing Modern Historical Documents." *Bulletin of the Institute of Historical Research* 3 (1925): 13–26.

apparatus; editing, general; transcription

This later report of the Anglo-American Historical Committee concentrates on the treatment of postmedieval documents.

A15. ARNOLD, DOUGLAS M. "Debating the Federal Constitution." *Documentary Editing* 7 (June 1985): 14–18.

annotation; selection; transcription

A review of *Commentaries on the Constitution: Public and Private*, vols. 1 and 2, ed. John P. Kaminski, Gaspare J. Saladino, and Richard Leffler.

A16. Aziz, Maqbool. "Editing James: The Question of Copy-Text." In *Editing British and American Literature, 1880–1920*, edited by Eric W. Domville, 31–47.

copy-text; James, Henry; serialization

Aziz discusses the problem of establishing a copy-text for an author whose work was first printed serially and who revised extensively.

B

B1. Badaracco, Claire. "The Editor and the Question of Value: Proposal." *Text* 1 (1984): 41–43.

types of editing

Badaracco suggests that the distinction between "textual" and "documentary" editing is more useful than that between "literary" and "historical" editing. See also Fredson Bowers, "The Editor and the Question of Value: Another View," immediately following.

B2. Badaracco, Claire M. "Pitfalls and Rewards of the Solo Editor: Sophia Peabody Hawthorne." *Resources for American Literary Study* 11 (Spring 1981): 91–100.

Hawthorne, Nathaniel; Hawthorne, Sophia Peabody; solo editing

Badaracco discusses Sophia Hawthorne's editing of Nathaniel's notebooks and her own editing of Sophia's Cuba journal.

B3. Baender, Paul. "The Meaning of Copy-Text." *Studies in Bibliography* 22 (1969): 311–18.

copy-text

Baender discusses the history of the term "copy-text" and argues that it may now require redefinition. See also G. Thomas Tanselle, "The Meaning of Copy-Text: A Further Note."

B4. BAENDER, PAUL. "Reflections upon the CEAA by a Departing Editor." *Resources for American Literary Study* 4 (1974): 131–44.

authorial intention; CEAA

Baender examines CEAA editions, offers criticism of their theory and practice, responds to their major critics, and concludes that they are worthwhile.

B5. BAENDER, PAUL, AND WILLIAM B. TODD. *Rules and Procedures for the Mark Twain Edition*. Iowa City: University of Iowa, 1965.

handbook; nineteenth century; Twain, Mark

A syllabus explaining how to edit a nineteenth-century text.

B6. BAILYN, BERNARD. "Boyd's Jefferson: Notes for a Sketch." *New England Quarterly* 33 (1960): 380–400.

annotation; Boyd, Julian; format; Jefferson, Thomas

In this review of vols. 7–15 of *The Papers of Thomas Jefferson*, Bailyn praises the project and discusses its contribution to understanding Jefferson.

B7. BAILYN, BERNARD. "Butterfield's Adams: Notes for a Sketch." *William and Mary Quarterly* 19 (1962): 238–56.

Adams papers; Butterfield, Lyman; public relations

Bailyn describes the publicity surrounding the publication of the first volume of Butterfield's edition of the Adams papers.

He also reviews the first four volumes and assesses their contribution to our understanding of John Adams.

B8. BAIRD, JOHN D., ED. *Editing Texts of the Romantic Period: Papers Given at the Conference on Editorial Problems, University of Toronto, November 1971.* Toronto: Hakkert, 1972.

romanticism

See articles by Burns, J. H.; Coburn, Kathleen; Owen, W. J. B.; Reiman, Donald H. ("Editing Shelley"); and Whalley, George.

B9. BALD, R. C. "Editorial Problems: A Preliminary Survey." *Studies in Bibliography* 3 (1950–51): 3–17. Reprinted in *Art and Error: Modern Textual Editing,* edited by Ronald Gottesman and Scott Bennett (Bloomington: Indiana University Press, 1970), 37–53.

audience; editing, general; transcription

Bald discusses the importance of properly edited texts; distinguishes modern-spelling editions, old-spelling editions, facsimile editions,and diplomatic editions; and surveys problems facing editors of texts from the Renaissance onward.

B10. BARNES, WARNER. "Eighteenth- and Nineteenth-Century Editorial Problems: A Selective Bibliography." *Papers of the Bibliographical Society of America* 62 (1968): 59–67.

bibliographies; eighteenth century; nineteenth century

An annotated listing that includes material on bibliography not included in the present volume.

B11. BARNES, WARNER. "Nineteenth-Century Editorial Problems: A Selective Bibliography." In *Editing Nineteenth-Century Texts,* edited by John M. Robson, 123–32.

bibliographies; nineteenth century

This bibliography, with abstracts, includes prefaces and introductions to editions, which are not included in the present bibliography.

B12. BASLER, ROY P. "Collecting the 'Collected Works.'" *Autograph Collector's Journal* 5 (1953): 37–38.

Hamilton, Alexander; search

Basler relates the difficulties he encountered when he tried to collect manuscripts for his edition of the papers of Alexander Hamilton.

B13. BATESON, F. W. "The Application of Thought to an Eighteenth-Century Text: *The School for Scandal.*" In *Evidence in Literary Scholarship*, edited by René Wellek and Alvaro Ribeiro, 321–35. Oxford: Clarendon Press, 1979.

authorial intention; Sheridan, Richard Brinsley; transmission of texts

Bateson argues for choosing the *best* reading, whether early, middle, or late, using Sheridan's *School for Scandal* as an example. Stemmatics, he contends, does not deal adequately with authorial revisions.

B14. BATESON, F. W. "Textual Criticism." In his *The Scholar-Critic,* 126–46. London: Routledge & Kegan Paul, 1972.

bibliography; editing, general

Bateson discusses the need to apply both bibliographical and critical approaches in textual editing.

B15. BATTESTIN, MARTIN C. "Fielding's Novels and the Wesleyan Edition: Some Principles and Problems." In *Editing Eighteenth-Century Novels*, edited by G. E. Bentley, Jr., 9–30.

copy-text; eighteenth century; Fielding, Henry; transcription

Battestin discusses establishing the text of Fielding's novels and provides examples illustrating the importance of reproducing the original typography. He also discusses the completion of the Wesleyan edition of *Tom Jones*.

B16. BATTESTIN, MARTIN C. "A Rationale of Literary Annotation: The Example of Fielding's Novels." *Studies in Bibliography* 34 (1981): 1–22. Reprinted in *Literary & Historical Editing*, edited by George L. Vogt and John Bush Jones, 57–79.

annotation; Fielding, Henry

Battestin lists the variables affecting annotation and then discusses its purpose and procedures.

B17. BEALE, HOWARD K. "Is the Printed Diary of Gideon Welles Reliable?" *American Historical Review* 30 (1925): 547–52.

transcription; Welles, Gideon

Beale compares the manuscript and printed versions of the diary, focusing on Welles's own alterations and his son's editing.

B18. BEALES, ROSS W., JR. "Historical Editing and Undergraduate Teaching: A Rationale and a Model." *Teaching History: A Journal of Methods* 3 (Spring 1978): 3–8.

training

Beales describes a one-semester undergraduate seminar and offers suggestions on materials, methodology, and format.

B19. BEALES, ROSS W., JR., AND RANDALL K. BURKETT. *Historical Editing for Undergraduates*. Worcester, Mass.: College of the Holy Cross, 1977.

handbook; training

This thirty-eight page booklet has four sections and two appendices, one containing a bibliography and the other the NHPRC's policy statement on selection and annotation. The four sections focus on an overview of the historical editing profession and a method of training undergraduates in editing.

B20. BEARD, JAMES FRANKLIN, AND JAMES P. ELLIOTT. *The Cooper Edition: Editorial Principles and Procedures* [*The Writings of James Fenimore Cooper: A Statement of Editorial Principles and Procedures*]. Worcester, Mass.: Clark University Press, 1977.

Cooper, James Fenimore; handbook

Aiming "to provide preliminary practical guidance, to establish some critical directions, for present and prospective Cooper editors," the authors present this working handbook. Topics covered are format; front matter; presentation, selection, and preparation of text; annotation; and apparatus.

B21. BEAURLINE, L. A. "The Director, the Script, and Author's Revisions: A Critical Problem." In *Papers in Dramatic Theory and Criticism*, edited by D. M. Knauf, 78–91. Iowa City: University of Iowa, 1969.

copy-text; drama

Beaurline discusses the problems of editing and establishing a copy-text for plays, which may exist in versions with revisions by the author, director, and others.

B22. BEBB, BRUCE, AND HERSHEL PARKER. "Freehafer on Greg and the CEAA: Secure Footing and 'Substantial Shortfalls.' " *Studies in the Novel* 7 (1975): 391–94.

CEAA

A response to John Freehafer's "Greg's Theory of Copy-Text and the Textual Criticism in the CEAA Editions." See also articles by Vinton A. Dearing ("Textual Criticism Today"), Thomas L. McHaney ("The Important Questions"), Morse Peckham ("Notes on Freehafer"), and G. Thomas Tanselle ("Two Basic Distinctions"), all in the same issue.

B23. BECKER, ROBERT STEPHEN. "Challenges in Editing Modern Literary Correspondence: Transcription." *Text* 1 (1984): 257–70.

letters; Moore, George; transcription; twentieth century

Becker reports on his survey of modern editions of letters, a questionnaire he sent to editors of modern letters, and his own work on George Moore. He concludes with seven recommendations on transcription, emphasizing the treatment of eccentricities.

B24. BEEMAN, RICHARD R. Review of *The Papers of James Madison*, vols. 11 and 12. *Virginia Magazine of History and Biography* 88 (1980): 104–5.

apparatus; Madison, James

After reviewing the content of the volumes and discussing the editorial policies of the papers of the Founding Fathers, Beeman concludes that the editor's "current decision to simplify the editorial apparatus while at the same time retain[ing] the commitment to completeness is the best possible course."

B25. BELL, ALAN. "The Letters of Sir Walter Scott: Problems and Opportunities." In *Editing Correspondence*, edited by J. A. Dainard, 63–80.

control; letters; microfiche; publishing; Scott, Sir Walter; search

A description of the Survey of the Letters of Sir Walter Scott and a discussion of future plans.

B26. BELL, WHITFIELD J., JR. "Editing a Scientist's Papers." *Isis* 53 (1962): 14–20.

copy-text; Franklin, Benjamin; history of science

Bell discusses the incorporation of Franklin's scientific papers into the complete papers, as well as the method for presenting different versions of the scientific papers.

B27. BELL, WHITFIELD J., JR. "Editors and Great Men." *Aspects of Librarianship*, no. 23 (1960): 1–8.

Hazard, Ebenezer; history of editing; NHPC; Sparks, Jared

Bell traces the history of documentary editing, notes criticism of the field, and remarks on its practical difficulties.

B28. BELL, WHITFIELD J., JR. "Franklin's Papers and *The Papers of Benjamin Franklin*." *Pennsylvania History* 22 (1955): 1–17.

control; Franklin, Benjamin; selection; transcription

Bell discusses the history and publication of the papers of Benjamin Franklin.

B29. BELL, WHITFIELD. Review of *The Papers of Benjamin Henry Latrobe*, ser. 1, vols. 1 and 2. *William and Mary Quarterly* 36 (January 1979): 134–37.

indexing; Latrobe, Benjamin Henry; microforms

A discussion of the compilation of the papers and the choice of form of publication, as well as the indexing system.

B30. BEMIS, SAMUEL FLAGG. "The Adams Family and Their Manuscripts." *Proceedings of the Massachusetts Historical Society* 73 (1961): 134–49.

Adams papers; Butterfield, Lyman

Bemis discusses Lyman Butterfield's work with the Adams papers.

B31. BENDER, T. K. "Literary Text in Electronic Storage: The Editorial Potential." *Computers and the Humanities* 10 (1976): 193–99.

computers

Bender discusses how electronic technology can help retain the essence of a work and notes the advantages of electronic storage of text.

B32. BENEDICT, MICHAEL LES. "Historians and the Continuing Controversy over Fair Use of Unpublished Manuscript Materials." *American Historical Review* 91 (1986): 859–81.

copyright

Benedict reviews the history of copyright law on unpublished works, as well as interpretations of the current (1976) copyright law as it applies to photocopying and quoting from unpublished works. He ends with recommendations for interpreting the law that would protect both scholarship and authorial rights.

B33. BENISON, SAUL. Letter to the Editor. *American Historical Review* 85 (1980): 272–73.

annotation; Henry, Joseph; history of science; selection

A response to John C. Burnham's review of *The Papers of Joseph Henry*, vol. 2. See also Burnham's response, 273–74.

B34. BENTLEY, G. E., JR. "The Great Illustrated-Book Publishers of the 1790's and William Blake." In *Editing Illustrated Books*, edited by William Blissett, 57–96.

Blake, William; eighteenth century; England; engraving; illustrations

An account of the development of engraving and book illustration in late eighteenth-century England.

B35. BENTLEY, G. E., JR. "The People of the Book: Eine Kleine Himmelfahrt." In *Editing and Editors: A Retrospect*, edited by Richard Landon, 15–27.

history of editing

After arguing "that the first editor was God," Bentley provides a history of the Toronto Conference on Editorial Problems.

B36. BENTLEY, G. E., JR. "William Blake's Protean Text." In *Editing Eighteenth-Century Texts*, edited by D. I. B. Smith, 44–58.

Blake, William; copy-text; search

Bentley discusses the limited information available on Blake's personality and the unique form of his writings. He then describes specific problems encountered in collecting the manuscripts, establishing a text, and editing.

B37. BENTLEY, G. E., JR., ED. *Editing Eighteenth-Century Novels: Papers on Fielding, Lesage, Richardson, Sterne, and Smollett Given at the Conference on Editorial Problems, University of Toronto, November 1973.* Toronto: Hakkert, 1975.

eighteenth century; novels

See articles by Battestin, Martin ("Fielding's Novels"); Brack, O M, Jr. (" 'Of Making Many Books' "); Carroll, John; Laufer, Roger; and New, Melvyn.

B38. BERGERON, PAUL H. "True Valor Seen: Historical Editing." *American Archivist* 34 (1971): 259–64.

editing, general; professional status

Bergeron describes the tasks of the historian as editor and of the editor as historian. The article concludes with a discussion of the rewards for historical editors.

B39. BERKELEY, FRANCIS L., JR. "History and Problems of the Control of Manuscripts in the United States." *Proceedings of the American Philosophical Society* 98 (1954): 171–78.

finding aids; Historical Records Survey

Berkeley addresses the problems of the mass and dispersion of U.S. historical documents and recommends the creation of a union catalog of manuscripts.

B40. BERLIN, IRA, JOSEPH P. REIDY, BARBARA J. FIELDS, AND LESLIE ROWLAND. "Writing *Freedom's* History." *Prologue* 14 (Fall 1982): 129–39.

black history; *Freedom*; military history

The authors provide a history of the Freedmen and Southern Society Project, including the collection of documents, and describe the plans for publishing *Freedom: A Documentary History of Emancipation, 1861–1867.* They then outline the issues facing black soldiers in the Union army and include seven relevant documents.

B41. BESTERMAN, THEODORE. "Twenty Thousand Voltaire Letters." In *Editing Eighteenth-Century Texts,* edited by D. I. B. Smith, 7–24.

annotation; format; letters; search; selection; Voltaire

The author, editor of Voltaire's correspondence, discusses the problems presented by his project, many of which arise from its size. His discussion covers the search, selection, design, annotation, and other editorial procedures.

B42. BESTOR, ARTHUR E., JR. "The Transformation of American Scholarship, 1875–1917." *Library Quarterly* 23 (1953): 164–79.

archives; history of editing

Bestor describes the changes in scholarship due to the establishment of research libraries and accessible archives.

B43. BEVINGTON, DAVID. "Drama Editing and Its Relation to Recent Trends in Literary Criticism." In *Editing Early English Drama*, edited by A. F. Johnston, 17–32.

anthologies; drama; history of editing; literary criticism; Middle Ages

In describing his compilation of *Medieval Drama*, Bevington discusses how anthologies are shaped by current criticism and how they shape future study. He also discusses the problem of including stage directions.

B44. BEVINGTON, DAVID. "Editorial Indications of Stage Business in Old-Spelling Editions." In *Play-Texts in Old Spelling*, edited by G. B. Shand and Raymond C. Shady, 105–12.

drama; Renaissance

Bevington reviews the practices of editors of Renaissance drama with regard to stage directions and offers recommendations.

B45. BICKFORD, CHARLENE N. "An Agenda for Professional Survival." *Documentary Editing* 8 (December 1986): 1–5.

ADE; funding; professional status

In her 1986 presidential address, Bickford reviews the accomplishments of the Association for Documentary Editing and stresses the importance of establishing a firm financial base for documentary editing projects through the establishment of a National Trust for Our Documentary Heritage (see Billings, Warren M., and Raymond W. Smock, "A Proposal").

B46. BICKFORD, CHARLENE BANGS. "The Documentary History of the First Federal Congress." *Prologue* 18 (Fall 1986): 173–79.

First Federal Congress project; history of editing; search

Bickford outlines the problems facing the First Congress, the history of the project, the difficulty of collecting materials, and the contents of existing volumes and those under way.

B47. BICKFORD, CHARLENE N., AND KENNETH R. BOWLING. "The First Federal Congress: A Second Sitting of the Federal Convention." *Manuscripts* 39 (Fall 1987): 301–8.

First Federal Congress project; project organization

The authors describe the project and the impact it has had on historical understanding of the First Congress.

B48. BICKFORD, CHARLENE B., GORDON DENBOER, JOHN P. KAMINSKI, RICHARD LEFFLER, MAEVA MARCUS, AND GASPARE J. SALADINO. "Documentary Editing: Its History and Meaning." *Prologue* 18 (Fall 1986): 147–51.

history of editing

The authors outline the development of federal support for documentary projects.

B49. BILLIAS, GEORGE ATHAN. Review of *Naval Documents of the American Revolution*, vol. 2. *American Historical Review* 73 (October 1967): 216–17.

search; selection

Billias criticizes the volume for an inadequate search and inappropriate selection standards.

B50. BILLIAS, GEORGE ATHAN. Review of *Naval Documents of the American Revolution*, vol. 5. *American Historical Review* 77 (June 1972): 831.

background research; copy-text

Billias criticizes the reproduction of documents from secondary sources and reliance on colonial newspapers.

B51. BILLINGS, WARREN M. "Veritas ex Documentis: What Truth?" *Documentary Editing* 10 (December 1988): 1–4.

ADE; public relations

Billings discusses the past and future of the Association for Documentary Editing and the documentary editing profession, encouraging members to ally with other groups and individuals that share its interests.

B52. BILLINGS, WARREN M., AND RAYMOND W. SMOCK. "A Proposal for a National Trust for Our Documentary Heritage." *Documentary Editing* 8 (June 1986): 19–21.

funding; NEH; NHPRC

The authors propose the creation of a national trust to support records preservation and documentary editions.

B53. BINDER, HENRY. "The *Red Badge of Courage* Nobody Knows." *Studies in the Novel* 10 (1978): 9–47.

copy-text; Crane, Stephen

Binder describes material cut from Crane's manuscript for the Appleton edition and explains the reasons for the cuts. He then offers a critical analysis of the manuscript version of the final chapter and a new reading of the story.

B54. BLACK, R. D. COLLISON. "Editing the Papers of W. S. Jevons." In *Editing Modern Economists*, edited by D. E. Moggridge, 19–42.

audience; economics; Jevons, William Stanley; letters; oral materials; search; selection

After discussing editorial problems peculiar to the writings of economists, Black describes the search for and selection of materials, as well as the editing of lectures transcribed by listeners. He closes with a brief discussion of publication and finance.

B55. BLACKWELL, KENNETH. " 'Perhaps you will think me fussy. . .': Three Myths in Editing Russell's *Collected Papers.*" In *Editing Polymaths: Erasmus to Russell,* edited by H. J. Jackson, 99–142.

accidentals; annotation; copy-text; philosophy; Russell, Bertrand; selection

The three myths are that (1) "only Russell's major writings are worth preservation and study"; (2) his works require little textual work; and (3) the choice of copy-text is obvious. Blackwell refutes the myths and discusses choice of copy-text, selection, annotation, and treatment of accidentals.

B56. BLAND, LARRY I. "The Editor and Word Processing Equipment." *Newsletter of the Association for Documentary Editing* 2 (May 1980): 4–5.

computers

Bland describes the role of word processing in editing.

B57. BLAND, LARRY I. *Publishing The Papers of George Catlett Marshall.* Lexington, Va.: George C. Marshall Research Foundation, 1985.

handbook; Marshall, George C.; publishing

This 84-page booklet provides selected correspondence between the director of the project and the publisher of the first volume, along with the project's *Editorial and Technical Manual*, which covers selection, format, annotation, and typesetting.

B58. BLEGEN, THEODORE C. "Our Widening Province." *Mississippi Valley Historical Review* 31 (1944): 3–20.

archives; finding aids; history of editing; Mississippi Valley Historical Association

Blegen discusses the history and role of the Mississippi Valley Historical Association. He calls for an inventory of archives and manuscript collections and a program of documentary publication.

B59. BLISSETT, WILLIAM, ED. *Editing Illustrated Books: Papers Given at the Fifteenth Annual Conference on Editorial Problems, University of Toronto, 2–3 November 1979.* New York: Garland, 1980.

illustrations

See articles by Bentley, G. E., Jr. ("The Great Illustrated-Book Publishers"); Eleen, Luba; Garry, Charlene; Knox, George; and Lange, Thomas V.

B60. BOEHM, ERIC H. "Current Emphases in the Dissemination of Information about Manuscripts." In *The Publication of American Historical Manuscripts*, edited by Leslie W. Dunlap and Fred Shelley, 57–68.

computers; finding aids; form of publication; microforms

A discussion of form of publication, the use of computers, and the need for a national catalogue of archival material.

B61. BOEWE, CHARLES. "Editing Rafinesque Holographs: The Case of the Short Letters." *Filson Club History Quarterly* 54 (1980): 37–49.

history of science; letters; Rafinesque, Constantine; transcription

Boewe discusses the importance of the papers of Rafinesque, a nineteenth-century botanist, to the history of science. He describes the difficulties created by Rafinesque's spelling and punctuation. The article also includes a list of letters printed in 1938.

B62. BORN, LESTER K. "The National Union Catalog of Manuscript Collections: Progress." *American Archivist* 23 (1960): 311–14.

NUCMC

Born updates the progress report begun by Robert H. Land, "The National Union Catalog of Manuscript Collections," 1954.

B63. BOWERS, FREDSON. "Current Theories of the Copy-text with an Illustration from Dryden." *Modern Philology* 68 (1950): 12–20. Reprinted in his *Essays in Bibliography, Text, and Editing,* 277–88.

copy-text

A comparison of the theories of McKerrow and Greg.

B64. BOWERS, FREDSON. "The Ecology of American Literary Texts." *Scholarly Publishing* 4 (1972–73): 133–40.

CEAA

Bowers illustrates the critical problems created by corrupt texts and explains the importance of the CEAA editions.

B65. BOWERS, FREDSON. "Editing a Philosopher: The Works of William James." *Analytical & Enumerative Bibliography* 4 (1980): 3–36.

apparatus; audience; history of editing; James, William; philosophy

Bowers argues for the importance of applying critical editorial principles and methods to the work of philosophers and explains what such work can be expected to accomplish. He also explains the rationale and value of the William James edition's apparatus.

B66. BOWERS, FREDSON. "The Editor and the Question of Value: Another View." *Text* 1 (1984): 45–73.

types of editing

In this response to Claire Badaracco's "The Editor and the Question of Value: Proposal," Bowers discusses the difference between "diplomatic" and "critical" editing and insists as well on the distinction between literary and textual criticism.

B67. BOWERS, FREDSON. "The Education of Editors." *Newsletter of the Association for Documentary Editing* 2 (December 1980): 1–4.

professional status; training

Bowers calls for the integration of documentary editing into the university and the recognition of editors as historians.

B68. BOWERS, FREDSON. *Essays in Bibliography, Text, and Editing.* Charlottesville: University Press of Virginia, 1975.

bibliography; editing, general; textual criticism

See his "Current Theories of the Copy-text"; "Established Texts and Definitive Editions"; "Multiple Authority"; "Old Spelling Editions"; " 'Old Wine in New Bottles' "; "Practical Texts and Definitive Editions"; "Remarks on Eclectic Texts"; "Some Relations of Bibliography to Editorial Problems"; "The

Text of Johnson"; and "Textual Criticism and the Literary Critic."

B69. BOWERS, FREDSON. "Established Texts and Definitive Editions." *Philological Quarterly* 41 (1962): 1–17. Reprinted in his *Essays in Bibliography, Text, and Editing,* 359–74.

accidentals; copy-text; substantives

Bowers compares the establishment of a copy-text for manuscripts and printed books and offers a summary explanation of the theories of bibliography as they apply to printed texts.

B70. BOWERS, FREDSON. "Greg's 'Rationale of Copy-text' Revisited." *Studies in Bibliography* 31 (1978): 90–161.

accidentals; copy-text

Bowers provides an analysis of the textual conditions of the Renaissance, a discussion of parts of Greg's classic essay, and a survey of some of the problems that arise in applying Greg's principles to modern texts.

B71. BOWERS, FREDSON. "Mixed Texts and Multiple Authority." *Text* 3 (1987): 63–90.

copy-text

Bowers reviews the situations in which multiple authority may arise in both single and radiating texts.

B72. BOWERS, FREDSON. "Multiple Authority: New Problems and Concepts of Copy-Text." *The Library,* 5th ser., 27 (1972): 81–115. Reprinted in his *Essays in Bibliography, Text, and Editing,* 447–87.

copy-text; Crane, Stephen

Bowers addresses the problem of copy-text "when two extant texts are not genetically related to each other in a linear or derived manner but instead stem immediately from two independent lost documents and thus radiate in some manner from the lost archetypal manuscript."

B73. BOWERS, FREDSON. "The New Textual Criticism of Shakespeare." In his *Textual & Literary Criticism*, 67–116.

compositorial studies; handwriting; Shakespeare, William; spelling; transmission of texts

Bowers discusses various approaches to recovering and understanding the transmission of texts, including the analysis of handwriting, compositorial evidence, and substantive readings.

B74. BOWERS, FREDSON. "Notes on Editorial Apparatus." In *Historical & Editorial Studies in Medieval & Early Modern English*, edited by Mary-Jo Arn and Hanneke Wirtjes, 147–62. The Netherlands: Wolters-Noordhoff, 1985.

apparatus

Bowers describes the purpose and placement of the apparatus suitable for an unmodernized scholarly edition: a list of editorial emendations, historical collation, alterations in the manuscript, and a list of end-of-line hyphenations.

B75. BOWERS, FREDSON. "Old Spelling Editions of Dramatic Texts." In *Studies in Honor of T. W. Baldwin*, edited by Don Cameron Allen, 9–15. Urbana: University of Illinois Press, 1958. Reprinted in Bowers, *Essays in Bibliography, Text, and Editing*, 289–95.

drama; editing, general; old-spelling editions; sixteenth century

Bowers defines "critical edition," "established text," "old spelling," and "definitive edition."

B76. BOWERS, FREDSON. " 'Old Wine in New Bottles': Problems of Machine Printing." In *Editing Nineteenth-Century Texts*, edited by John M. Robson, 9–36. Reprinted in Bowers, *Essays in Bibliography, Text, and Editing*, 392–411.

Crane, Stephen; Hawthorne, Nathaniel; printing; proofreading

A discussion of the application of textual bibliographical techniques and principles to works produced by machine methods.

B77. BOWERS, FREDSON. *On Editing Shakespeare and the Elizabethan Dramatists.* Philadelphia: University of Pennsylvania Library, 1955.

bibliography; copy-text; drama; Shakespeare, William; textual criticism

Bowers reviews the nature of the dramatic texts of the Elizabethan period, the printing process, the use of bibliographical and critical approaches, and the method of producing a critical edition.

B78. BOWERS, FREDSON. "Practical Texts and Definitive Editions." In Charlton Hinman and Fredson Bowers, *Two Lectures on Editing: Shakespeare and Hawthorne*, 21–70. Columbus: Ohio State University Press, 1969. Reprinted in Bowers, *Essays in Bibliography, Text, and Editing*, 412–39.

apparatus; audience; copy-text; Hawthorne, Nathaniel; practical editions; transcription

Bowers distinguishes between the scholarly definitive edition and the practical edition, comparing the preparation of the Riverside and Centenary editions of Hawthorne as an example.

B79. BOWERS, FREDSON. "Principle and Practice in the Editing of Early Dramatic Texts." In his *Textual & Literary Criticism*, 117–50.

audience; drama; facsimiles; history of editing; old-spelling editions; seventeenth century; sixteenth century; transcription

Bowers discusses the purpose and value of a critical edition. He first differentiates between the editorial methods of the eighteenth and nineteenth centuries and those of the twentieth. He then discusses the advantages and problems of facsimile editions and complete and partial modernization. He closes by arguing for critical old-spelling editions and provides some general guidelines for such editions.

B80. BOWERS, FREDSON. "Remarks on Eclectic Texts." *Proof* 4 (1974): 31–76. Reprinted in his *Essays in Bibliography, Text, and Editing,* 488–528.

accidentals; apparatus; copy-text

Bowers defines "eclectic text," provides examples of the varieties of works that may require eclectic treatment, and concludes with a "categorizing of the main kinds of single and of multiple authority, and a brief analysis of the eclectic editorial treatment appropriate for the different categories."

B81. BOWERS, FREDSON. Review of vol. 1 of *John Locke: An Essay Concerning Human Understanding,* ed. Peter H. Nidditch. *The Library,* 5th ser., 31 (1976): 395–405.

apparatus; copy-text; Locke, John; philosophy

In this lengthy review, Bowers discusses the reaction of philosophers to the edition, the application of copy-text theory to philosophical texts, emendation, and apparatus. His most extensive comments are directed toward the complications of apparatus that result from the choice of a revised edition as copy-text.

B82. BOWERS, FREDSON. "Scholarship and Editing." *Papers of the Bibliographical Society of America* 70 (1976): 161–88.

apparatus; copy-text; editing, general; proofreading

Bowers offers three criteria for definitive editions ("a rationally principled text," "full apparatus," and "formal analysis of the documents in which the text is preserved") and discusses the appropriate standards for each. He also offers an addendum on the issuing of revised editions of definitive texts.

B83. BOWERS, FREDSON. "Some Principles for Scholarly Editions of Nineteenth-Century American Authors." *Studies in Bibliography* 17 (1964): 223–28. Reprinted in *Art and Error: Modern Textual Editing*, edited by Ronald Gottesman and Scott Bennett (Bloomington: Indiana University Press, 1970), 54–61; and in *Bibliography and Textual Criticism*, edited by O M Brack, Jr., and Warner Barnes (Chicago: University of Chicago Press, 1969), 194–201.

apparatus; copy-text; nineteenth century; transcription

In this discussion of applying Greg's theory of copy-text to American literature, Bowers argues against modernization and in favor of critical (as opposed to reprint) editions. He then outlines the procedures for establishing a text and providing an editorial apparatus.

B84. BOWERS, FREDSON. "Some Relations of Bibliography to Editorial Problems." *Studies in Bibliography* 3 (1950–51): 37–62. Reprinted in his *Studies in Bibliography, Text, and Editing*, 15–36.

bibliography; compositorial studies; textual criticism

A discussion of the relationship between analytical and textual criticism, and of the nature and uses of bibliographical evidence.

B85. BOWERS, FREDSON. "The Text of Johnson." *Modern Philology* 61 (1964): 298–309. Reprinted in his *Essays in Bibliography, Text, and Editing*, 375–91.

annotation; copy-text; Johnson, Samuel; transcription

In this review of the second volume of the Yale edition of Johnson, Bowers discusses the editors' divergent theories of copy-text, transcription, and annotation.

B86. BOWERS, FREDSON. *Textual and Literary Criticism.* Cambridge: Cambridge University Press, 1959.

textual criticism

See his "The New Textual Criticism of Shakespeare," "Principle and Practice in the Editing of Early Dramatic Texts," "Textual Criticism and the Literary Critic," and "The Walt Whitman Manuscripts of 'Leaves of Grass' (1860)."

B87. BOWERS, FREDSON. "Textual Criticism." In *The Aims and Methods of Scholarship in Modern Languages and Literatures,* edited by James Thorpe, 23–42. New York: MLA, 1963.

apparatus; copy-text; editing, general

Bowers reviews the aims of textual criticism; the varieties of editions (facsimile, critical, modernized, or old-spelling); the establishment of the text through documentary evidence and collation; and preparation of a definitive text.

B88. BOWERS, FREDSON. "Textual Criticism and the Literary Critic." In his *Textual & Literary Criticism,* 1–34. Reprinted in his *Essays in Bibliography, Text, and Editing,* 296–325.

editing, general; professional status; transmission of texts

Bowers discusses the importance to any literary critic of beginning with a reliable text and offers a summary of the sources of error, as well as the ways textual scholars recover an accurate text. He offers numerous examples from several centuries.

B89. BOWERS, FREDSON. "Transcription of Manuscripts: The Record of Variants." *Studies in Bibliography* 29 (1976): 212–64.

apparatus; transcription

Bowers proposes a system for transcribing and for recording corrections and revisions in both clear text editions and editions in which such corrections are placed within the transcribed text.

B90. BOWERS, FREDSON. "The Walt Whitman Manuscripts of 'Leaves of Grass' (1860)." In his *Textual & Literary Criticism*, 35–65.

dating; poetry; Whitman, Walt

Bowers discusses the discovery of the manuscripts of 'Leaves of Grass' and their biographical and literary significance. He describes in detail the process of dating and ordering the poems as well as the light the manuscripts shed on Whitman's process of composition and revision.

B91. BOWLING, KENNETH R. "Documentary Editing and the Bicentennial of the First Federal Congress: Will the Former Impact the Latter?" *Documentary Editing* 7 (December 1985): 7–11.

First Federal Congress project

Bowling describes the First Federal Congress project and its significance.

B92. BOWLING, KENNETH R. Review of *The Correspondence and Miscellaneous Papers of Benjamin Henry Latrobe*, vol. 1. *Journal of Southern History* 52 (1986): 295–97.

Latrobe, Benjamin Henry; microforms; transcription

Bowling praises the edition's "middle course" on transcription in view of the availability of a microfiche edition.

B93. BOWLING, KENNETH R. Review of *The Papers of James Madison*, vol. 14, and *The Papers of Thomas Jefferson*, vol. 20. *Virginia Magazine of History and Biography* 92 (1984): 108–10.

annotation; Boyd, Julian; Jefferson, Thomas; Madison, James

Bowling contrasts the Madison edition's spare annotation with the expansive annotation of the Jefferson series.

B94. BOYD, JULIAN P. " 'God's Altar Needs Not Our Pollishings.' " *New York History* 39 (1958): 3–21.

history of editing

The editor of the Thomas Jefferson papers discusses the history of historical editing in the United States, beginning with colonial ministers. Boyd also describes the cooperation among modern historical editors and calls for support of documentary projects.

B95. BOYD, JULIAN P. "Historical Editing in the United States: The Next Stage?" *Proceedings of the American Antiquarian Society* 72 (1962): 309–28.

NHPC; professional status

This article discusses the future of scholarly editing. Boyd describes the role of the NHPC and its plans. He also discusses the problems within the historical profession regarding the status of documentary editors.

B96. BOYD, JULIAN P. "A Modest Proposal to Meet an Urgent Need." *American Historical Review* 70 (1965): 329–49.

Adams, Herbert Baxter; Jameson, J. Franklin

Boyd relates the history of U.S. history. The modest proposal of the title is a call for a national center to support the study of history.

B97. BOYD, JULIAN P. "Some Animadversions on Being Struck by Lightning." *Daedalus* 86 (1955): 49–56.

editing, general; history of editing

Boyd contrasts the work of modern editors with that of their predecessors. He also addresses the question of the jurisdiction of historical editors.

B98. BOYD, JULIAN P. "A Zeal at His Heart." In *Butterfield in Holland: A Record of L. H. Butterfield's Pursuit of the Adamses Abroad in 1959,* 1–14. Cambridge, Mass.: privately printed, 1961.

Butterfield, Lyman H.

A note on Butterfield's life and personality.

B99. BOYD, STEVEN R. "Form of Publication: A Key to the Widespread Availability of Documents." *AHA Newsletter* 10 (1972): 24–27.

form of publication; letterpress; microfilm

Boyd discusses the expense and time involved in preparing a letterpress edition, suggests that microfilm editions could make the works of the common person more accessible, and urges expanded NHPRC support of microfilm projects.

B100. BOYDSTON, JO ANN. "A Critical Chronicle." *Documentary Editing* 10 (September 1988): 16–17.

editing, general; history of editing

A review of G. Thomas Tanselle's *Textual Criticism Since Greg: A Chronicle, 1950–1985.*

B101. BOYDSTON, JO ANN. "Editing the Library of America." *Scholarly Publishing* 16 (1984–85): 121–32.

Library of America; proofreading; selection

An expanded version of Boydston's "The Library of America."

BI02. BOYDSTON, JO ANN. "Editing the Poems of John Dewey." *Documentary Editing* 7 (March 1985): 1–6.

authentication; Dewey, John; poetry; search

Boydston discusses the search for John Dewey documents and the problems involved in the collection. She explains how the authorship of the poems was confirmed and the editorial procedures used in the edition.

BI03. BOYDSTON, JO ANN. "The Language of Scholarly Editing." *Documentary Editing* 7 (December 1985): 1–6.

professional status; types of editing

A plea for unity, common definitions of terms among editors in all disciplines, and the development of professional standards.

BI04. BOYDSTON, JO ANN. "The Library of America." *Newsletter of the Association for Documentary Editing* 4 (December 1982): 1–5. An expanded version of this article appears as "Editing the Library of America" in *Scholarly Publishing.*

Library of America; proofreading; selection

Boydston's article begins with a discussion of the long-term movement that led to the creation of the Library of America. The Library's editorial policy and selection and proofreading procedures are explained.

BI05. BOYDSTON, JO ANN. "The Press and the Project: A Study in Cooperation." *Scholarly Publishing* 15 (1983–84): 301–12.

Dewey, John; funding; publishing

Boydston describes the cooperation between the Dewey project and the Southern Illinois University Press that facilitated
the work of the project.

B106. BOYLE, LEONARD E., O. P. " 'Epistulae Venerant Parum Dulces':
The Place of Codicology in the Editing of Medieval Latin
Texts." In *Editing and Editors: A Retrospect*, edited by Richard
Landon, 29–46.

codicology; Latin; Middle Ages

Boyle explains the importance of examining the codex itself,
taking into account its physical setting, when establishing and
editing medieval texts.

B107. BRACK, O M, JR. "The Centenary Hawthorne Eight Years
Later: A Review Article." *Proof* 1 (1971): 358–67.

accidentals; copy-text; Hawthorne, Nathaniel; practical editions

Brack reviews the first five volumes of *The Centenary Edition*,
tracing the modification of textual practices. He also notes the
failure of reprint publishers to use the Centenary texts.

B108. BRACK, O M, JR. "Introduction." In *Bibliography and Textual
Criticism*, edited by O M Brack, Jr., and Warner Barnes, 3–22.
Chicago: University of Chicago Press, 1969.

history of editing

A brief review of the history of bibliographical and textual
editing methods, and of some of the key works in the field.

B109. BRACK, O M, JR. "The Ledgers of William Strahan." In *Editing
Eighteenth-Century Texts*, edited by D. I. B. Smith, 59–77.

ledgers; Strahan, William

Brack describes the contents and organization of Strahan's ledgers, the problems in preparing the edition, and its potential usefulness.

B110. BRACK, O M, JR. " 'Of making many books there is no end': Editing Smollett." In *Editing Eighteenth-Century Novels*, edited by G. E. Bentley, Jr., 91–115.

collation; copy-text; Smollett, Tobias

A discussion of the bibliographical research and collation involved in establishing the copy-texts for an edition of Smollett.

B111. BRADFORD, JAMES C. "New Naval Project Launched." *Documentary Editing* 9 (March 1987): 9–11.

history of editing; naval history; selection

In this review of *The Naval War of 1812: A Documentary History*, Bradford reviews the history of Navy Department documentary publications and compares the volume in question with other projects.

B112. BRADFORD, JAMES C. "The Papers of John Paul Jones." In *Editing Naval Documents: An Historical Appreciation*, 27–41.

authentication; Jones, John Paul; letters; naval history; search; selection; translation

Bradford explains the search, selection, and translation of Jones documents, and describes the numerous forgeries of Jones letters that the project had to deal with.

B113. BRASWELL, LAUREL NICHOLS. *Western Manuscripts from Classical Antiquity to the Renaissance: A Handbook*, 329–58.

bibliographies

Although this bibliography is devoted in the main to paleography and bibliography, the last section covers textual criticism. It lists many works on classical and medieval manuscripts that are not included in the present volume, as well as material not written in English.

B114. BRAUNMULLER, A. R. "Editing Elizabethan Letters." *Text* 1 (1984): 185–99.

letters; seventeenth century; sixteenth century

Braunmuller focuses on "letter-books," collections of letters sent (and sometimes those received), belonging to diplomats or other officials and to civilians.

B115. BRAY, ROBERT C. "Tom Sawyer Once and for All." *Review* 3 (1981): 75–93.

annotation; apparatus; CEAA; copy-text; Twain, Mark

In this review of volume 4 of *The Works of Mark Twain*, edited by Paul Baender, Terry Firkins, and John C. Gerber, Bray criticizes excessive annotation and apparatus but praises the editors' establishment of the text.

B116. BROEKER, GALEN. "Jared Sparks, Robert Peel and the State Papers Office." *American Quarterly* 13 (1961): 140–52.

access; England; Peel, Robert; Sparks, Jared

An account of Sparks's difficulties in using papers in the British State Papers Office.

B117. BROOKE, CHRISTOPHER N. L. "The Teaching of Diplomatic." *Journal of the Society of Archivists* 4, 1 (1970): 1–9.

authentication; Middle Ages; training

Brooke discusses the need for all historians, including undergraduate students, to be taught diplomatic—the study of documents which includes their authentication and understanding the workings of the bureaucracy that generated them.

B118. BROOKE, JOHN. "The Prime Ministers' Papers." *Journal of the Society of Archivists* 3 (April 1969): 467–69.

calendaring; Great Britain; selection

Brooke explains the selection decisions of the Royal Commission on Historical Manuscripts in publishing the papers of nineteenth-century prime ministers. He discusses the objections to calendaring and to complete publication.

B119. BROWN, ARTHUR. "Editorial Problems in Shakespeare." *Studies in Bibliography* 8 (1956): 15–26.

practical editions; Shakespeare, William

A discussion of the "problems confronting the editor of a semi-popular edition of Shakespeare," including choice of copy-text, modernization of spelling and punctuation, act and scene divisions, collation, and annotation.

B120. BROWN, ARTHUR. "The Rationale of Old-Spelling Editions of the Plays of Shakespeare and His Contemporaries: A Rejoinder." *Studies in Bibliography* 13 (1960): 69–76.

facsimiles; old-spelling editions

Brown discusses problems in using photographic facsimiles and responds to the criticism of old-spelling editions expressed in John Russell Brown's "The Rationale of Old-Spelling Editions."

B121. BROWN, HOWARD M. " 'Lord, have mercy upon us': Early Sixteenth-Century Scribal Practice and the Polyphonic Kyrie." *Text* 2 (1985): 93–110.

music; sixteenth century

Brown considers the relationship of text to music, specifically the issue of text underlay: "which phrases of text were meant to be sung to which phrases of music." He discusses the practices of the scribes who wrote out the settings of the mass.

B122. BROWN, JOHN RUSSELL. "The Rationale of Old-Spelling Editions of the Plays of Shakespeare and His Contemporaries." *Studies in Bibliography* 13 (1960): 49–67.

facsimiles; old-spelling editions; punctuation; Shakespeare, William; transcription

Brown differentiates between type facsimiles and old-spelling critical editions. He discusses the advantages of photographic facsimiles over both forms and argues for the readability of critically modernized spelling. See also Arthur Brown's response, immediately following in the same issue.

B123. BROWN, RALPH ADAMS. Review of *The Adams Papers*, ser. 3, *Papers of John Adams*, vols. 1 and 2. *Pennsylvania Magazine of History and Biography* 102 (1978): 244–46.

Adams papers; search

Brown discusses the collection and editorial methodology of the Adams papers project.

B124. BROWNE, HENRY J. "A New Historical Project: Editing the Papers of Archbishop John Carroll." *American Ecclesiastical Review* 127 (1952): 341–50.

annotation; Carroll, John; history of religion; transcription

A discussion of the history of the project, with a sample edited document and its annotations.

B125. BRUBAKER, ROBERT L. "The Publication of Historical Sources: Recent Projects in the United States." *Library Quarterly* 37 (1967): 193–225.

history of editing; NHPC

Brubaker analyzes the role of the National Historical Publications Commission, its programs, achievements, and future.

B126. BRUCCOLI, MATTHEW J. "A Few Missing Words." *PMLA* 86 (1971): 587–89.

CEAA

A brief description of the founding and purpose of the CEAA.

B127. BRUCCOLI, MATTHEW J. " 'A Might Collation': Animadversions on the Text of F. Scott Fitzgerald." In *Editing Twentieth-Century Texts*, edited by Francess G. Halpenny, 28–50.

collation; copyright; Fitzgerald, F. Scott

Bruccoli discusses the errors in existing editions of Fitzgerald and includes a collation of some Fitzgerald editions. He also discusses the problem of publishing new editions of works protected by copyright.

B128. BRUNER, KATHARINE FROST. "On Editing a Series of Letters." *Scholarly Publishing* 9 (1977): 41–53.

annotation; Hart, Sir Robert; letters

The editor of the letters of Sir Robert Hart describes her work. The article includes discussions of the preparation of the edition and editorial procedures, emphasizing annotation.

B129. BRUNS, ROGER A. "The NHPRC—In Search of the Fountain of Funding." *Documentary Editing* 10 (December 1988): 11–14.

funding; NHPRC

Bruns discusses the prospects of finding private funding for documentary editing projects and offers suggestions for approaching government agencies, private foundations, and corporations.

B130. BULLION, JOHN L. Review of *The Adams Papers*, ser. 3, *Papers of John Adams*, vols. 5 and 6. *Pennsylvania Magazine of History and Biography* 108 (1984): 237–39.

Adams papers; selection

Bullion comments on the problems of selection, noting that the editors' concerns included repetition of documents published elsewhere and whether the document "was merely a matter of official routine, or was simply representative of a general type, without any intrinsic interest or importance of its own."

B131. BURG, B. RICHARD. "The Autograph Trade and Documentary Editing." *Manuscripts* (1970): 247–54.

access; autograph collectors

Burg describes the history of autograph collecting. He also addresses the issue of editors' access to private collections.

B132. BURKE, FRANK G. "Automation and Documentary Editing." *British Journal for the History of Science* 20 (January 1987): 73–79.

computers

Burke reports the results of a 1983 survey on the use of computer technology by documentary editing projects. He discusses advantages and disadvantages of electronic manuscripts and notes the results of increased computer use.

B133. BURKE, FRANK G. "The Historian as Editor: Progress and Problems." *The Public Historian* 4 (Spring 1982): 5–19.

funding; history of editing; NHPRC; training

A discussion of the recent history, problems, and prospects of the profession.

B134. BURKE, FRANK G. "Rebuttal to 'Great Documents Deluge.'"
*Newsletter of the Society for Historians of American Foreign
Relations,* June 1976, pp. 11–14.

funding; professional status

In this response to Thomas H. Etzold's "The Great Documents
Deluge," Burke discusses the economics of documentary editing and scholarly publishing. See also Joseph Siracusa, "Reply."

B135. BURKETT, RANDALL K. "Historical Editing and Researching Local History in an Undergraduate Black Studies Seminar."
Teaching History: A Journal of Methods 3 (1978): 9–13.

black history; history of religion; training

Burkett describes and evaluates the use of a documentary editing project to teach black history.

B136. BURKHARDT, FREDERICK. "Editing the Correspondence of
Charles Darwin." *Studies in Bibliography* 41 (1988): 149–59.

Darwin, Charles; letters

Burkhardt describes the types of documents used in the project, the practices adopted in selecting and transcribing the documents, and problems encountered.

B137. BURKHARDT, FREDERICK. "In Response." *Documentary Editing*
10 (September 1988): 22–24.

Darwin, Charles

A response to Nathan Reingold, "The Darwin Industry Encounters Tanselle and Bowers."

B138. BURKHARDT, FREDERICK. Letter to the Editor. *Times Literary
Supplement,* 5 August 1977, p. 962.

philosophy; types of editing

A response to John Passmore's "A Philosopher of the Particulars."

B139. BURNETTE, O. LAWRENCE, JR. "Preservation and Dissemination of Historical Evidence." In his *Beneath the Footnote: A Guide to the Use and Preservation of American Historical Sources*, 340–78. Madison: State Historical Society of Wisconsin, 1969.

editing, general; history of editing; preservation

Burnette discusses the editorial processes connected with documentary editing, the history of documentary editing, and the forms and methods of documentary reproduction. He also describes the care and preservation of original documents.

B140. BURNHAM, JOHN C. Letter to the Editor. *American Historical Review* 85 (1980): 273–74.

annotation; indexing

A response to Saul Benison's letter, ibid., 272–73.

B141. BURNHAM, JOHN C. Review of *The Papers of Joseph Henry*, vol. 2. *American Historical Review* 84 (1979): 547–48.

annotation; Henry, Joseph

Burnham criticizes the volume for excessive, antiquarian annotation. See also Saul Benison's letter to the editor (1980) and Burnham's response.

B142. BURNS, J. H. "The Bentham Project." In *Editing Texts of the Romantic Period*, edited by John D. Baird, 73–87.

Bentham, Jeremy; copy-text

Burns enumerates the difficulties of editing Bentham, with detailed examples.

B143. BUTT, JOHN. "Editing a Nineteenth-Century Novelist (Proposals for an Edition of Dickens)." *English Studies Today*, 2d ser. (1961): 187–95. Reprinted in *Art and Error: Modern Textual Editing*, edited by Ronald Gottesman and Scott Bennett (Bloomington: Indiana University Press, 1970), 155–66.

apparatus; copy-text; Dickens, Charles; illustrations

Butt describes Dickens's proofreading and revising habits and their implications for the editor; makes a case for including Dickens's working notes, illustrations, and cover-designs; and suggests necessary editorial apparatus.

B144. BUTTERFIELD, LYMAN H. "The Adams Papers." *Daedalus* 86 (1955): 62–71.

Adams papers; search; selection

Butterfield discusses the collection of the Adams papers and the need for selectivity.

B145. BUTTERFIELD, LYMAN H. "The Adams Papers: 'Whatever you write preserve.' " *American Heritage* 10 (April 1959): 26–33; 88–93.

Adams papers

A short version of Butterfield's longer article, "The Papers of the Adams Family."

B146. BUTTERFIELD, LYMAN H. "Archival and Editorial Enterprise in 1850 and 1950: Some Comparisons and Contrasts." *Proceedings of the American Philosophical Society* 98 (1954): 159–70.

control; funding; history of editing; search; transcription

Butterfield's comparison of the profession in 1850 and 1950 focuses on collection and control, editorial practice, and sources of financial support.

B147. BUTTERFIELD, LYMAN H. "Bostonians and Their Neighbors as Pack Rats." *American Archivist* 24 (1961): 141–59.

history of editing; Massachusetts

Butterfield discusses the collection and publication of documents and personal papers in Massachusetts, beginning in the eighteenth century. He also discusses the lack of state, as opposed to private, programs for collecting, preserving, and storing records.

B148. BUTTERFIELD, LYMAN H. "Butterfield in Holland." In *Butterfield in Holland: A Record of L. H. Butterfield's Pursuit of the Adamses Abroad in 1959*, 15–36. Cambridge, Mass.: privately printed, 1961.

Adams papers; search

Butterfield's diary and letters during his 1959 European travels in search of Adams papers.

B149. BUTTERFIELD, LYMAN H. "Editing American Historical Documents." *Proceedings of the Massachusetts Historical Society* 78 (1966): 81–104.

history of editing

In describing the history of documentary editing, Butterfield emphasizes the search for comprehensiveness and care in collection, authentication, transcription, and annotation.

B150. BUTTERFIELD, LYMAN H. "Historical Editing in the United States: The Recent Past." *Proceedings of the American Antiquarian Society* 72 (1962): 283–308.

history of editing

Butterfield discusses the history of documentary editing from J. Franklin Jameson to Julian P. Boyd.

BI51. BUTTERFIELD, LYMAN H. "The Papers of the Adams Family: Some Account of Their History." *Proceedings of the Massachusetts Historical Society* 71 (1953–57): 328–56.

Adams papers

Butterfield describes the history of the Adams papers, including the work of Charles Francis Adams, Worthington Chauncey Ford, and Samuel Flagg Bemis.

BI52. BUTTERFIELD, LYMAN H. "The Papers of Thomas Jefferson: Progress and Procedures in the Enterprise at Princeton." *American Archivist* 12 (1949): 131–45.

annotation; apparatus; control; indexing; Jefferson, Thomas; search

Butterfield describes the history of Boyd's Jefferson edition, the search for Jefferson documents, and how those documents were processed. He also describes Boyd's plans for annotation and editorial apparatus.

BI53. BUTTERFIELD, LYMAN H. "The Scholar's One World." *American Archivist* 29 (1966): 343–61.

archives; history of editing; microfilm

Butterfield discusses archival administration, relations between archivists and historians, and the importance of various microfilm editions.

BI54. BUTTERFIELD, LYMAN H. "The Tenth Anniversary of the Gift of the Adams Papers." *Proceedings of the Massachusetts Historical Society* 78 (1966): 159–63.

Adams papers

The editor of the Adams papers describes how the Massachusetts Historical Society acquired the papers and reports on the project's progress.

B155. BUTTERFIELD, LYMAN H. " 'Vita sine literis, mors est': The Microfilm Edition of the Adams Papers." *Library of Congress Quarterly Journal of Current Acquisitions* 18 (1961): 53–58.

Adams papers; microfilm

The editor of the Adams papers describes the microfilm edition of the papers. He discusses their history, lists some relevant statistics, and describes the content of the papers.

B156. BUTTERFIELD, LYMAN H. "Worthington Chauncey Ford, Editor." *Proceedings of the Massachusetts Historical Society* 83 (1971): 46–82.

Ford, Worthington Chauncey

Butterfield describes and evaluates the life and career of Worthington Chauncey Ford.

C

C1. CALDWELL, JOHN. *Editing Early Music.* Oxford: Clarendon Press, 1985.

annotation; apparatus; copy-text; emendation; music; transcription

Caldwell discusses transcribing and editing medieval, Renaissance, baroque, and classical music. Topics include choice of copy-text, emendation, and annotation (for sources and methods of performance), layout, and apparatus for indicating variants.

C2. CALLCOTT, GEORGE H. "Antiquarianism and Documents in the Age of Literary History." *American Archivist* 21 (1958): 17–29.

history of editing

Callcott contrasts the popularity of documentary history in colonial times and the early nineteenth century with its lack of popularity today. He lists some reasons for this change, focusing on the attitudes of Americans in the earlier periods.

C3. CALLCOTT, GEORGE H. "The Sacred Quotation Mark." *The Historian* 21 (1959): 409–20.

history of editing

Callcott discusses criticism of earlier scholars for altering quotations and for plagiarism.

C4. CAMPION, EDMUND J. "Practical Solutions to the Problems Involved in Editing Seventeenth-Century French Plays." *Text* 2 (1985): 187–96.

drama; French; seventeenth century

Campion offers solutions to four problems facing editors of seventeenth-century plays: the lack of accepted standards; the difficulty of determining how many editions must be collated, locating them, and choosing a base text; the problems of annotation; and the lack of interest among publishers.

C5. CAPPON, LESTER J. "American Historical Editors before Jared Sparks: 'they will plant a forest. . . .'" *William and Mary Quarterly* 30 (1973): 375–400.

history of editing

This article discusses historical editors before Jared Sparks, including Ebenezer Hazard, William Hening, Hezekiah Niles, and James Savage. Cappon also notes the role of learned societies in promoting documentary editing.

C6. CAPPON, LESTER J. "The Historian as Editor." In *In Support of Clio: Essays in Memory of Herbert A. Kellar*, edited by

William B. Hesseltine and Donald R. McNeil, 173–93. Madison: State Historical Society of Wisconsin, 1958.

editing, general; history of editing; professional status; training

A general essay on the gifts, skills, and instincts required of historical editors, as well as the tasks and responsibilities they face. Cappon includes book and magazine editors in his discussion.

c7. CAPPON, LESTER J. " 'The Historian's Day'—From Archives to History." In *The Reinterpretation of Early American History: Essays in Honor of John Elwin Pomfret,* edited by Ray Allen Billington, 233–51. San Marino, Calif.: Huntington Library, 1966.

archives; editing, general; finding aids; local records; microfilm

A review of sources for early U.S. history and media for publication.

c8. CAPPON, LESTER J. "Jared Sparks: The Preparation of an Editor." *Proceedings of the Massachusetts Historical Society* 90 (1978): 3–21.

history of editing; Sparks, Jared

Cappon relates Sparks's early career as a writer and literary editor to his later work as a documentary editor.

c9. CAPPON, LESTER J. "A New Generation of Editors." *Newsletter of the Association for Documentary Editing* 1 (March 1979): 3–4.

archives; history of editing; professional status

Cappon provides a short history of the recent past of historical editing and the training of archivists. He also discusses the role of editors within the historical profession.

C10. CAPPON, LESTER J. "A Rationale for Historical Editing Past and Present." *William and Mary Quarterly* 23 (1966): 56–75.

editing, general; history of editing; training

Cappon discusses the responsibilities and functions of historical editors and the history of documentary editing. He calls for editorial creativity and interpretation.

C11. CAPPON, LESTER J. "Reference Works and Historical Texts." *Library Trends* 5 (1957): 369–79.

archives; finding aids; microfilm

Cappon explains the need for finding aids and describes manuscript projects under way.

C12. CAPPON, LESTER J. "Tardy Scholars Among the Archivists." *American Archivist* 21 (1958): 3–16.

archives; computers; National Archives; NHPC; state records

Cappon describes archivists as historical scholars and reviews the history of archival publications. The importance of selection and familiarity with documents is discussed, as are the impact of the new technology, the National Archives, and the NHPC. The article concludes with a discussion of state records and the role of the Society of American Archivists.

C13. CARLSON, LARRY A. " 'The Gift of Tongues': Elizabeth Palmer Peabody's Letters and the Life of New England." *Documentary Editing* 10 (March 1988): 6–10.

annotation; indexing; Peabody, Elizabeth Palmer; selection

Carlson praises *Letters of Elizabeth Palmer Peabody: American Renaissance Woman*, but questions the editor's selection criteria and annotation policy and criticizes the index.

C14. CARPENTER, WILLIAM N. "Editing Naval Documents." *Documentary Editing* 8 (March 1986): 12–15.

naval history

Carpenter's review of *Editing Naval Documents: An Historical Appreciation* summarizes the volume.

C15. CARROLL, JOHN. "On Annotating *Clarissa*." In *Editing Eighteenth-Century Novels*, edited by G. E. Bentley, Jr., 49–66.

annotation; novels; Richardson, Samuel

A discussion of the annotation of quotations and allusions in Samuel Richardson's *Clarissa*.

C16. CARTER, CLARENCE E. *Historical Editing*. Bulletins of the National Archives, no. 7. Washington, D.C.: Government Printing Office, 1952.

editing, general; handbook; microfilm

In this 51-page booklet, Carter discusses all phases of historical editing from the search for documents to the preparation of indexes. He supplements his discussion with examples from his own work and the work of other editors. He also includes a section on preparing microfilm editions and a description of how to prepare manuscripts for typesetting and printing.

C17. CARTER, CLARENCE E. "The Territorial Papers of the United States." *American Archivist* 8 (1945): 122–35.

selection; Territorial Papers

Carter recounts the history of the Territorial Papers project and describes selection procedures and editorial policies.

C18. CARTER, CLARENCE E. "The Territorial Papers of the United States: A Review and a Commentary." *Mississippi Valley Historical Review* 42 (1955): 510–24.

history of editing; Territorial Papers; transcription

Carter describes the history of the Territorial Papers project, its editorial procedures, and its future.

C19. CARTER, CLARENCE E. "The United States and Documentary Historical Publication." *Mississippi Valley Historical Review* 25 (1938): 3–24.

history of editing; NHPC

Carter discusses the role of the federal government in supporting documentary editing from Ebenezer Hazard forward and urges the historical profession to support the work of the NHPC.

C20. CARTER, EDWARD C., II. "The Papers of Benjamin Henry Latrobe and the Maryland Historical Society, 1885–1971: Nature, Structure and Means of Acquisition." *Maryland Historical Magazine* 66 (1971): 436–55.

Latrobe, Benjamin Henry; search; visual material

Carter describes the history, procedures, and schedule of the project, emphasizing the collection process and the presentation of graphic material.

C21. CASTELLANI, ARRIGO. "Transcription Errors." In *Medieval Manuscripts and Textual Criticism*, edited by Christopher Kleinhenz, 167–73. Originally published as "Indagine sugli errori di trascrizione," in *Studi e problemi di critica testuale*, edited by Raffaele Spongano (Bologna: Commissione per i Testi di Lingua, 1961), 35–40.

transcription

Castellani discusses ways of avoiding or correcting errors in transcription.

C22. CENTER FOR EDITIONS OF AMERICAN AUTHORS. *Statement of Editorial Principles and Procedures: A Working Manual for Editing Nineteenth-Century Texts*, rev. ed. New York: MLA, 1972.

bibliographies; handbook; nineteenth century

The CEAA statement of principles covers in 25 pages questions of copy-text, collation, emendation, apparatus, annotation, and production, along with CEAA procedures. A bibliographical note includes some articles on bibliography and collation not included in the present bibliography.

C23. CENTER FOR SCHOLARLY EDITIONS. *The Center for Scholarly Editions: An Introductory Statement.* New York: MLA, 1977; *PMLA* 92 (1977): 583–97.

bibliographies; CEAA; CSE

An account of the history and purpose of the CSE, a general statement of editorial standards, and a bibliography.

C24. CHESNUTT, DAVID R. "Comprehensive Text Processing and the Papers of Henry Laurens." *Newsletter of the Association for Documentary Editing* 2 (May 1980): 12–14.

computers; Laurens, Henry

Chesnutt describes the use of computers in his project.

C25. CHESNUTT, DAVID R. "Comprehensive Text Processing and the Papers of Henry Laurens, part 2." *Newsletter of the Association for Documentary Editing* 2 (September 1980): 3–5.

computers; indexing; Laurens, Henry

Chesnutt discusses the coding scheme for his project and the indexing procedures used.

c26. CHESNUTT, DAVID R. "Optical Scanning and CINDEX: Tools for Creating a Cumulative Index to the Laurens Papers." *Newsletter of the Association for Documentary Editing* 5 (May 1983): 8–11.

computers; indexing; Laurens, Henry

Chesnutt describes CINDEX, a computer-assisted indexing program, and discusses how the program was used on the Laurens project.

c27. CHOUEKA, YAOCOV. "Computerized Full-Text Retrieval Systems and Research in the Humanities: The Responsa Project." *Computers and the Humanities* 14 (November 1980): 153–69.

computers

The Responsa project involved a full-text retrieval system. Choueka describes the database, testing of the system, and other details.

c28. CLANIN, DOUGLAS E. "A Phoenix Rising from the Ashes: The William Henry Harrison Papers Project." *Documentary Editing* 10 (June 1988): 6–10.

Harrison, William Henry; microfilm; search

Although many of Harrison's papers were destroyed in a fire in 1858, the project was able to reconstruct the documentary record. The article describes in detail the search for documents and explains the decision to publish a microfilm edition of transcripts with sparse notes and a full index.

c29. CLAUSSEN, MARTIN P. "Revisiting America's State Papers, 1789–1861: A Clinical Examination and Prognosis." *American Archivist* 36 (1973): 523–36.

American State Papers; microforms

In this review essay on the New American State Papers, Claussen describes the history of the publication of the ASP and criticizes the New ASP as "a shoddy but costly government-reprint potboiler, archivally myopic, bibliographically redundant, quantitatively subfractional, editorially substandard, misleadingly huckstered and impertinently copyrighted."

c30. Coburn, Kathleen. "Editing the Coleridge Notebooks." In *Editing Texts of the Romantic Period*, edited by John D. Baird, 7–25.

annotation; Coleridge, Samuel Taylor; dating; notebooks; transcription

A discussion of editorial problems raised in editing Coleridge's notebooks, with the solutions adopted.

c31. Cohen, I. Bernard. "The Thrice-Revealed Newton." In *Editing Texts in the History of Science and Medicine*, edited by Trevor H. Levere, 117–84.

editing, general; history of science; Newton, Isaac

Cohen discusses Newton's own selection of his work to be published, the changes in our understanding wrought by the nineteenth-century publication of a biography and new texts, and the results of the sale of Newton's manuscripts in 1936, including the growth of interest and scholarship since the 1950s. He then describes the existing Newton manuscripts and the problems of editing them.

c32. "Committee on Scholarly Editions: Aims and Policies." *PMLA* 100 (1985): 444–47.

CSE

An explanation of the purpose and functions of the Committee on Scholarly Editions, and a general statement of its editorial standards.

C33. CONDON, M. M., AND ELIZABETH M. HALLAM. "Government Printing of the Public Records in the Eighteenth Century." *Journal of the Society of Archivists* 7 (October 1984): 348–88.

eighteenth century; England; public records

The authors outline the history of the editing and publication of the Foedera, Rotuli Parliamentorum, and Domesday Book.

C34. COOK, DON L. "Bowers Does Fielding." *Review* 1 (1979): 13–27.

accidentals; annotation; Fielding, Henry; proofreading

In this review of several Fielding volumes issued by the Oxford and Wesleyan University Presses, Cook praises the edition but criticizes flaws resulting from carelessness and regularization of accidentals.

C35. COOK, DON L. "Practical Editions: The Writings of William Dean Howells." *Proof* 2 (1972): 293–300.

Howells, William Dean; practical editions

Cook reviews the availability and quality of Howells's works.

C36. COOK, DON L. "Precise Editing in a Book Club Format." *Documentary Editing* 10 (September 1988): 6–10.

annotation; Norris, Frank

Cook reviews *Frank Norris: Collected Letters*, compiled and edited by Jesse S. Crisler. He describes the dearth of Norris letters and reviews their discovery and printing. He praises the edition's transcription but is critical of the absence of both a statement of editorial practices and an index.

C37. COOK, DON L. "The Short Happy Thesis of G. Thomas Tanselle." *Newsletter of the Association for Documentary Editing* 3 (February 1981): 1–4.

editing, general; types of editing

Cook draws six propositions from G. Thomas Tanselle's "The Editing of Historical Documents." His discussion focuses on points of agreement between Tanselle and historical editors.

c38. COOK, DON L. "Textual Ignorance as a Threat to Scholarship." *Documentary Editing* 9 (March 1987): 5–8.

authorial intention; types of editing

In this review of Hershel Parker's *Flawed Texts and Verbal Icons*, Cook comments on Parker's ideas about completeness of information and the place of authorial intention. He also discusses the role of theory in editing.

c39. CORRIGAN, BEATRICE. "Italian Renaissance Plays: Problems and Opportunities." In *Editing Renaissance Dramatic Texts*, edited by Anne Lancashire, 57–68.

annotation; copy-text; drama; history of editing; Italian; Renaissance; transcription

A discussion of a range of editorial problems—establishing a text, transcribing and annotating it—as they occur in Italian Renaissance drama.

c40. COX, HENRY BARTHOLOMEW. "Private Letters and the Public Domain." *American Archivist* 28 (1965): 381–88.

copyright; letters

Cox reviews the copyright status of unpublished letters under the pre-1976 copyright law and recommends limitations on the duration of copyright for unpublished materials.

c41. COX, HENRY BARTHOLOMEW. "Publication of Manuscripts: Devaluation or Enhancement?" *American Archivist* 32 (1969): 25–32.

autograph collectors; manuscripts

Cox discusses the debate over what happens to the value of a manuscript after it is published, based on interviews with lawyers, historians, editors, dealers, librarians, collectors, and curators.

C42. Cox, LaWanda. "From Great White Men to Blacks Emerging from Bondage, with Innovations in Documentary Editing." *Reviews in American History* 12 (1984): 31–39.

black history; editing, general; *Freedom*

In this review of *Freedom: A Documentary History of Emancipation, 1861–1876,* Cox raises the question of differentiating between documentary collections and documentary histories. The volume under review is highly selective and divided into topical chapters introduced by interpretive essays, with minimal annotation.

C43. Crawford, Michael J. "Dangerous to Documentary Editing: Copyright Office Report on Section 108." *Newsletter of the Association for Documentary Editing* 5 (May 1983): 6–7.

copyright

Section 108 of the 1976 Copyright Act permits libraries and archives to copy works for reasons of security, preservation, or transfer to other public collections. According to Crawford, the copyright office's report might make libraries hesitate to make copies for researchers.

C44. Crawford, Michael J. "Good Intentions: The Microfilm Edition of the Papers of John Paul Jones." *Documentary Editing* 10 (March 1988): 11–15.

facsimiles; Jones, John Paul; microfilm; transcription

Crawford describes the apparatus and transcription policy of the edition, which combines facsimiles with transcriptions and translations. He is highly critical of the execution of these policies, noting extensive typographical errors, uneven quality of translations, inaccurate annotation, and oddities in the index.

c45. CREASY, WILLIAM C. "A Microcomputer Editorial Procedure." In William C. Creasy and Vinton A. Dearing, *Microcomputers & Literary Scholarship*, 1–22. Los Angeles: William Andrews Clark Memorial Library, University of California, Los Angeles, 1986.

collation; computers

Creasy describes his editing of Thomas à Kempis's *Imitatio Christi* using an Apple II microcomputer and specially written programs for collation, concordance, and formatting.

c46. CRONON, E. DAVID. Review of *The Papers of Woodrow Wilson*, vols. 29–31. *Journal of Southern History* 46 (1980): 448–49.

transcription; Wilson, Woodrow

Cronon notes that recent volumes of the series have become more selective and less heavily annotated, and that vol. 31 "includes a lengthy explanation of the editors' policy of avoiding so far as possible the textual correction of documents and their increasingly strict adherence to the rule of verbatim et literatim."

c47. CROSS, J. E. "The Poem in Transmitted Text: Editor and Critic." *Essays and Studies*, n.s. 27 (1974): 84–97.

Old English; poetry

Cross illustrates the need to understand the entire text of a poem when settling even small editorial questions, especially when the only available texts have been transmitted through earlier editors.

c48. CROW, JOHN. "Editing and Emending." *Essays and Studies* 8 (1955): 1–20.

editing, general

An informal discussion of the problems of emendation based on the assumption that 'the editor of a text desires . . . to come as close as he can to what the author wrote—not what he should have written."

c49. CULLEN, CHARLES T. "Desktop Typesetting." *Documentary Editing* 6 (December 1984): 13–16.

computers

A description of TYXTEX, a typesetting program that can be run on a microcomputer.

c50. CULLEN, CHARLES T. "Principles of Annotation in Editing Historical Documents; or, How to Avoid Breaking the Butterfly on the Wheel of Scholarship." In *Literary & Historical Editing*, edited by George L. Vogt and John Bush Jones, 81–95.

annotation

Cullen summarizes the controversy surrounding annotation and then discusses the scope and relevance of notes.

c51. CULLEN, CHARLES T. Review of *The Papers of Daniel Webster, Correspondence*, vol. 1. *New England Quarterly* 50 (1977): 349–51.

form of publication; selection; Webster, Daniel

Cullen discusses problems raised by dividing the documents between a letterpress and a microfilm edition and by the organization of the letterpress edition. He also questions the decision to omit many personal letters from the letterpress edition.

C52. CULLEN, CHARLES T. Review of *The Papers of James Iredell*, vols. 1 and 2. *Journal of American History* 65 (September 1978): 412–13.

apparatus; Iredell, James; letters; transcription

Cullen criticizes the edition for its transcription and apparatus.

C53. CULLEN, CHARLES T. "Some Reflections on the Soft Money Generation." *Newsletter of the Association for Documentary Editing* 5 (December 1983): 1–4.

funding; professional status

Cullen focuses on the changes in the profession of documentary editing between the first generation of editors, used to working part-time and without federal funding, and the second generation of full-time editors, responsible for raising money for themselves and their staffs. See also Helen C. Aguera, "In Response."

C54. CULLEN, CHARLES T. "Twentieth-Century Technology and the Jefferson Papers." *Scholarly Publishing* 13 (1981–82): 45–53.

computers; indexing; Jefferson, Thomas

Cullen discusses the advantages of using a computer, particularly for indexing.

C55. CUNNINGHAM, NOBLE E. Review of *The Papers of Alexander Hamilton*, vols. 25 and 26. *Journal of Southern History* 46 (1980): 293–95.

annotation; calendaring; Hamilton, Alexander

Cunningham attributes the project's rapid completion to the calendaring of routine coorespondence, general avoidance of lengthy annotation, and long service by capable assistant and associate editors.

c56. CURRY, KENNETH. "The Text of Robert Southey's Published Correspondence: Misdated Letters and Missing Names." *Papers of the Bibliographical Society of America* 75 (1981): 127–46.

dating; Southey, Robert

Curry reviews the reasons for misdatings by earlier editors and the reasons for their omitting names. He then lists the corrected dates and names.

c57. CUTLER, WAYNE. "The 'Authentic' Witness: The Editor Speaks for the Document." *Newsletter of the Association for Documentary Editing* 4 (February 1982): 8–9.

types of editing

Cutler's article is a response to an earlier article ("The 'Perfect' Text: The Editor Speaks for the Author") in which David J. Nordloh criticized the James K. Polk project's editorial methods. Cutler cites differences in language used by himself and Nordloh and claims that there is a major difference between historical and literary editing in the way that the reader uses the material.

D

d1. DAINARD, J. A., ED. *Editing Correspondence: Papers Given at the Fourteenth Annual Conference on Editorial Problems, University of Toronto, 3–4 November 1978.* New York: Garland, 1979.

letters

See articles by Bell, Alan; Leigh, Ralph A.; Lewis, Wilmarth S.; Matthews, John; and Walker, John A.

D2. DANIEL, PETE, AND STUART B. KAUFMAN. "The Booker T. Washington Papers and Historical Editing at Maryland." *Maryland Historian* 1 (1970): 23–29.

training; Washington, Booker T.

The authors describe the Booker T. Washington papers project and the training of editors in the graduate history program at the University of Maryland.

D3. DAVIS, R. H. C. "Record Societies in England." *History: The Journal of the Historical Association* 60 (1975): 239–46.

annotation; England; history of editing; public records

Davis lists the societies in England that edit and publish records, reviews their work (with special reference to the extent of annotation and commentary), and suggests avenues for future activity.

D4. DAVIS, TOM. "The CEAA and Modern Textual Editing." *The Library*, 5th ser., 32 (1977): 61–74.

CEAA; copy-text

Davis reviews the history and criticism of the CEAA and its editions and discusses Greg's theory of copy-text, which underlies these editions. He is critical of rigid adherence to the accidental/substantive distinction and of the failure to encourage "liberty of editorial judgment."

D5. DAVIS, TOM. "Textual Criticism: Philosophy and Practice." *The Library*, 6th ser., 6 (1984): 386–97.

editing, general; Hardy, Thomas; Lawrence, D. H.

In this review of several volumes of the Cambridge edition of D. H. Lawrence and of two volumes of the Clarendon Press edition of Thomas Hardy, Davis discusses the "paradoxes" that have risen from issues of textual criticism and applies his conclusions to the works in question. In so doing, he offers a definition of the editor's role.

D6. DAVIS, TOM, AND SUSAN HAMLYN. "What Do We Do When Two Texts Differ? *She Stoops to Conquer* and Textual Criticism." In *Evidence in Literary Scholarship,*, edited by René Wellek and Alvaro Ribeiro, 263–79. Oxford: Clarendon Press, 1979.

copy-text; drama; Goldsmith, Oliver

The authors discuss the problem of choosing between a written text of a play and an acting version, equally authoritative.

D7. DAVISON, PETER. "Editing Orwell: Eight Problems." *The Library*, 6th ser., 6 (1984): 217–28.

editing, general; Orwell, George; translation

Davison describes his editing of Orwell's works and discusses the aim of the project, the choice of copy-text, the attribution of revisions, the editing of translations, and the problem of an author's request for posthumous changes.

D8. DEARING, VINTON A. "Concepts of Copy-text Old and New." *The Library* 28 (1973): 281–93.

copy-text; emendation

A summary and discussion of Greg's and Bowers's approaches to copy-text and emendations.

D9. DEARING, VINTON A. "Methods of Textual Editing." *William Andrews Clark Memorial Library Seminar Papers* (1962): 1–34. Reprinted in *Bibliography and Textual Criticism*, edited by O M Brack, Jr., and Warner Barnes, 73–101. Chicago: University of Chicago Press, 1969.

collation; computers; copy-text; editing, general; emendation; finding aids; planning

Dearing breaks textual criticism into eight processes: "exploring the implications of the project; collecting the texts; choosing a base text for comparison; comparing the texts; determining the archetype or copy text; emending; normalizing; writing the textual notes." As he describes each process, he also discusses the expense and time required, and the use of the computer.

DIO. DEARING, VINTON A. "Personal Computers and Literary Research." In William C. Creasy and Vinton A. Dearing, *Microcomputers & Literary Scholarship*, 23–41. Los Angeles: William Andrews Clark Memorial Library, University of California, Los Angeles, 1986.

computers

Dearing reviews the uses of PCs in word processing; literary analysis; compiling concordances, bibliographies, chronologies, and indexes; scansion of poetry; content analysis; and statistical analysis.

DII. DEARING, VINTON A. *Principles and Practice of Textual Analysis*. Berkeley: University of California Press, 1974.

Bible; computers; editing, general; history of editing; statistical analysis

Dearing presents a method of analysis derived from textual criticism of the Greek New Testament. He defines textual analysis as determining "the genealogical relationships between different forms of the same message." He enumerates seven steps of textual analysis and describes the use of mathematical probability in the process. Chapter 5, "Editing Texts and Documents," summarizes the process from planning and fundraising to compilation of apparatus. Dearing provides examples of both literary and historical research and, in two appendices, describes labor-saving devices (key sorting) and computer programs for proofreading, collating, compiling concordances, performing probabilistic studies, diagramming textual and bibliographical trees, locating the archetype in a preliminary diagram, and using the binary-tree method of sorting and searching data.

DI2. DEARING, VINTON A. "Textual Analysis: A Kind of Textual Criticism." *Text* 2 (1985): 13–23.

textual criticism; transmission of texts

Dearing distinguishes between genealogy of texts and genealogy of media and discusses the importance and reliability of genealogical analysis. He then explains the application of genealogical reasoning.

DI3. DEARING, VINTON A. "Textual Criticism Today: A Brief Survey." *Studies in the Novel* 7 (1975): 394–98.

CEAA; editing, general

Dearing reviews the procedures for editing a critical text and the approaches of different schools to various problems. His suggestions for the future include more extensive explanations of editorial decisions. See also articles by John Freehafer ("Greg's Theory"), Bruce Bebb and Hershel Parker, Thomas L. McHaney ("The Important Questions"), Morse Peckham ("Notes on Freehafer"), and G. Thomas Tanselle ("Two Basic Distinctions") in the same issue.

DI4. DEBATTISTA, MICHAEL. "Tape Proofreading: An Adaptation for Part-Time Staff." *Scholarly Publishing* 6 (1974–75): 147–50.

proofreading

DeBattista describes a proofreading method that uses tape-recorded readings.

DI5. DENBOER, GORDON. "The Documentary History of the First Federal Elections." *Prologue* 18 (Fall 1986): 163–71.

First Federal Elections project

DenBoer describes the project and the first federal elections.

DI6. DENBOER, GORDON. "The First Federal Elections: A Bridge from the Ratification Conventions to the First Federal Congress." *Manuscripts* 39, 4 (Fall 1987): 293–300.

First Federal Elections project

DenBoer describes the project, the importance of the first federal elections, and the sorts of documents that have been found.

DI7. DEWANI, LAKSHMAN. "Selected Works of Jawaharlal Nehru: An Introduction." *Newsletter of the Association for Documentary Editing* 4 (December 1982): 8–9.

annotation; India; Nehru, Jawaharlal; translation

A description of the project, which began in 1968.

DI8. DINE, SARAH BLANK. "The Diary of Elizabeth Drinker: An American Legacy." *Documentary Editing* 9 (June 1987): 1–5.

Drinker, Elizabeth Sandwith; journals; women's history

A description of the diary of a Quaker woman in Philadelphia, kept from 1758 to 1807.

DI9. DODGE, CHARLYNE. "Photographic Copies vs. Original Documents." *Papers of the Bibliographical Society of America* 71 (1977): 223–26.

photocopying

A brief note on the necessity of consulting original documents rather than photocopies, with examples from the preparation of *The Correspondence of Harold Frederic.*

D20. DOMVILLE, ERIC W., ED. *Editing British and American Literature, 1880–1920: Papers Given at the Tenth Annual Conference on Editorial Problems, University of Toronto, November 1974.* New York: Garland, 1976.

nineteenth century; twentieth century

See articles by Aziz, Maqbool; Farmer, David; Katz, Joseph (" 'Novelists of the Future' "); MacKenzie, Norman H.; and Sidnell, Michael.

D21. DONALD, DAVID HERBERT. Review of *The Papers of Jefferson Davis,* vol. 1. *American Historical Review* 77 (December 1972): 1506–8.

annotation; Davis, Jefferson; selection

Donald criticizes the volume for including unimportant documents rather than calendaring them, and for excessive annotation.

D22. DOWD, DAVID L. "The French Departmental Archives and the Fulbright Microfilm Project." *American Archivist* 16 (1953): 241–49.

finding aids; France

Dowd describes the microfilming of inventories of French archival collections and their usefulness.

D23. DRAKE, STILLMAN. "Dating Unpublished Notes, Such As Galileo's on Motion." In *Editing Texts in the History of Science and Medicine,* edited by Trevor H. Levere, 13–37.

dating; Galileo; history of science; notebooks

Drake outlines a method for dating notes and gives examples from his work on Galileo.

D24. DUDLEY, WILLIAM S. "The Naval War of 1812: A Documentary History." In *Editing Naval Documents: An Historical Appreciation*, 3–18.

annotation; naval history; selection; War of 1812

Dudley explains the background, selection process, and contents of the first volume of *The Naval War of 1812: A Documentary History*.

D25. DUNLAP, LESLIE W., AND FRED SHELLEY, EDS. *The Publication of American Historical Manuscripts*. Iowa City: University of Iowa Libraries, 1976.

editing, general

This volume is the report of a three-day conference held in 1975. See also entries for Boehm, Eric H.; Idzerda, Stanley J.; Jackson, Donald ("The Editor's Other Functions"); Jensen, Merrill; Klyberg, Albert T.; McCown, Robert A.; Reed, Daniel J.; Tompkins, E. Berkeley; and Van Dusen, Albert E.

E

E1. EASSON, ANGUS. "Reviewing Editions: Letters, Journals, Diaries." In *Literary Reviewing*, edited by James O. Hoge (Charlottesville: University Press of Virginia, 1987), 44–67.

reviewing

Easson discusses the purposes of reviewing editions as well as the duties of the reviewer, including evaluating literary value, understanding the problems specific to the material edited, assessing the contents of all prefatory material, and assessing and evaluating transcription, bibliographical information, annotation, and the index.

E2. *Editing Naval Documents: An Historical Appreciation.* Selected Papers from the Sixth Naval History Symposium, U.S. Naval Academy, Annapolis, Maryland, 29 September 1983. Washington, D.C.: Naval Historical Center, Department of the Navy, 1984.

naval history

See articles by Bradford, James C. ("Papers of John Paul Jones"); Dudley, William S.; Hattendorf, John B.; and Morgan, William James. See also Carpenter, William N., "Editing Naval Documents," a review.

E3. EDWARDS, PHILIP. "The Function of Commentary." In *Play-Texts in Old Spelling,* edited by G. B. Shand and Raymond C. Shady, 97–104.

annotation

Edwards discusses what should and should not be annotated in a scholarly edition, the importance of decisiveness, the placement of notes, and the use of glossaries and indexes.

E4. EISENBERG, DANIEL. "On Editing *Don Quixote.*" *Cervantes: Bulletin of the Cervantes Society of America* 3 (1983): 3–34.

Cervantes Saavedra, Miguel de; compositorial studies

Eisenberg describes three possible editions of *Don Quixote*— one for students, one for scholars, and a definitive edition for Cervantes specialists. He discusses at length the limitations of compositorial studies and provides information about Juan de la Cuesta, who printed the novel.

E5. ELEEN, LUBA. "Cycles of New Testament Illustration in the Thirteenth Century." In *Editing Illustrated Books,* edited by William Blissett, 15–34ff.

Bible; illustrations; Middle Ages

A discussion of how editors can reconstruct the sources and evolution of an illustration, including the interpretation of "error."

E6. ELIAS, ROBERT H. "Eighteenth-Century Thorns, Twentieth-Century Secretaries, & Other Prickly Matters." *Text* 3 (1987): 347–53.

letters; transcription; twentieth century

Elias discusses the problem of editing texts that have been produced by a secretary using a typewriter.

E7. ERWIN, JOHN SEYMOUR. Letter to the Editor. *Journal of American History* 70 (June 1983): 224–25.

authenticity; Erwin, Margaret Johnson

A response to John Simon's "In Search of Margaret Johnson Erwin."

E8. ETZOLD, THOMAS H. "The Great Documents Deluge." *Newsletter of the Society for Historians of American Foreign Relations* 8 (1976): 14–21.

editing, general

Etzold asks whether documentary editing is scholarship and whether it is worth the money spent on it. He answers both questions in the negative. See also Frank Burke's "Rebuttal" and Joseph Siracusa's "Reply."

E9. EVANS, FRANK B. "Manuscripts on Microfilm: American Personal Papers." *Quarterly Journal of the Library of Congress* 24 (1967): 147–51.

finding aids; microfilm; NHPC

Evans reports on the microfilm program of the NHPC and compares it to those of its predecessors and contemporaries. He explains the program's procedures and finding aids.

E10. EVANS, FRANK B. "Publication Programs and Historical Editing." In *Modern Archives and Manuscripts: A Select Bibliography*, 97–101. Chicago: Society of American Archivists, 1975.

bibliographies

An unannotated bibliography.

E11. EVANS, FRANK B. *The Selection and Preparation of Records for Publication on Microfilm*. National Archives Staff Information Paper no. 19. Washington, D.C.: National Archives, 1970.

microfilm

This staff information paper provides National Archives employees with specific instructions for microfilming. Among the topics covered are which records to microfilm, how to prepare records for filming, how to describe the records, and how to add the necessary inserts.

E12. EVANS, G. BLAKEMORE. "Shakespeare Restored—Once Again!" In *Editing Renaissance Dramatic Texts*, edited by Anne Lancashire, 39–56.

compositorial studies; copy-text; drama; punctuation; Shakespeare, William; transcription

A description of the preparation of the Riverside Shakespeare, emphasizing the problems of working on a much-edited text— "the burden of the past."

E13. EXNER, RICHARD. "Editing Hofmannsthal: Some Remarks Concerning a New Edition." In *Editing Twentieth-Century Texts*, edited by Francess G. Halpenny, 51–76.

format; Hofmannsthal, Hugo von; organization of editions; selection

A discussion of preliminary plans for a critical edition of Hofmannsthal's collected works.

F

F1. FAHY, CONOR. "The View from Another Planet: Textual Bibliography and the Editing of Sixteenth-Century Italian Texts." *Italian Studies* 34 (1979): 71–92.

bibliography; Italian; sixteenth century

Fahy discusses the applicability of Anglo-American bibliographical approaches to Italian sixteenth-century printing, the special difficulties of Italian bibliography, and the advisability of adopting Anglo-American practices in editing Italian sixteenth-century texts.

F2. FALLETA, T. S. "Word Processing Interface to Typesetting." *Scholarly Publishing* 11 (1979–80): 171–78.

computers

Falleta describes the types of word processing and the connection between word processing and typesetting.

F3. FARMER, DAVID. "Women in Love: A Textual History and Premise for a Critical Edition." In *Editing British and American Literature, 1880–1920*, edited by Eric W. Domville, 77–92.

censorship; copy-text; Lawrence, D. H.

A discussion of the problems that arise in establishing a copy-text when changes have occurred as a result of censorship and threatened libel action.

F4. FAULKNER, ROBERT K. Review of *The Papers of John Marshall*, vol. 1. *William and Mary Quarterly* 33 (1976): 154–56.

calendaring; Marshall, John; selection

Faulkner suggests the calendaring of a variety of material.

F5. FAULKNER, ROBERT K. Review of *The Papers of John Marshall*, vol. 2. *William and Mary Quarterly* 36 (1979): 646–48.

calendaring; Marshall, John; selection

Faulkner suggests the calendaring of a variety of material.

F6. FELLER, DANIEL. "Compromising Clay." *Documentary Editing* 8 (September 1986): 1–6.

annotation; Clay, Henry; selection; transcription

Feller criticizes the editorial compromise of summarizing, excerpting, and paraphrasing; finds the transcription generally "faithful yet readable"; and, while praising the annotation policy, finds that it has not been well executed.

F7. FELLER, DANIEL. " 'What Good Are They Anyway?' A User Looks at Documentary Editions of Statesmen's Papers." *Documentary Editing* 9 (December 1987): 10–15.

annotation; audience; calendaring; editing, general; transcription

Feller argues that, to make their work more usable, editors must produce editions expeditiously and present documents in accessible form. To improve the record, he suggests leaner annotation, elimination of lengthy summaries in favor of calendaring, and expanded transcription.

F8. FERGUSON, E. JAMES. Review of *The Papers of Alexander Hamilton*, vol. 26. *Journal of American History* 66 (March 1980): 919–20.

editing, general; Hamilton, Alexander; publishing

Ferguson suggests that the last volume in this series "may afford a model and at the same time provide useful instruction as to the inner propensities of historical editing."

F9. FIFER, C. N. "Editing Boswell: A Search for Letters." *Manuscripts* 6 (1953): 2–5.

Boswell, James; letters; search

Fifer discusses the problems in putting together a definitive edition of James Boswell's letters.

F10. FINKENBINE, ROY E. "Garveyism and the 'New Documentary Editing.'" *Documentary Editing* 7 (March 1985): 7–11.

annotation; black history; Garvey, Marcus; indexing; search; selection; transcription

A review of *The Marcus Garvey and Universal Negro Improvement Association Papers*, vols. 1 and 2, ed. Robert A. Hill, Carol A. Rudisell, Emory J. Tolbert, and Deborah Forczek.

F11. FIRTH, EDITH G. "The Editing and Publishing of Documents." *Canadian Archivist Newsletter* 1 (1963): 3–12.

annotation; copy-text; dating; selection; transcription

Firth reviews the process of editing historical documents, concentrating on transcription, the choice of which version of a letter or document to use as copy-text; and annotation. She also discusses the selection process as a source of bias.

F12. FISHER, JOHN H. "The MLA Editions of Major American Authors." *Professional Standards and American Editions: A Response to Edmund Wilson*, 20–26. New York: MLA, 1969.

CEAA

Fisher offers a justification of the CEAA program in response to Edmund Wilson's "The Fruits of the MLA."

FI3. FLORES, R. M. "The Need for a Scholarly, Modernized Edition of Cervantes' Works." *Cervantes: Bulletin of the Cervantes Society of America* 2 (1982): 69–87.

Cervantes Saavedra, Miguel de; compositorial studies; spelling

Flores describes the alteration by early compositors of Cervantes' spelling and style and argues that this gives urgency to the task of producing a scholarly, critical, modernized edition. He then summarizes proposed editorial policies for such an edition.

FI4. FOLEY, JOHN MILES. "Editing Oral Epic Texts: Theory and Practice." *Text* 1 (1984): 75–94.

epic; oral materials; Serbo-Croatian

Foley discusses the theoretical difficulty of transforming an oral performance into a written text. He provides examples from the Serbo-Croatian oral tradition.

FI5. FORD, WORTHINGTON CHAUNCEY. "The Editorial Function in United States History." *American Historical Review* 23 (1918): 273–86.

history of editing; professional status

Ford reviews the development of documentary editing in the United States.

FI6. FORD, WORTHINGTON CHAUNCEY. "On Calendaring Manuscripts." *Papers of the Bibliographical Society of America* 4 (1909): 45–56.

calendaring

Ford reviews the advantages of alphabetical and chronological calendaring, and the combination of the two arrangements in the Library of Congress. He discusses the desirable extent of a calendar, the need for qualified personnel, and costs.

F17. FORSTER, G. C. F. "Record Publishing in the North-West in Retrospect and Prospect." *Northern History* 14 (1978): 243–51.

England; history of religion; public records; selection; social history

A history of record publishing in northwestern England (Lancashire, Cumberland, Westmorland, and Cheshire), including a description of the records collected and published and suggestions for principles of selection.

F18. "FOUNDING FATHERS." *Times Literary Supplement,* 6 July 1962, pp. 485–86.

Adams papers; Hamilton, Alexander; history of editing

This review essay compares the papers of the Adams family with those of Alexander Hamilton. It also contrasts Charles Francis Adams's editing of John Adams's papers with Henry Cabot Lodge's editing of Hamilton's.

F19. FOXON, D. F. "Greg's 'Rationale' and the Editing of Pope." *The Library,* 5th ser., 33 (1978): 119–24.

compositorial studies; Pope, Alexander

Foxon discusses the limited applicability of Greg's preferred treatment of accidentals to eighteenth-century authors. He urges thorough study of each author's practices in writing, revising, and proofreading, as well as contemporary compositorial practices.

F20. FRANK, ISTVÁN. "The Art of Editing Lyric Texts." In *Medieval Manuscripts and Textual Criticism,* edited by Christopher

Kleinhenz, 123–38. First published as "De l'art d'éditer les textes lyriques," in *Recueil de travaux offert à M. Clovis Brunel*, Mémoires et Documents XII (Paris: Société de l'Ecole des Chartes, 1955), 1:463–75.

Middle Ages; oral materials

In this discussion of the lyric *chansonniers* of the Middle Ages, Frank describes the problems of variants, stemmatics, and contamination, and discusses the applicability of the selective and combinatory methods of establishing an archetype.

F21. FRANKLIN, R. W. *The Editing of Emily Dickinson: A Reconsideration.* Madison: University of Wisconsin Press, 1967.

authorial intention; Dickinson, Emily; history of editing

Franklin describes in detail the nineteenth-century editing of Dickinson's poems. He then discusses the compiling of the 1955 variorum edition by Thomas H. Johnson and the difficulties a future editor would face in dealing with material that the author herself did not prepare for publication.

F22. FRANKLIN, WAYNE. "The 'Library of America' and the Welter of American Books." *Iowa Review* 15 (1985): 176–94.

CEAA; Library of America; Wilson, Edmund

A discussion of the 1968 debate over CEAA editions, and a history and appraisal of the Library of America.

F23. FREEHAFER, JOHN. "Greg's Theory of Copy-Text and the Textual Criticism in the CEAA Editions." *Studies in the Novel* 7 (1975): 375–88.

accidentals; annotation; CEAA; copy-text

Freehafer discusses the shortcomings of CEAA editions, attributing many of them to the routine, unimaginative application of Greg's theory of copy-text and to the failure to use sources outside the text. See also responses by Bruce Bebb and Hershel Parker, Vinton A. Dearing ("Textual Criticism Today"), Thomas L. McHaney ("The Important Questions"), Morse Peckham ("Notes on Freehafer"), and G. Thomas Tanselle ("Two Basic Distinctions") in the same issue.

F24. FREEHAFER, JOHN. "How Not to Edit American Authors: Some Shortcomings of the CEAA Editions." *Bulletin of the New York Public Library* 75 (November 1971): 419–23.

CEAA; copy-text

Freehafer expands on Donald Pizer's criticisms of CEAA editions ("On the Editing of Modern American Texts"). He is especially critical of the absence from CEAA editions of critical commentary and explanatory notes, and of their "unimaginative" application of Greg's theory of copy-text. See also articles by Norman S. Grabo and Hershel Parker ("In Defense"), as well as Pizer's final response, in the same volume.

F25. FREEHAFER, JOHN. "*The Marble Faun* and the Editing of Nineteenth-Century Texts." *Studies in the Novel* 2 (1970): 487–503.

CEAA; Hawthorne, Nathaniel

Freehafer criticizes the Centenary Edition of *The Marble Faun* for "cumbersome and repetitious" apparatus; "tendentious and narrow analysis of internal bibliographic evidence, without regard to pertinent external evidence; inattention to pertinent linguistic and lexicographic evidence; 'normalization' of variants which often runs counter to Hawthorne's artistic and linguistic intentions; and adherence to a predetermined editorial practice which is not adequate to deal successfully with special problems in editing *The Marble Faun*."

F26. FREEMAN, ARTHUR. "Inaccuracy and Castigation: The Lessons of Error." In *Editing Renaissance Dramatic Texts*, edited by Anne Lancashire, 97–120.

drama; Kyd, Thomas; proofreading; Renaissance

A discussion of the sources of "minor error in the editing or reproduction of texts" and how to deal with them.

F27. FRIEDEL, FRANK. "Editing and Printing." In *Harvard Guide to American History*, edited by Frank Friedel, 1: 27–36. Rev. ed. Cambridge: Harvard University Press, 1974.

editing, general; transcription

This chapter offers a brief overview of documentary editing methods, with an emphasis on transcription.

F28. FRIEDMAN, ARTHUR. "Principles of Historical Annotation in Critical Editions of Modern Texts." *English Institute Annual, 1941*, 115–28. New York: Columbia University Press, 1942.

annotation

Friedman offers principles for notes whose purpose is to set a work in its historical context, either by supplying information no longer available to readers or by explaining the work's relationship to earlier works.

F29. FRIEDMAN, ARTHUR. "The Problem of Indifferent Readings in the Eighteenth Century, with a Solution from *The Deserted Village*." *Studies in Bibliography* 13 (1960): 143–47.

copy-text; statistical analysis

Friedman offers a method of distinguishing authorial revision from compositorial error based on the percentage of changes occurring in reprints.

F30. FROST, WILLIAM. "On Editing Dryden's Virgil." In *Editing Poetry from Spenser to Dryden*, edited by A. H. de Quehen, 99–126.

Dryden, John; poetry; translation; visual material

Frost notes that contemporary politics impinged upon Dryden's Virgil, and discusses both Dryden's "Notes and Observations" and the choice of illustrations. He then sets Dryden's translation in the context of other translations.

G

G1. GABLER, HANS WALTER. Review of *James Joyce, Ulysses: A Facsimile of the Manuscript. The Library* 32 (1977): 177–82.

facsimile; Joyce, James

Gabler discusses the editorial decisions required in producing a facsimile edition, as well as textual issues surrounding the novel.

G2. GABLER, HANS WALTER. "The Synchrony and Diachrony of Texts: Practice and Theory of the Critical Edition of James Joyce's *Ulysses.*" *Text* 1 (1984): 305–26.

authorial intention; Joyce, James; Milton, John

Gabler discusses the editorial treatment of textual variants that result from authorial revision and are integral elements of the text. Examples are drawn from Milton and Joyce.

G3. GABLER, HANS WALTER. "The Text as Process and the Problem of Intentionality." *Text* 3 (1987): 107–16.

authorial intention

Gabler discusses the implications for the editor of viewing authorial intention as dynamic rather than static.

G4. GAINES, BARRY. "Textual Apparatus—Rationale and Audience." In *Play-Texts in Old Spelling*, edited by G. B. Shand and Raymond C. Shady, 65–71.

apparatus; collation

Gaines discusses the value of historical collations, emendation of accidentals, and textual introductions, calling into question the value of the first two kinds of apparatus.

G5. GAIR, REAVLEY. "In Search of 'the mustie fopperies of antiquity.'" In *Play-Texts in Old Spelling*, edited by G. B. Shand and Raymond C. Shady, 123–30.

annotation

Gair illustrates the development of annotation with examples from an incomplete play by Sir Thomas Salusbury.

G6. GALAMBOS, LOUIS. "The Eisenhower Papers: Editing Modern Public Documents." *Documentary Editing* 6 (June 1984): 5–7.

Eisenhower, Dwight; privacy

Galambos deals with the problems associated with editing the papers of a modern public person, ranging from the sheer number of documents available to respecting the privacy of individuals mentioned in the documents.

G7. GALLOWAY, PATRICIA. "Dearth and Bias: Issues in the Editing of Ethnohistorical Materials." *Newsletter of the Association for Documentary Editing* 3 (May 1981): 1–6.

annotation; Native Americans; selection

The author, head of the Mississippi Provincial Archives, discusses the study of Native Americans. The two main problems she encountered were the scarcity of documents and the bias of European writers. She discusses the use of selection and annotation to overcome these difficulties.

G8. GARRATY, JOHN A. Review of *The Letters of Theodore Roosevelt*, vols. 7 and 8. *American Quarterly* 6 (1954): 281–84.

letters; Roosevelt, Theodore; selection

Garraty discusses the issues of selectivity versus completeness, the reprinting of letters published elsewhere, the grounds for selection, and the inclusion of letters to Roosevelt.

G9. GASKELL, PHILIP. *From Writer to Reader: Studies in Editorial Method.* Oxford: The Clarendon Press, 1978.

annotation; authorial intention; copy-text; format; handbook; transcription

After a brief introduction, Gaskell works through the editing of a dozen examples ranging in time from the sixteenth century through 1974.

G10. GASKELL, PHILIP. "*Night and Day*: The Development of a Play Text." In *Textual Criticism and Literary Interpretation*, edited by Jerome J. McGann, 162–79.

drama; Stoppard, Tom

Gaskell traces the development of the text of Stoppard's *Night and Day* from before rehearsal, through several series of performances, and in five printed editions.

G11. GASKELL, PHILIP. "Textual Bibliography." In his *A New Introduction to Bibliography*, 336–60. New York: Oxford University Press, 1972.

accidentals; collation; compositorial studies; copy-text; transmission of texts

Gaskell reviews the basic principles of copy-text and treatment of accidentals, along with a summary of compositorial practices.

G12. GEHRING, CHARLES. "New York's Dutch Records: A Historiographical Note." *New York History* 56 (1975): 347–54.

Dutch; New York

Gehring discusses the history of the publication of the records of the Dutch in New York.

G13. GEORGE, JULIETTE L., MICHAEL F. MARMOR, AND ALEXANDER L. GEORGE. Letter to the Editor. *Journal of American History* 70 (March 1984): 955–56.

annotation; objectivity; Wilson, Woodrow

A response to a letter by Arthur S. Link et al. in the same issue.

G14. GEORGE, JULIETTE L., MICHAEL F. MARMOR, AND ALEXANDER L. GEORGE. Letter to the Editor. *Journal of American History* 71 (June 1984): 198–212.

selection; Wilson, Woodrow

A further response to the letter by Arthur S. Link et al.

G15. GEORGE, JULIETTE L., MICHAEL F. MARMOR, AND ALEXANDER L. GEORGE. "Research Note: Issues in Wilson Scholarship: References to Early 'Strokes' in the Papers of Woodrow Wilson." *Journal of American History* 70 (March 1984): 845–53.

annotation; objectivity; Wilson, Woodrow

The authors criticize the inclusion of references to strokes in editorial notes as compromising the edition's objectivity. See also the letter to the editor by Arthur S. Link et al. and responses by George, Marmor, and George in the March and June 1984 issues of the same journal.

G16. GERBER, JOHN C. "Practical Editions: Mark Twain's *The Adventures of Tom Sawyer* and *Adventures of Huckleberry Finn*." *Proof* 2 (1972): 285–92.

practical editions; Twain, Mark

Gerber reviews the textual history of *Tom Sawyer* and *Huckleberry Finn* and evaluates the available practical editions of the novels.

G17. GIBSON, WILLIAM M. "The Center for Editions of American Authors." *Professional Standards and American Editions: A Response to Edmund Wilson*, 1–6. New York: MLA, 1969.

CEAA

Gibson describes the CEAA, its editorial standards, purpose, and procedures. He then responds to the arguments made by Edmund Wilson in "The Fruits of the MLA."

G18. GIBSON, WILLIAM M., AND EDWIN H. CADY. "Editions of American Writers, 1963: A Preliminary Survey." *PMLA* 78, no. 4, pt. 2 (1963): 1–8.

CEAA

The authors review progress in the publication of authoritative editions of American writers, suggest future projects, recall the purpose of such volumes, and list practical problems.

G19. GIBSON, WILLIAM M., ET AL. *A Statement of Editorial Principles: Center for Editions of American Authors*. New York: MLA, 1967.

CEAA

The CEAA's suggestions for developing editions that meet its criteria.

G20. GILMAN, WILLIAM H. "How Should Journals Be Edited?" *Early American Literature* 6 (Spring 1971): 73–83.

CEAA; Emerson, Ralph Waldo; Irving, Washington; journals; Shelley, Percy Bysshe; transcription

In this review essay on the CEAA-sponsored edition of Washington Irving's *Journals and Notebooks*, Gilman discusses the CEAA *Manual* as it applies to private manuscripts. He uses as examples *Shelley and His Circle* and the *Emerson Journals* as well.

G21. GILMORE, WILLIAM J. Review of *The Letters of John Greenleaf Whittier*, edited by John P. Pickard. *Journal of American History* 63 (1976): 672–73.

letters; selection; transcription; Whittier, John Greenleaf

Gilmore discusses the selection of documents and transcription policy, particularly with regard to capitalization.

G22. GIRLING, HARRY KNOWLES. "A Toot of the Trumpet Against the Scholarly Regiment of Editors." *Bulletin of Research in the Humanities* 81 (1978): 297–323.

authorial intention; CEAA; compositorial studies; James, Henry

According to Girling, "modern editors . . . are demonstrably engaged in reproducing nineteenth-century printing-house practices which in the original editions had regularized and thus misrepresented the system of punctuation by which authors had intended to indicate semantic and stylistic distinctions. Scholars are thus expending their devoted labours in perpetuating the original flouting of authorial intentions." He draws examples from Thoreau, Crane, Dorothy Richardson, and—in detail—Henry James.

G23. GNEUSS, HELMUT. "Guide to the Editing and Preparation of Texts for the Dictionary of Old English." In *A Plan for the Dictionary of Old English*, edited by Roberta Frank and Angus Cameron, 9–24. Toronto: University of Toronto Press, 1973.

apparatus; handbook; Old English

Gneuss sets out guidelines for editing Old English texts, including the preparation of introductory material, selection, transcription, presentation of text, and apparatus.

G24. GODDEN, MALCOLM. "Old English." In *Editing Medieval Texts*, edited by A. G. Rigg, 9–33.

dating; history of editing; Middle Ages; Old English

A discussion of the state of editorial work on Old English texts and the work that remains to be done.

G25. GONDOS, VICTOR J. *J. Franklin Jameson and the Birth of the National Archives, 1906–1926*. Philadelphia: University of Pennsylvania Press, 1981.

history of editing; Jameson, J. Franklin; National Archives

A biography.

G26. "GOODBYE GUTENBERG." *Newsletter of the Association for Documentary Editing* 3 (September 1981): 1–2.

computers

This short article is a summary of the 1981 Modern Technology and Historical Editing / NHPRC Word Processing Conference.

G27. GOODMAN, PAUL. Review of *Documentary History of the First Federal Congress*, vol. 1. *William and Mary Quarterly* 30 (1973): 508–10.

annotation; First Federal Congress project

Goodman discusses the value of the edition and praises its annotation for facilitating research.

G28. GOTTESMAN, RONALD. "Some Implications to *The Literary Manuscripts of Upton Sinclair:* A Preview Article." *Proof* 3 (1973): 395–410.

finding aids; Sinclair, Upton

Gottesman describes the procedures, contents, and significance of *The Literary Manuscripts of Upton Sinclair*, the second volume in the series Calendars of American Literary Manuscripts.

G29. GOTTESMAN, RONALD, AND DAVID NORDLOH. "The Quest for Perfection: or Surprises in the Consummation of *Their Wedding Journey*." *CEAA Newsletter* 1 (March 1968): 12–13.

proofreading

The authors recommend checking repro proofs and folded-and-gathered sheets, using the Hinman Collator.

G30. GRABO, NORMAN S. "Pizer vs Copy-Text." *Bulletin of the New York Public Library* 75 (April 1971): 171–73.

CEAA; copy-text

A response to Donald Pizer's "On the Editing of Modern American Texts." See also articles by John Freehafer ("How Not to Edit") and Hershel Parker ("In Defense"), as well as Pizer's final response, in the same volume.

G31. GRAF, LEROY P. "Editing the Andrew Johnson Papers." *Mississippi Quarterly* 15 (1962): 113–19.

funding; Johnson, Andrew; planning; selection

Graf discusses the problems of what material to include, who the edition's readers should be, and how to get the project funded.

G32. GRAFF, HENRY F., AND A. SIMONE REAGOR. *Documentary Editing in Crisis: Some Reflections and Recommendations*. Washington, D.C.: NHPRC, 1981.

editing, general; funding; NHPRC

A report on the development of documentary editing under the guidance of the NHPRC, including recommendations for financial support, use of new technologies, establishment of coherent editorial principles, and other measures for quality control.

G33. GRAHAM, JOHN W. "Editing a Manuscript: Virginia Woolf's *The Waves*." In *Editing Twentieth-Century Texts*, edited by Francess G. Halpenny, 77–92.

annotation; apparatus; format; transcription; Woolf, Virginia

Graham explains the principles he used in editing Woolf's two early manuscript drafts of the novel.

G34. GRAHAM, VICTOR E. "Editing French Lyric Poetry of the Sixteenth Century." In *Editing Sixteenth-Century Texts*, edited by R. J. Schoeck, 27–42.

annotation; collation; dating; Desportes, Philippe; French; poetry; search

A discussion of how the author located, collated, dated, edited, and annotated the works of Philippe Desportes.

G35. GRAYBILL, RONALD D. " 'Proofreading' and Collating by Computer." *Documentary Editing* 10 (December 1988): 24–25.

computers; proofreading

A review of "Compare Rite," a program that compares two text files and highlights the differences.

G36. GREASER, C. U. "Writers, Editors, and Compositors." *Scholarly Publishing* 12 (1980–81): 123–30.

computers

Greaser describes how the Rand Corporation uses computers in editing and publishing. The article also discusses the advantages of using computers for editing.

G37. GREENE, DONALD. "No Dull Duty: The Yale Edition of the Works of Samuel Johnson." In *Editing Eighteenth-Century Texts*, edited by D. I. B. Smith, 92–123.

annotation; authentication; Johnson, Samuel; project organization

Greene discusses the problems in preparing a comprehensive edition of Johnson's papers, particularly the difficulty in establishing what he wrote. The article also discusses the staff involved, editorial decisions made, content of the volumes, and annotation policies.

G38. GREENE, JACK P. "The Publication of the Official Records of the Southern Colonies: A Review Article." *William and Mary Quarterly* 14 (1957): 268–80.

colonial records

Greene reviews the publication of the colonial and revolutionary records of Georgia, Maryland, North Carolina, South Carolina, and Virginia with regard to editorial standards and scholarship. He also provides brief histories and descriptions.

G39. GREG, W. W. "The Rationale of Copy-text." *Studies in Bibliography* 3 (1950–51): 19–36. Reprinted in *Bibliography and Textual Criticism*, edited by O M Brack, Jr., and Warner Barnes (Chicago: University of Chicago Press, 1969), 41–58; and in *Art and Error: Modern Textual Editing*, edited by Ronald Gottesman and Scott Bennett (Bloomington: Indiana University Press, 1970), 17–36.

accidentals; authorial intention; copy-text; substantives

A classic statement of the establishment of practical rules for the selection of the copy-text; of the distinction between substantives and accidentals; and of the relationship between the establishment of copy-text and textual criticism. Much of the debate over CEAA editions centers around the application of Greg's theory to nineteenth-century authors. See entries indexed under CEAA for examples.

G40. GRODEN, MICHAEL. "Editing Joyce's 'Ulysses': An International Effort." *Scholarly Publishing* 12 (1980–81): 37–54.

computers; Joyce, James

This article discusses the changes made in Joyce's *Ulysses* and how the TU-STEP program helped recreate Joyce's original writing.

G41. GROVER, WAYNE C. "Toward Equal Opportunities for Scholarship." *Journal of American History* 52 (1966): 715–24.

microfilm; National Archives

Grover describes the history and significance of the National Archives Microfilm Publication Program.

G42. GRUBER, IRA D. Review of *Naval Documents of the American Revolution*, vol. 1. *William and Mary Quarterly* 22 (1965): 660–63.

authentication; naval history; search; selection

Gruber criticizes the volume's selection as "neither balanced nor comprehensive," relying too heavily on the collections of the Naval History Division. He is also critical of the establishment of texts, editorial omissions, and the index.

G43. GUNTHER, GERALD. Review of *The Adams Papers: Diary and Autobiography of John Adams. Harvard Law Review* 75 (1961–62): 1669–80.

finding aids; legal history; microforms; NHPC; Presidential Papers Program; selection

Gunther uses this review as an opportunity to evaluate the multivolume comprehensive editions sponsored by the NHPC. He argues that completeness is impossible, given the lack of cataloguing of manuscripts, and urges the inclusion of microfilm editions of "complete" collections along with printed descriptions of omitted material (especially since legal papers are frequently omitted). He criticizes the NHPC's "preoccupation" with printed volumes and lack of priorities in endorsements. He would prefer that the NHPC concentrate on microform reproduction and the improvement of finding aids.

H

H1. HABICH, ROBERT D. " 'Without Doubt a Poet': Emerson's Poetry Notebooks." *Documentary Editing* 9 (September 1987): 21–24.

apparatus; Emerson, Ralph Waldo; notebooks; poetry; transcription

In this review of *The Poetry Notebooks of Ralph Waldo Emerson*, Habich praises the genetic text and textual analysis of the edition.

H2. HAGERMANN, CHARLES. "Generic Encoding for Phototypesetting. I. Some Consequences of Literal Transcription and Computer Translation." *Documentary Editing* 9 (March 1987): 14–16.

computers; transcription

Hagermann explains the process of encoding data for layout and style.

H3. HAGERMANN, CHARLES. "Generic Encoding for Phototypesetting. II. Creating and Using a Generic Code System." *Documentary Editing* 9 (June 1987): 18–19, 24.

computers

Hagermann explains how to develop an encoding system for typesetting documents, based on the assumption of literal transcription.

H4. HAGERMANN, CHARLES. "Oberon International Omni-Reader." *Documentary Editing* 8 (September 1986): 16–17.

computers; optical scanners

A review of the Oberon International Omni-Reader, a hand-operated optical character reader.

H5. HAGERMANN, CHARLES. "Word Processor Formats: How to Share Your Files." *Documentary Editing* 10 (March 1988): 20–22.

computers

Hagermann explains how to share files with colleagues using the same hardware and software, and different hardware and software.

H6. HAIG, JUDITH G. "Wielding Occam's Razor: Bertrand Russell's Quest for Certainty." *Documentary Editing* 8 (June 1986): 10–14.

annotation; format; illustrations; indexing; philosophy; Russell, Bertrand; transcription

A review of *The Collected Papers of Bertrand Russell*, vol. 1, ed. Kenneth Blackwell et al., and vol. 7, ed. Elizabeth Ramsden Eames, in collaboration with Kenneth Blackwell.

H7. HAIGHT, GORDON S. "The Reader's Convenience." In *Editing the Victorians*, edited by N. John Hall, 137–39.

apparatus; letters

A brief discussion of the use and misuse of abbreviations, apparatus, notes, and numbering.

H8. HALL, BERT S. "Editing Texts in the History of Early Technology." In *Editing Texts in the History of Science and Medicine*, edited by Trevor H. Levere, 69–100.

history of science; Middle Ages; Renaissance; visual materials

Hall reviews the variety of technological treatises written in the Middle Ages and Renaissance and points out the importance of dealing sensitively with drawings as well as verbal materials.

H9. HALL, DONALD. "Robert Frost Corrupted." *Atlantic Monthly* (March 1982): 60–64.

authorial intention; Frost, Robert; poetry; punctuation

In this review of Edward Conery Lathem's edition of Frost's poetry, Hall describes the corruption of the text that occurred through repunctuation.

H10. HALL, KERMIT L. "John Marshall the Lawyer." *Documentary Editing* 10 (June 1988): 20–23.

annotation; legal history; Marshall, John; organization of editions; selection

In this review of the fifth volume of *The Papers of John Marshall*, Hall discusses the dearth of materials and praises the selection and organization of material, as well as the annotation. He criticizes the editors' failure to include the arguments of Marshall's adversaries in appellate cases.

HII. HALL, N. JOHN, ED. *Editing the Victorians. Browning Institute Studies* 9. New York: Browning Institute and City University of New York, 1981.

nineteenth century

See articles by Haight, Gordon S.; Kelley, Philip, and Ronald Hudson; Robson, John M. ("A Mill for Editing"); Schweik, Robert C., and Michael Priet; and Shillingsburg, Peter L. ("Editorial Problems").

HI2. HALPENNY, FRANCESS G. "Press Editors and Project Editors." In *Editor, Author, and Publisher*, edited by William J. Howard, 47–58. Toronto: University of Toronto Press, 1969.

funding; publishing

Halpenny elucidates the relationship between publisher and scholarly editor, emphasizing the distinction between publishing and directing research. She suggests ways that the two can best cooperate on editorial projects.

HI3. HALPENNY, FRANCESS G., ED. *Editing Canadian Texts: Papers Given at the Conference on Editorial Problems, University of Toronto, November 1972.* Toronto: Hakkert, 1975.

Canada

See articles by Nesbitt, Bruce; New, William H.; Pacey, Desmond; and Savard, Pierre.

HI4. HALPENNY, FRANCESS G., ED. *Editing Twentieth-Century Texts: Papers Given at the Editorial Conference, University of Toronto, November 1969.* Toronto: University of Toronto Press, 1972.

twentieth century

See articles by Bruccoli, Matthew J. (" 'A Might Collation' "); Exner, Richard; Graham, John W.; Jones, Eldred; and Meriwether, James B. ("A Proposal").

H15. HALSBAND, ROBERT. "Editing the Letters of Letter-Writers." *Studies in Bibliography* 11 (1958): 25–37. Reprinted in *Art and Error: Modern Textual Editing,* edited by Ronald Gottesman and Scott Bennett (Bloomington: Indiana University Press, 1970), 124–39.

annotation; authentication; letters; selection; transcription

Halsband compares nineteenth- and twentieth-century editions of letters. He then reviews the problems of selection (especially the decision whether to include letters to the subject), arrangement, transcription, provenance, and annotation.

H16. HAM, EDWARD B. "Textual Criticism and Common Sense." *Romance Philology* 12 (1958–59): 198–215.

copy-text; French; training

Ham reviews "some of the familiar attractions and pitfalls" of editorial dissertations and tries "to counteract some of the needless complications which textual theorists have been multiplying." He includes extensive suggestions for reading in editorial theory and in the editing of French manuscripts of the Middle Ages and later.

H17. HAMBY, ALONZO L., AND EDWARD WELDON. *Access to the Papers of Recent Public Figures: The New Harmony Conference.* Bloomington, Ind.: OAH, 1977.

access; archives; presidential papers; privacy; twentieth century

The report of a conference at which historians and archivists discussed the problems involved in using papers of contemporary public figures, generally federal government officials.

The conflicting interests of archivists, historians, and donors were aired. Specific topics discussed included the Freedom of Information Act, national security, and the procedures of presidential libraries. The conference concluded with a series of resolutions.

H18. HAMER, PHILIP M. " '. . . authentic Documents tending to elucidate our History.' " *American Archivist* 25 (1962): 3–13.

form of publication; Hazard, Ebenezer; history of editing; NHPC

Hamer offers a brief history of documentary editing, with special attention to the NHPC. He also assesses the relative merits of microfilm and letterpress editions and suggests the characteristics of a good historical editor.

H19. HAMER, PHILIP M. "Henry Laurens of South Carolina—The Man and His Papers." *Proceedings of the Massachusetts Historical Society* 77 (1965): 3–14.

editing, general; Laurens, Henry

Hamer describes the life of Henry Laurens, as well as the history of his papers.

H20. HAMILTON, A. C. "The Philosophy of the Footnote." In *Editing Poetry from Spenser to Dryden,* edited by A. H. de Quehen, 127–63.

annotation; poetry

Hamilton discusses the history and purpose of annotating poetry.

H21. HANCHER, MICHAEL. "The Text of 'The Fruits of the MLA.' " *Papers of the Bibliographical Society of America* 68 (1974): 411–12.

CEAA; editing, general

A satirical textual analysis of Edmund Wilson's "The Fruits of the MLA."

H22. HANCHER, MICHAEL. "Three Kinds of Intention." *Modern Language Notes* 87 (1972): 827–51.

authorial intention

Hancher analyzes the issues involved in the concept of authorial intention.

H23. HANNA, BLAKE T. "The Critical Edition of Diderot's *Oeuvres complètes.*" In *Editing Polymaths: Erasmus to Russell,* edited by H. J. Jackson, 41–75.

apparatus; Diderot, Dénis; format; selection; transcription

Hanna describes the history and procedures of the Diderot edition sponsored by the Centre National de Recherche Scientifique. He includes discussions of selection, transcription, annotation, and organization. He also reviews criticisms of the edition.

H24. HANNA, RALPH, III. "A New Edition of Chaucer." *Review* 1 (1979): 61–74.

annotation; apparatus; audience; Chaucer, Geoffrey; spelling

Hanna's major criticism of John H. Fisher's *Complete Poetry and Prose of Geoffrey Chaucer* is its failure to define an audience. This failure, says Hanna, is reflected in the bibliography, orthography, annotation, and critical essays.

H25. HARKNESS, BRUCE. "Bibliography and the Novelistic Fallacy." *Studies in Bibliography* 12 (1959): 59–73.

Fitzgerald, F. Scott; novels; textual criticism

Harkness discusses the failure of editors, reprinters, publishers, scholars, and bibliographers to engage in bibliographic study of the novel. He illustrates the results of such neglect with examples from *The Great Gatsby*.

H26. HARLAN, LOUIS R. "Booker T. Washington: The Labyrinth and the Thread." *Newsletter of the Association for Documentary Editing* 5 (December 1983): 5–9.

biography; selection; Washington, Booker T.

Harlan discusses the problems and benefits of being both biographer and editor. He also deals with the problems in handling as complex a person as Booker T. Washington and in selecting papers for the edition.

H27. HARLAN, LOUIS R., AND RAYMOND W. SMOCK. "The Booker T. Washington Papers." *Maryland Historian* 6 (1975): 55–59.

black history; form of publication; selection; Washington, Booker T.

The editors of the Booker T. Washington papers discuss the significance and problems of their project.

H28. HARLAN, LOUIS R., AND RAYMOND W. SMOCK. "What We Would Have Done Differently Now That It Is Too Late." *Newsletter of the Association for Documentary Editing* 2 (May 1980): 9–12.

access; annotation; computers; microfilm; transcription; Washington, Booker T.

The editors of the Booker T. Washington papers discuss their mistakes and successes, warning other editors about possible pitfalls. The two also provide specific information about their project.

H29. HARMAN, ELEANOR. "Hints on Proofreading." *Scholarly Publishing* 6 (1974–75): 151–57.

proofreading

Harman provides practical hints for proofreaders.

H30. HARRIS, C. M. Review of *The Papers of Henry Clay*, vols. 6 and 7. *Virginia Magazine of History and Biography* 92 (1984): 110–11.

annotation; Clay, Henry; format

Harris criticizes the change in editorial policy under which headings were modernized, closings dropped, and annotation largely eliminated.

H31. HARRIS, CHARLES M. Review of *The Papers of James Madison*, vol. 13. *Pennsylvania Magazine of History and Biography* 105 (1981): 497–98.

dating; form of publication; Madison, James

Harris comments on the value of comprehensive documentary editions as opposed to microforms.

H32. HART, JOHN A. "Pope as Scholar-Editor." *Studies in Bibliography* 23 (1970): 45–59.

history of editing; Pope, Alexander; Shakespeare, William

Hart reevaluates Pope's editing of Shakespeare, discussing Pope's word definition and textual collation. He argues that Pope's collation was "careful and considerate," and that his errors or failures as a scholar are attributable to his goals and approach to editing.

H33. HARTH, PHILLIP. Review of *John Dryden: Four Comedies* and *John Dryden: Four Tragedies*. *Modern Philology* 67 (1970): 379–82.

annotation; copy-text; Dryden, John; spelling

Harth compares the California and Chicago editions of Dryden and discusses both the analysis and the alteration of spellings.

H34. HATTENDORF, JOHN B. "Purpose and Contribution in Editing Naval Documents: A General Appreciation." In *Editing Naval Documents: An Historical Appreciation*, 43–61.

Great Britain; history of editing; microforms; naval history

Hattendorf reviews the history of editing naval documents in the United States and Great Britain. He describes six categories of naval documents, with examples of each.

H35. HAY, LOUIS. "Does 'Text' Exist?" *Studies in Bibliography* 41 (1988): 64–76. Translated by Matthew Jocelyn.

France; history of editing; textual criticism

After reviewing historical notions of text, Hay describes in detail "genetic criticism," a critical approach that began in the 1970s based on extensive empirical study of manuscripts to understand the genesis of an author's works.

H36. HAY, LOUIS. "Genetic Editing, Past and Future: A Few Reflections by a User." *Text* 3 (1987): 117–33. Translated by J. M. Luccioni and Hans Walter Gabler.

computers; facsimile editions; history of editing

Hay reviews the development of genetic editing, current problems and trends, the use of computer technology, and possibilities for the future.

H37. HEMLOW, JOYCE. "Letters and Journals of Fanny Burney: Establishing the Text." In *Editing Eighteenth-Century Texts*, edited by D. I. B. Smith, 25–43.

Burney, Fanny; journals; letters

Hemlow describes the task of deciphering—and presenting—manuscripts heavily edited both by Burney herself and by her descendants and publishers.

H38. HEMPHILL, W. EDWIN. "The Calhoun Papers Project: One Editor's Valedictory." *Proceedings of the South Carolina Historical Association*, 1977, 28–36.

Calhoun, John C.; editing, general

Hemphill describes the project's history and accomplishments, as well as his own career, with reflections on the various roles a documentary editor must play.

H39. HEWITT, DAVID S. "Burns and the Argument for Standardisation." *Text* 1 (1984): 217–29.

Burns, Robert; Scots; spelling

Hewitt proposes an edition of Burns that standardizes spelling and grammar, with standards determined by historical evidence.

H40. HIGGINBOTHAM, DON. "The Vicissitudes of Solo Editing." *Newsletter of the Association for Documentary Editing* 1 (March 1979): 4–5.

solo editing

The author describes the problems of being the sole editor of the Iredell papers.

H41. HIGGINS, BRIAN, AND HERSHEL PARKER. "The Chaotic Legacy of the New Criticism and the Fair Augury of the New Scholarship." In *Ruined Eden of the Present: Hawthorne, Melville, and Poe*, edited by G. R. Thompson and Virgil L. Lokke, 27–45. West Lafayette, Ind.: Purdue University Press, 1981.

CEAA; literary criticism; Melville, Herman

The authors discuss the weakness of the New Critics in handling documentary evidence and then describe the "New Scholarship," which combines "rigorous textual analysis with . . . creativity theory and reading conventions."

H42. HILL, ELIZABETH L. "Descriptive Guides for Publications on Microfilm." *American Archivist* 34 (1971): 318–23.

finding aids; microfilm

Hill reviews guides to 17 microfilm editions.

H43. HILL, W. SPEED. "The Calculus of Error, or Confessions of a General Editor." *Modern Philology* 75 (1977/78): 247–60.

editing, general; Hooker, Richard; Renaissance

Hill discusses proofreading errors, errors of transcription, erroneous citation or quotation, and other types of error in this article on the degree of accuracy possible in a scholarly edition. He draws examples from his editing of the *Works* of Richard Hooker.

H44. HINDLE, BROOKE. Review of *The Papers of Benjamin Franklin*, ed. William B. Willcox et al., vols. 16 and 17. *Journal of American History* 60 (1974): 1071–73.

annotation; Franklin, Benjamin

Hindle discusses the difficulty of annotating the papers of a figure involved in a wide variety of endeavors.

H45. HINMAN, CHARLTON. "Basic Shakespeare: Steps Toward an Ideal Text of the First Folio." In Charlton Hinman and Fredson Bowers, *Two Lectures on Editing*, 7–19. Columbus: Ohio State University Press, 1969.

apparatus; facsimiles; Shakespeare, William

Hinman describes the text of the First Folio and his efforts to prepare a text that is clear and readable, with "through line numbering."

H46. *Historical Editing: A Guide for Departments of History.* Bloomington, Ind.: Organization of American Historians, 1984.

editing, general; history of editing; training

This 34-page pamphlet describes the varieties of historical editing, surveys the history of the field, and surveys training programs.

H47. HOBSON, CHARLES F. "Sotheby's Sale of John Marshall Letters." *Documentary Editing* 9 (March 1987): 1–4.

Marshall, John; search; Washington, Bushrod

Hobson describes the acquisition of nine letters from Marshall to Washington, including an account of their provenance.

H48. HOCKEY, SUSAN. *A Guide to Computer Applications in the Humanities.* Baltimore: Johns Hopkins University Press, 1980.

computers

Hockey's book is based on a series of lectures at Oxford that dealt with the use of computers in the humanities.

H49. HOEMANN, GEORGE H. "The Perils of a Full-Court Press." *Documentary Editing* 9 (June 1987): 9–12.

legal history; selection; Supreme Court; transcription

In this review of volume 1 of *The Documentary History of the Supreme Court of the United States, 1789–1800,* Hoemann criticizes the edition for its selection policy, its overly literal transcription, and for its claims to be a "documentary history."

H50. HOLLAND, PATRICIA G. "The Papers of Elizabeth Cady Stanton and Susan B. Anthony: Reconstructing the Record." *Documentary Editing* 6 (September 1984): 9–13.

Anthony, Susan B.; search; Stanton, Elizabeth Cady

The author, co-editor of the Stanton and Anthony papers, discusses the history and collection of the papers.

H51. HOLMES, D. M., AND H. D. JANZEN. "A Note on Editing Jacobean Drama." In *Editing Seventeenth-Century Prose*, edited by D. I. B. Smith, 25–30.

background research; drama; transcription

Examples of the creation and perpetuation of error owing to inadequate preparation and understanding.

H52. HOLMES, OLIVER W. "Documentary Publication in the Western Hemisphere." *Archivum* 16 (1966): 79–96; "National Documentary Publication Programming: Documentary Publication in the Western Hemisphere." *National Archives Accessions*, no. 60 (1967): 13–27 (without appended summary and discussion).

Canada; history of editing; Latin America

Holmes outlines the interests of those in the Western Hemisphere in European documents of the ages of discovery, exploration, colonization, and liberation of the New World. He then surveys recent efforts at publishing records and documents in Latin America, the United States, and Canada.

H53. HOLMES, OLIVER W. "Recent Writings Relevant to Documentary Publication Programs." *American Archivist* 26 (1963): 137–42.

bibliographies; history of editing

A bibliography of documentary publication projects from about 1950 until 1962.

H54. HONIGMANN, E. A. J. "The Date and Revision of *Troilus and Cressida.*" In *Textual Criticism and Literary Interpretation,* edited by Jerome J. McGann, 38–54.

dating; Shakespeare, William

Honigmann discusses the dating of the play, its genre, and its textual history.

H55. HONIGMANN, ERNEST A. J. "Shakespeare as a Reviser." In *Textual Criticism and Literary Interpretation,* edited by Jerome J. McGann, 1–22.

drama; Shakespeare, William

Honigmann discusses recent work and his own theories as to how much of the revision of Shakespeare's plays was done by Shakespeare himself.

H56. HOPKINS, JAMES F. "Editing the Henry Clay Papers." *American Archivist* 20 (1957): 231–38.

authentication; Clay, Henry; funding; search; selection; transcription

Hopkins describes the editorial procedures used and special problems encountered in editing Henry Clay's papers. He emphasizes the selection and acquisition processes.

H57. HORNBERGER, THEODORE. Review of *The Papers of Thomas Jefferson,* vols. 1 and 2. *American Quarterly* 3 (1951): 87–90.

annotation; copy-text; Jefferson, Thomas; selection; transcription

Hornberger compares the Boyd and Ford editions, finding the Boyd edition superior because of its inclusivity, more literal transcription, and more helpful annotation.

H58. HORNSBY, ALTON, JR. "The Hope Papers Project: Problems and Prospects." *Maryland Historian* 6 (1975): 51–54.

black history; Hope, John and Lugenia Burns

Hornsby reviews the history of the Hope Papers project and the contribution of the Hopes to American society.

H59. HOUSMAN, A. E. "The Application of Thought to Textual Criticism." *Proceedings of the Classical Association* 18 (1921): 67–84. Reprinted in idem, *Selected Prose*, edited by John Carter (Cambridge: Cambridge University Press, 1962), 131–50; and in *Art and Error: Modern Textual Editing*, edited by Ronald Gottesman and Scott Bennett (Bloomington: Indiana University Press, 1970), 1–16.

editing, general; textual criticism

Housman defines textual criticism, suggests some reasons why it is difficult, and gives examples of its being done without adequate application of thought. He concludes that to be a textual critic "one thing beyond all others is necessary; and that is to have a head, not a pumpkin, on your shoulders, and brains, not pudding, in your head."

H60. HOWARD, WILLIAM J. "Literature in the Law Courts, 1770–1800." In *Editing Eighteenth-Century Texts*, edited by D. I. B. Smith, 78–91.

copyright; legal history

A discussion of the evolution of British copyright law in the last half of the eighteenth century and the effect of the law on contemporary literature.

H61. HOWARD-HILL, T. H. "Computer and Mechanical Aids to Editing." *Proof* 5 (1977): 217–35.

computers

In this sequel to his "Practical Scheme for Editing Critical Texts," Howard-Hill reviews the problems that literary scholars face in using computers and then discusses in some detail the specifics of hardware and software, including optical character recognition devices and photocomposition machines.

H62. HOWARD-HILL, T. H. "A Practical Scheme for Editing Critical Texts with the Aid of a Computer." *Proof* 3 (1973): 335–56.

computers

Howard-Hill summarizes the attributes desirable in a system of computerized editing and describes such a system in terms of the headings of the CEAA *Statement of Editorial Principles and Procedures*. He emphasizes computer use for collation, choice of copy-text, emendation, reporting of emendations and variant readings, and proofreading.

H63. HOWSON, SUSAN. "Economists as Policy-Makers: Editing the Papers of James Meade, Lionel Robbins, and the Economic Advisory Council." In *Editing Modern Economists*, edited by D. E. Moggridge, 129–52.

annotation; economics; Meade, James; organization of editions; Robbins, Lionel; selection

Howson outlines the work of the Economic Advisory Council in the 1930s and discusses the editorial problems posed by the papers relating to the EAC, chiefly organization, selection, and annotation.

H64. HOY, CYRUS. "On Editing Elizabethan Plays." *Renaissance and Reformation* 8 (1972): 90–99.

compositorial studies; copy-text; drama; textual criticism

Hoy reviews the procedures of editing a play (choosing a copy-text, collating, handling accidentals, assembling apparatus, writing an introduction) and points out the inconsistency he considers inevitable in a team-produced edition. He also argues that analytical bibliography is of limited use unless supplemented with philological, historical, and critical knowledge and sensitivities.

H65. HOY, SUELLEN, ED. "Historical Editing." In *The Craft of Public History: An Annotated Select Bibliography*, edited by David F. Trask and Robert W. Pomeroy III, 171–227. Westport, Conn.: Greenwood Press, 1983.

bibliographies

The documentary editing section of this bibliography contains entries with relatively lengthy summaries for 143 items, most of which are included in the present work.

H66. HRUBÝ, ANTONÍN. "A Quantitative Solution of the Ambiguity of Three Texts." *Studies in Bibliography* 18 (1965): 147–82.

copy-text; statistical analysis

Hrubý suggests a method of using statistics and probability calculus to determine the descent of three texts from a common ancestor.

H67. HRUBÝ, ANTONÍN. "Statistical Methods in Textual Criticism." *General Linguistics* 5, no. 3, supp. 1962, 77–136.

copy-text; statistical analysis

Hrubý offers a statistical method to establish stemmata.

H68. HUDSON, ANNE. "Middle English." In *Editing Medieval Texts*, edited by A. G. Rigg, 34–57.

history of editing; Lollard movement; Middle Ages; Middle English

A discussion of some recent approaches to editing Middle English works and of tasks remaining in the field.

H69. HUDSPETH, ROBERT N. "Hawthorne's Letters and the 'Darksome Veil of Mystery.'" *Documentary Editing* 8 (September 1986): 7–11.

annotation; Hawthorne, Nathaniel; indexing; letters; transcription

In this review of *Nathaniel Hawthorne: The Letters*, Hudspeth praises the edition's text and explanatory notes, reserving criticism for the index and textual notes "at its periphery."

H70. HUGGINS, NATHAN IRVIN. Review of *The Correspondence of W. E. B. DuBois*, vol. 1. *American Historical Review* 80 (1975): 512–13.

DuBois, W. E. B.; selection

Huggins questions the rationale for selection and the lack of information about documents excluded.

H71. HUNNISETT, R. F. *Editing Records for Publication.* Archives and the User Series, no. 4. London: British Records Association, 1977.

handbook

A booklet for documentary editors.

H72. HURLEBUSCH, KLAUS. "Conceptualisations for Procedures of Authorship." *Studies in Bibliography* 41 (1988): 100–35.

Germany; history of editing

In this "attempt to investigate the ways editors see their role, by analysing their conceptualisations of authorial writing," Hurlebusch examines contrasting concepts of the critical edition. These concepts differ on issues of presentation of text and apparatus and of authorial intention. Examples are drawn from German editions.

H73. HURLEBUSCH, KLAUS. " 'Relic' and 'Tradition': Some Aspects of Editing Diaries." *Text* 3 (1987): 143–53.

journals; Klopstock, Friedrich Gottlieb; transcription

Hurlebusch discusses the ways in which diaries differ from letters and from works intended for publication. He then describes his editing of Klopstock's "work journal," including the presentation of text, annotation, and handling of coded material.

I

I1. IDZERDA, STANLEY J. "The Editor's Training and Status in the Historical Profession." In *The Publication of American Historical Manuscripts*, edited by Leslie W. Dunlap and Fred Shelley, 11–29.

history of editing; professional status; training

Idzerda sets the social, cultural, and academic importance of documentary editing in contrast to the historical profession's lack of interest in—and esteem for—the field. He urges that all students of history be trained in editing, whether they plan to work as editors or not.

I2. IRVINE, DALLAS D. "The Genesis of the *Official Records*." *Mississippi Valley Historical Review* 24 (1937): 221–29.

Civil War; history of editing; military history; *Official Records of the Union and Confederate Armies*

Irvine discusses the history and significance of the *Official Records* of the Civil War.

J

J1. JACK, IAN. "A Choice of Orders: The Arrangement of 'The Poetical Works.'" In *Textual Criticism and Literary Interpretation*, edited by Jerome J. McGann, 127–43.

anthologies; organization of editions; poetry

Jack discusses the issues to be considered in arranging a poet's work in a collected edition.

J2. JACKSON, DONALD. "The Editor's Other Functions." In *The Publication of American Historical Manuscripts*, edited by Leslie W. Dunlap and Fred Shelley, 69–76.

access; administration; funding

Jackson touches upon the administrative and fundraising duties of the editor and discusses at greater length the problem of requests for assistance and information that documentary projects receive.

J3. JACKSON, DONALD. "The Papers of George Washington." *Manuscripts* 22 (1970): 3–11.

search; Washington, George

Jackson criticizes the Fitzpatrick edition of Washington's papers. He also describes the search for manuscripts.

14. JACKSON, DONALD. "Some Advice for the Next Editor of Lewis and Clark." *Bulletin of the Missouri Historical Society* 24 (1967): 52–62.

Clark, William; journals; Lewis, Meriwether; search; selection

Jackson summarizes the history of the publication of accounts of the Lewis and Clark expedition. He then comments on three issues an editor of these works would have to address: the completeness of the record, the principles of selection; and the background of the documents.

15. JACKSON, DONALD. "Starting in the Papers Game." *Scholarly Publishing* 3 (1971): 28–38.

project organization; Washington, George

The editor of the *Papers of George Washington* describes the history of the project.

16. JACKSON, DONALD. "What I Did for Love—of Editing." *Western Historical Quarterly* 13 (1982): 1–5.

editing, general

A speech recounting the pleasures and problems of an editorial career.

17. JACKSON, H. J., ED. *Editing Polymaths: Erasmus to Russell: Papers Given at the 18th Annual Conference on Editorial Problems, University of Toronto, 5–6 November 1982.* Toronto: Committee for the Conference on Editorial Problems, 1983.

See articles by Blackwell, Kenneth; Hanna, Blake T.; Petry, Michael J.; and Sowards, J. K.

18. JAMBECK, KAREN K. "The *Fables* of Marie de France: Base Text and Critical Text." *Text* 2 (1985): 83–91.

France, Marie de; French; Middle Ages

Jambeck analyzes Karl Warnke's 1898 critical edition of the *Fables*. She argues that, because of Warnke's assumptions about the corruption of his base text and about the author's language, his edition is flawed and needs to be replaced.

J9. JAMESON, J. FRANKLIN. "The Functions of State and Local Historical Societies with Respect to Research and Publication." *Annual Report of the American Historical Association for the Year 1897*, 53–59. Washington, D.C.: Government Printing Office, 1898.

local historical societies; state historical societies

This article describes the defects of local and state historical societies with regard to publishing manuscripts. Jameson discusses some reasons for the defects and gives suggestions for improvements.

J10. JAMESON, J. FRANKLIN. "Gaps in the Published Records of United States History." *American Historical Review* 11 (1905–6): 817–31.

editing, general

Jameson's essay was written to encourage an orderly, systematic approach to publishing the nation's documents. Beginning with the colonial period, he lists the areas of U.S. history that need to be documented for the nation as a whole, and for the colonies and states. He discusses the need to publish documents from English, French, and Spanish archives as well.

J11. JANZEN, HENRY D. "Preparing a Diplomatic Edition: Heywood's *The Escapes of Jupiter*." In *Play-Texts in Old Spelling*, edited by G. B. Shand and Raymond C. Shady, 73–79.

handwriting; Heywood, Thomas; transcription

Janzen describes his preparation of a diplomatic edition of a Renaissance play from a holograph in "atrocious" handwriting. He explains the modernizations he adopted.

J12. JARRETT, BEVERLY. "In Search of Margaret Johnson Erwin: A Response." *Journal of American History* 69 (March 1983): 942–45.

authenticity; Erwin, Margaret Johnson

A response to John Simon's "In Search of Margaret Johnson Erwin." See also John Seymour Erwin's letter to the editor and Simon's letter to the editor, June 1983.

J13. JEFFREY, THOMAS E. "The Education of Editors: Current Status and Future Prospects." *Documentary Editing* 7 (March 1985): 12–17.

training

This article focuses on the response to an ADE questionnaire concerning the education of editors. Jeffrey also gives his views on the future education of editors and provides a list of universities offering relevant courses.

J14. JEFFREY, THOMAS E. "Microform Editions of Documentary Collections: Where Do We Stand? And Where Do We Go from Here?" *Newsletter of the Association for Documentary Editing* 4 (September 1982): 1–5.

microforms

An introduction to microform publishing that concentrates on the uses of this form of publication rather than on its technical aspects.

J15. JEFFREY, THOMAS E. "Raiders of the Lost Archives: A Scholarly Detective Story." *Documentary Editing* 8 (March 1986): 16–19.

access; microfilm; security

An account of the theft and recovery of numerous items from the Edison National Historic Site. Jeffrey recommends microfilming of collections as a security measure.

J16. JENKINS, REESE V. "Words, Images, Artifacts and Sound: Documents for the History of Technology." *British Journal for the History of Science* 20 (1987): 39–56.

artifacts; Edison, Thomas Alva; sound; visual materials

Jenkins discusses the motivations for technical creativity and the design and exploitation of technologies, with illustrations from Edison's career. His purpose is to demonstrate the importance of nonverbal documents in the history of technology.

J17. JENKINS, REESE V., AND THOMAS E. JEFFREY. "Worth a Thousand Words: Nonverbal Documents in Editing." *Documentary Editing* 6 (September 1984): 1–8.

annotation; Edison, Thomas A.; history of science; microfilm; visual materials

The editors of the *Thomas A. Edison Papers* discuss the importance of visual material in documentary publications and the ways such materials have traditionally been treated. Jenkins and Jeffrey also describe the problems and advantages of using nonverbal documents in Edison's papers. The differences between microfilm and printed editions are described, as is the process of annotating nonverbal documents.

J18. JENKINSON, HILARY. "The Representation of Manuscripts in Print." *The London Mercury* 30 (1934): 429–38.

audience; transcription; types of editing

Jenkinson examines the question "What, if any, is the difference between the task of [a literary editor] and that of one editing texts in the Historical or some other scholastic or scientific interest?" He calls for agreement on a recognized method of editing documents in all fields, and for consideration of the interests of a variety of readers and scholars.

J19. JENSEN, MERRILL. "The Bicentennial and Afterwards." In *The Publication of American Historical Manuscripts*, edited by Leslie W. Dunlap and Fred Shelley, 47–55.

history of editing; NHPRC

Jensen describes the celebrations of the bicentennial of independence, including both ephemeral events and the lasting contribution to documentary editing.

J20. JENSEN, MERRILL, SAMUEL FLAGG BEMIS, AND DAVID DONALD. "The Life and Soul of History." *New England Quarterly* 34 (1961): 96–105.

Adams papers; microfilm

This article incorporates three essays, one on each generation of the Adams family and the importance of their contribution as reflected in the contents of the microfilms of the Adams papers.

J21. JOHNSON, HERBERT A. Review of *Plymouth Court Records*, vols. 1–3. *William and Mary Quarterly* 38 (1981): 730–35.

calendaring

Johnson comments on the accuracy and value of the volumes and praises the method of inclusive calendaring.

J22. JOHNSON, LUDWELL H. Review of *The Papers of John C. Calhoun*, vol. 2. *William and Mary Quarterly* 21 (1964): 315–17.

Calhoun, John C.; selection

Johnson criticizes the decision to abstract letters rather than exercise careful selection and calendar what was not included.

J23. JOHNSON, THOMAS H. "Establishing a Text: The Emily Dickinson Papers." *Studies in Bibliography* 5 (1952–53): 21–32. Reprinted in *Art and Error: Modern Textual Editing*, edited by Ronald Gottesman and Scott Bennett (Bloomington: Indiana University Press, 1970), 140–54.

dating; Dickinson, Emily; handwriting

Johnson sets out the difficulties of establishing the chronology of Dickinson's poems and letters and describes the analysis of paper and handwriting to resolve these issues.

J24. JOHNSTON, ALEXANDRA F. "The *York Cycle* and the *Chester Cycle*: What Do the Records Tell Us?" In *Editing Early English Drama*, edited by A. F. Johnston, 121–43.

drama; local records; Middle Ages; practical editions

Johnston reviews what has been learned about the mystery play cycles from the texts and from records outside the texts. She also compares the problems of editing medieval drama with those of editing Elizabethan drama and discusses the development of teaching editions.

J25. JOHNSTON, A. F., ED. *Editing Early English Drama: Special Problems and New Directions: Papers Given at the Nineteenth Annual Conference on Editorial Problems, University of Toronto, 4–5 November 1983.* New York: AMS Press, 1987.

drama

See articles by Bevington, David ("Drama Editing"); Johnston, Alexandra F.; Meredith, Peter; Parry, David; and Somerset, J. A. B.

J26. JOHNSTON, CAROL. "Single-Editor Editions from Manuscript: The Journals of Theodore Parker." *Newsletter of the Association for Documentary Editing* 5 (May 1983): 4–5.

handwriting; Parker, Theodore; solo editing; transcription

Johnston discusses the career and importance of Theodore Parker. She explains the reasons for editing the manuscripts and how she interpreted and transcribed difficult handwriting. She also notes the value of an editorial manual even for one-person projects.

J27. JONES, ELDRED D. "A Note on Editing *The Interpreters*, a Novel by Wole Soyinka." In *Editing Twentieth-Century Texts*, edited by Francess G. Halpenny, 93–101.

annotation; Soyinka, Wole

Jones sets out some of the difficulties a reader encounters in Soyinka's novels and explains how annotation was used to make the text more accessible.

J28. JONES, H. G. *For History's Sake: The Preservation and Publication of North Carolina History, 1663–1903*. Chapel Hill: University of North Carolina Press, 1966.

North Carolina; preservation; state records

Jones provides a book-length treatment of the creation, preservation, use, and publication of North Carolina's records.

J29. JONES, H. G. "The Publication of Documentary Sources, 1934–1968." In *The Records of a Nation: Their Management, Preservation, and Use*, 117–33. New York: Atheneum, 1969.

Jameson, J. Franklin; NHPC

Jones focuses on the history of the National Historical Publications Commission. Jones emphasizes the response of the federal government to changes in historical publications and discusses J. Franklin Jameson's role in the history of the NHPC.

J30. JONES, JOHN BUSH. "Editing Victorian Playwrights: Some Problems, Priorities, and Principles." *Theatre Survey* 17 (1976): 106–23.

drama; nineteenth century

Jones discusses the value of editing Victorian playwrights, the choice of which to edit, the degree of completeness desirable, and principles of selection. He compares the rationales for critical editions, microforms, photo-offset reprints, and practical texts. He then discusses the principles for a critical edition, including the choice of copy-text, emendation, and apparatus.

J31. JONES, JOHN BUSH. "Galley Proofs in America: A Historical Survey." *Proof* 4 (1975): 153–64.

printers' practices

From his study of printers' manuals and trade journals, Jones concludes that galleys first appeared in the United States in 1859 and came into widespread use by 1870.

J32. JONES, JOHN BUSH. "Introduction: The Literary Editor's View." In *Literary & Historical Editing,* edited by George L. Vogt and John Bush Jones, 7–12.

professional status; types of editing

A brief discussion of the need for communication among editors of various sorts, and between editors and teachers.

J33. JONES, JOHN BUSH. "Victorian 'Readers' and Modern Editors: Attitudes and Accidentals Revisited." *Papers of the Bibliographical Society of America* 71 (1977): 49–59.

accidentals; printers' practices

Jones surveys nineteenth-century printers' manuals to determine proofreaders' attitudes toward authors and their care in manuscript preparation. He concludes that printers' alteration of accidentals and assumptions about authorial indifference were far less uniform than James Thorpe suggests in *Principles of Textual Criticism*.

J34. JORDAN, PHILIP D. "A Dedication to the Memory of Clarence Edwin Carter, 1881–1961." *Arizona and the West* 10 (1968): 309–12.

Carter, Clarence Edwin; history of editing

A biographical sketch.

K

K1. KAHRL, STANLEY. "Editing Texts for Dramatic Performance." In *The Drama of Medieval Europe: Proceedings of the Colloquium Held at the University of Leeds, 10–13 September 1974*, 39–52; discussion, 53–65.

drama; history of editing; Middle Ages

Kahrl discusses the work of the Early English Text Society and its concern with the study of language. He suggests that editors of medieval plays share the concerns of editors of plays from other periods, particularly the need to help the reader visualize the production of the play. The article and subsequent discussion cover topics including modernization, stage directions, production, publishing, and teaching.

K2. KAMINSKI, JOHN P. "The Records of a Productive Summer." *Documentary Editing* 9 (September 1987): 16–20.

annotation; Farrand, Max; indexing

In this review of the reissue of volumes 1–3 of *The Records of the Federal Convention of 1787* edited by Max Farrand and the *Supplement* (vol. 4), Kaminski praises the durability of Farrand's editorial work, assesses the importance of the *Supplement*, and criticizes the design, annotation, and index of volume 4.

K3. KAMINSKI, JOHN P., RICHARD LEFFLER, AND GASPARE J. SALADINO. "The Documentary History of the Ratification of the Constitution." *Prologue* 18 (Fall 1986): 153–61.

history of editing; legal history; Ratification of the Constitution project

The authors outline the history of the project and describe its contents, uses, and value, emphasizing its usefulness for legal research.

K4. KAMMEN, MICHAEL. "Colonial Court Records and the Study of Early American History: A Bibliographical Review." *American Historical Review* 70 (1964): 732–39.

colonial records; legal history

Kammen reviews the colonial court records published since 1933 and discusses the impact of such publications on historians' views of colonial history.

K5. KANE, GEORGE. "Conjectural Emendation." In *Medieval Manuscripts and Textual Criticism*, edited by Christopher Kleinhenz, 211–25. Reprinted from *Medieval Literature and Civilization: Studies in Memory of G. N. Garmonsway*, edited by D. A. Pearsall and R. A. Waldron (London: Athlone Press, 1969), 155–69.

editing, general; emendation; textual criticism

Describing editing as "an intellectual responsibility," Kane advocates the correct practice of conjectural emendation (emendation not based on manuscript evidence) and reviews its theory and practice.

K6. KATZ, JOSEPH. "The *Maggie* Nobody Knows." *Modern Fiction Studies* 12 (1966): 200–212.

copy-text; Crane, Stephen

Katz compares the 1893 edition of *Maggie* (Crane's original text, printed at his expense) with the 1896 Appleton edition, revised by Crane and edited by the publisher.

K7. KATZ, JOSEPH. " 'Novelists of the Future': Animadversions Against the Rigidity of Current Theory in the Editing of Nineteenth-Century American Writers." In *Editing British and American Literature, 1880–1920,* edited by Eric W. Domville, 65–76.

authorial intention; CEAA; nineteenth century; Norris, Frank

An argument against the attempt to publish "definitive" editions of nineteenth-century authors.

K8. KATZ, JOSEPH. "Practical Editions: Stephen Crane's *The Red Badge of Courage.*" *Proof* 2 (1972): 301–18.

Crane, Stephen; practical editions

Katz surveyed fifteen practical editions of Crane's novel. After listing four tests for reliability to be applied to any practical edition, he reports that all fifteen editions failed at least one of them; several failed them all.

K9. KATZ, JOSEPH. "The Structure of Critical Editions." *The Editorial Quarterly* 1 (1975): 8–9.

apparatus; organization of editions

Katz discusses the structural division of critical editions into text and apparatus as an organizing principle. He also sets out the purpose of the historical and textual essays; textual and explanatory notes; tables of editorial emendations, end-line hyphenation, and historical collations; supplementary apparatus; and appendices.

K10. KAUFMAN, STUART BRUCE. "The Samuel Gompers Papers as Literature: Toward a Stream-of-Consciousness History." *Maryland Historian* 8 (1977): 54–59.

editing, general; Gompers, Samuel; training

The senior editor of the Gompers papers describes documentary editions as literature and suggests that they can provide interpretive insight. Kaufman also describes his work with students.

K11. KELLEY, MAURICE. "Considerations Touching the Right Editing of John Milton's *De Doctrina Christiana*." In *Editing Seventeenth-Century Prose*, edited by D. I. B. Smith, 31–50.

Milton, John; theology; transcription

A proposal of a new editorial approach to Milton's *De Doctrina Christiana*.

K12. KELLEY, PHILIP, AND RONALD HUDSON. "Editing the Brownings' Correspondence: An Editorial Manual." In *Editing the Victorians*, edited by N. John Hall, 141–60.

Browning, Elizabeth Barrett; Browning, Robert; handbook; letters

An abbreviated version of the handbook used by the editors of *The Brownings' Correspondence*.

K13. KENT, GEORGE O. "The German Foreign Ministry's Archives at Whaddon Hall, 1948–58." *American Archivist* 24 (1961): 43–54.

Germany; microfilm; selection; translation

Kent describes an international project to microfilm and translate the archives of the German Foreign Ministry collected at the end of World War II. See also articles by Francis L. Loewenheim and Dagmar Horna Perman.

K14. KERBER, LINDA K. Review of *The Papers of James Madison,* vols. 3 and 4. *William and Mary Quarterly* 35 (1978): 147–55.

annotation; Madison, James; selection

Kerber explains the two types of notes used in the edition. She expresses concern about duplication of letters published in the Founding Fathers projects and notes that documentary editions, despite their costs, are less expensive than such historical projects as museum exhibits and television productions.

K15. KERR, CHESTER. "Publishing Historical Sources: A Prejudiced View of the Problem of Finance." *Proceedings of the American Philosophical Society* 98 (1954): 273–78.

funding

Kerr discusses the problems of financing the publication of historical sources and lists possible sources of funding for documentary publications. The article also describes the kinds of savings, markets, and subsidies available for manuscript publication.

K16. KETCHAM, RALPH L. "The Madison Family Papers: Case Study in a Search for Historical Manuscripts." *Manuscripts* 11 (Summer 1959): 49–55.

Madison, James; search

Ketcham describes a search for Madison papers and some of the discoveries made.

K17. KEWER, ELEANOR D. "Case Histories in the Craft of the Publisher's Editor, Culminating in a Justification of Barbed Wire."

In *Editor, Author, and Publisher,* edited by William J. Howard, 65–73. Toronto: University of Toronto Press, 1969.

apparatus; format; letters

Kewer reviews some problems faced and decisions made by the editors at Harvard University Press and the editors of some editions they published. She emphasizes problems of presentation and apparatus, including symbols.

K18. KIMNACH, WILSON H. "Realities of the Sermon: Some Considerations for Editors." *Newsletter of the Association for Documentary Editing* 5 (February 1983): 5–10.

Edwards, Jonathan; oral material; sermons; transcription

The main problem in editing sermon manuscripts, according to Kimnach, is that sermons are both oral events and written manuscripts. Sermon manuscripts contain marks for the speaker, little (if any) punctuation, and revisions reflecting their repeated use.

K19. KING, T. J. "The Use of Computers for Storing Records in Historical Research." *Historical Methods* 14 (Spring 1981): 55–64.

computers

King discusses the use of computers, as well as editing commands and information about filing and storage.

K20. KIRKHAM, E. KAY. *How to Read the Handwriting and Records of Early America.* Salt Lake City: Deseret Book Company, 1965.

archives; handwriting; preservation

Kirkham explains in detail how to read early American and German-American handwriting, provides examples of handwriting and a glossary of legal terms and abbreviations, and offers information on obtaining copies of records and using archival materials.

K21. KITCHING, CHRISTOPHER. "Record Publication in England and Wales, 1957–1982." *Archives: The Journal of the British Records Association* 17 (April 1985): 38–46.

England; public records; Wales

Kitching analyzes the subject matter of the 469 documentary volumes published in England and Wales during this period and discusses some of the problems facing British documentary editors.

K22. KLEINHENZ, CHRISTOPHER, ED. *Medieval Manuscripts and Textual Criticism*. Chapel Hill: University of North Carolina Department of Romance Languages, 1976.

Middle Ages

See articles by Castellani, Arrigo; Frank, István; Kane, George; Roncaglia, Aurelio; Rossini, Egidio; and Vinaver, Eugène.

K23. KLINE, MARY-JO. *A Guide to Documentary Editing*. Baltimore: Johns Hopkins University Press, 1987.

handbook; history of editing

This handbook, prepared for the Association for Documentary Editing, provides information on virtually every aspect of the subject. It is meant to be descriptive rather than prescriptive, and to offer a variety of opinions and solutions.

K24. KLINGELHOFER, HERBERT E. "Dating the Elbridge Gerry Memorandum on Representation." *Manuscripts* 39 (Fall 1987): 320–26.

dating; Gerry, Elbridge

Klingelhofer dates the document by analyzing the discussions that took place during the Constitutional Convention.

K25. KLYBERG, ALBERT T. "Memoirs of a Quarter-Master General's Quartermaster: The Role of the Sponsoring Institution in an Historical Publication Project." In *The Publication of American Historical Manuscripts*, edited by Leslie W. Dunlap and Fred Shelley, 1–10.

administration; consortia; funding; Greene, Nathanael; project organization

Klyberg describes the establishment and administration of the Greene papers and suggests ways of cutting costs, including the publication of a handbook, cooperative searching, and a national catalogue of archival collections.

K26. KNIGHT, DAVID. "Background and Foreground: Getting Things in Context." *British Journal for the History of Science* 20 (January 1987): 3–12.

audience; history of science; illustrations

Knight discusses the problem of defining the audience for the history of science and some of the special difficulties the field presents, including those of annotation, indexing, and treatment of illustrations.

K27. KNOX, GEORGE. "Anthony and Cleopatra in Russia: A Problem in the Editing of Tiepolo Drawings." In *Editing Illustrated Books*, edited by William Blissett, 35–55.

authentication; illustrations

A reconstruction of a set of Tiepolo paintings from textual and illustrative evidence.

K28. KOCH, ADRIENNE. "The Historian as Scholar." *The Nation*, 24 November 1962, 357–61.

editing, general; NHPC; professional status

This article describes the projects of the NHPC. Koch also discusses the work of historical editors, its importance, and criticism of editors by their colleagues.

K29. KOHN, RICHARD H., AND GEORGE M. CURTIS III. "The Government, the Historical Profession, and Historical Editing: A Review." *Reviews in American History* 9 (June 1981): 145–55.

NEH; NHPRC; professional status; training

Kohn and Curtis review NHPRC and NEH funding of documentary editing projects and discuss four critical issues for historical editing: what to edit, what form to publish in, editorial standards, and who should do the editing. The authors recommend that editors be better integrated into the historical profession.

K30. KORTEPETER, CARL MAX. "German Zeitung Literature in the Sixteenth Century." In *Editing Sixteenth-Century Texts*, edited by R. J. Schoeck, 113–29.

Arabic; German; sixteenth century

A discussion of the development of Zeitung literature and its uses, along with some observations on the problems of editing Arabic documents.

K31. KRADITOR, AILEEN S. "Editing the Abolitionists." *Reviews in American History* 1 (1973): 519–23.

Garrison, William Lloyd; letters; selection

Kraditor discusses the advantages and disadvantages of excluding letters to Garrison. See also James Brewer Stewart, "Garrison Again. . . ."

K32. KRISTELLER, PAUL OSKAR. "Between the Italian Renaissance and the French Enlightenment: Gabriel Naude as an Editor." *Renaissance Quarterly* 32 (Spring 1979): 41–72.

Italian; Naude, Gabriel

Kristeller discusses the life and work of Gabriel Naude and the significance of the Italian writing he published.

K33. KRISTELLER, PAUL OSKAR. "The Lachmann Method: Merits and Limitations." *Text* 1 (1984): 11–20.

history of editing

Kristeller describes "the standard method of textual criticism formulated by Karl Lachmann in the early nineteenth century and consistently applied to the editing of classical Greek and Latin texts by Lachmann himself and by many other scholars." He discusses the revision of the method and its application to nonclassical texts.

K34. KRISTELLER, PAUL OSKAR. "Textual Scholarship and General Theories of History and Literature." *Text* 3 (1987): 1–9.

editing, general; literary criticism

Kristeller differentiates between "two layers of historical scholarship, the textual scholarship which we pursue and which is more modest but more certain, and the general theory of history and of literature which is more ambitious but also more conjectural."

K35. KURTZ, STEPHEN G. "The Papers of John Marshall." *Smithsonian Journal of History* 2 (1967): 76.

legal history; Marshall, John

The editor of the John Marshall papers discusses the contributions of the first chief justice.

L

L1. LABAREE, LEONARD W. "In Search of 'B Franklin.'" *William and Mary Quarterly* 16 (1959): 188–97.

authenticity; Franklin, Benjamin

Labaree discusses the search for manuscripts for his edition of the Franklin papers. He lists the various sources, from the National Archives to private collections, in which he found manuscripts and enumerates problems of forgery and uncooperative owners.

L2. LABAREE, LEONARD W. "The Papers of Benjamin Franklin." *Daedalus* 86 (1955): 57–62.

Franklin, Benjamin; organization of editions; project organization

The editor of Franklin's papers discusses historical editing as a cooperative enterprise. He presents the problems of assembling and organizing material and the basic editorial procedures his project adopted.

L3. LABAREE, LEONARD W. "The Papers of Benjamin Franklin: The Background and Objectives of a Great Project and an Appeal for Help and Cooperation." *Manuscripts* 7 (1954): 36–39.

autograph collectors; Franklin, Benjamin; search

The editor of Franklin's papers discusses his work and describes the objectives of the project and the sources of manuscripts. Labaree also issues an appeal to autograph collectors for their help in locating papers.

L4. LABAREE, LEONARD W. "Scholarly Editing in Our Times." *Ventures* 3 (1964): 28–31.

annotation; funding; search; selection; transcription

A summary of documentary editing practices.

L5. LABAREE, LEONARD W., AND WHITFIELD J. BELL, JR. "The Papers of Benjamin Franklin: A Progress Report." *Proceedings of the American Philosophical Society* 101 (1957): 532–34.

Franklin, Benjamin; search; selection

The editors of the Franklin papers discuss their project, emphasizing collection of manuscripts, including where both manuscripts and printed material were found. They also discuss their criteria for including a manuscript in the edition.

L6. LAFANTASIE, GLENN W. "Toward Better Reviewing of Local History Documentary Editions: A Nineteenth-Century Model." *Newsletter of the Association for Documentary Editing* 4 (February 1982): 1–5.

local history; reviewing

LaFantasie uses Samuel Gardner Drake's nineteenth-century review of Savage's edition of John Winthrop's journal and his complaints about made-to-order reviews to criticize modern reviews of documentary editions. LaFantasie notes the changes in local history writing and reviewing since Drake's time, but notes that Drake's review could still serve as a model.

L7. LANCASHIRE, ANNE, ED. *Editing Renaissance Dramatic Texts: English, Italian, and Spanish: Papers Given at the Eleventh Annual Conference on Editorial Problems, University of Toronto, 31 October-1 November 1975.* New York: Garland, 1976.

drama; Renaissance

See articles by Corrigan, Beatrice; Evans, G. Blakemore; Freeman, Arthur; Proudfoot, G. R.; and Reichenberger, Arnold G.

L8. LANCASHIRE, IAN. "Medieval Drama." In *Editing Medieval Texts*, edited by A. G. Rigg, 58–85.

drama; history of editing; Middle Ages

A review of the approaches taken in editing medieval drama and a discussion of the remaining problems.

L9. LAND, ROBERT H. "The National Union Catalog of Manuscript Collections." *American Archivist* 17 (1954): 195–207.

finding aids; NUCMC; search

Land describes how the NUCMC project was organized, its rules for cataloging, and progress.

L10. LANDON, RICHARD, ED. *Editing and Editors: A Retrospect: Papers Given at the Twenty-First Annual Conference on Editorial Problems, University of Toronto, 1–2 November 1985.* New York: AMS Press, 1988.

history of editing

See articles by Bentley, G. E., Jr. ("The People of the Book"); Boyle, Leonard E.; Metzger, Bruce M.; Nordloh, David J. ("Theory, Funding, and Coincidence"); Reiman, Donald H. ("Gentlemen Authors and Professional Writers"); and Wells, Stanley ("Revision in Shakespeare's Plays").

L11. LANGE, THOMAS V. "English Illustrated Books on Microfiche." In *Editing Illustrated Books*, edited by William Blissett, 97–112.

illustrations; microfiche; nineteenth century; search; selection

A description of the compilation of a microfiche edition of 100 illustrated English books.

L12. LANGWORTHY, CAROL ROLLOFF. "The Modern World of Neith Boyce." *Documentary Editing* 7 (June 1985): 1–7.

annotation; Boyce, Neith

Langworthy's article discusses the subjects covered in Neith Boyce's memoirs. The editing problems presented by the project are detailed, with emphasis on Boyce's policy of omitting names. Langworthy explains the procedures used to discover the missing names.

L13. LATHAM, ROBERT. "Publishing Pepys." *Scholarly Publishing* 6 (1974–75): 51–57.

annotation; apparatus; journals; Pepys, Samuel

Latham reviews the publishing history of Pepys's diary and describes the transcription and translation from shorthand, the annotation, and the apparatus of the edition he edited. It was possible to abbreviate the annotation by publishing a "Companion" volume of essays and glossaries.

L14. LAUFER, ROGER. "From Publishing to Editing *Gil Blas de Santillane:* An Evaluation of the Rival Claims of Practical and Ideal Editing." In *Editing Eighteenth-Century Novels,* edited by G. E. Bentley, Jr., 31–48.

accidentals; copy-text; French; Lesage, René; substantives

A description of an edition of *Gil Blas,* with an extensive discussion of the problem of accidentals versus substantives.

L15. LAWRENCE, DAN H. "A Bibliographical Novitiate: In Search of Henry James." *Papers of the Bibliographical Society of America* 52 (1958): 23–33.

editing, general; James, Henry; search

Lawrence offers his experience as a beginning bibliographer as a lesson for others, emphasizing the value of curiosity and the use of nontraditional sources.

L16. LEBRAVE, JEAN-LOUIS. "Rough Drafts: A Challenge to Uniformity in Editing." *Text* 3 (1987): 135–42.

computers; drafts

Lebrave discusses the ways in which editing rough drafts can provide insight into the writing process and suggests ways that computers could be used for this purpose.

L17. LEE, CHARLES E. "Documentary Reproduction: Letterpress Publication—Why? What? How?" *American Archivist* 28 (1965): 351–65.

archives; form of publication; selection; South Carolina

Lee describes how document publication has been a low priority for archivists and discusses the publishing activities of South Carolina's Archives. The article includes rules for what material to publish and how to publish it.

L18. LEECH, CLIFFORD. "A Note from a General Editor." In *Editing Sixteenth-Century Texts*, edited by R. J. Schoeck, 24–26.

drama; sixteenth century; transcription

Leech comments on S. Schoenbaum's remarks (in the same volume) on duplication of effort, modern spelling, and the inclusion of criticism in editions.

L19. LEECH, CLIFFORD. "On Editing One's First Play." *Studies in Bibliography* 23 (1970): 61–70.

annotation; collation; copy-text; drama

Leech suggests guidelines and procedures for an editor editing a play in a series that has a general editor.

L20. LEES, LORRAINE M., AND SANDRA GIOIA TREADWAY. "A Future for Our Diplomatic Past? A Critical Appraisal of the *Foreign*

Relations Series." *Journal of American History* 70 (December 1983): 621–29.

annotation; *Foreign Relations* series; publishing; selection; transcription

The reviewers criticize the series for its ambiguous editorial statement, unevenness of annotation, principles of selection, and slowness of publication. See also Marvin F. Russell's letter to the editor and Lees and Treadway's response, both in the June 1984 issue.

L21. LEES, LORRAINE M., AND SANDRA GIOIA TREADWAY. Letter to the Editor. *Journal of American History* 71 (June 1984): 216–17.

declassification; *Foreign Relations* series; National Archives

A brief response to Marvin F. Russell's letter in the same issue.

L22. LEFFLER, RICHARD. "The Case of George Mason's Objections to the Constitution." *Manuscripts* 39 (Fall 1987): 285–92.

Mason, George; Ratification of the Constitution project

Leffler recounts the textual history of Mason's objections to the Constitution.

L23. LEIGH, RALPH A. "Rousseau's Correspondence: Editorial Problems." In *Editing Correspondence,* edited by J. A. Dainard, 39–62.

annotation; letters; organization of editions; Rousseau, Jean-Jacques; transcription

A discussion of the special problems of editing Rousseau and their solutions, along with general advice.

L24. LEISINGER, ALBERT H., JR. "Selected Aspects of Microreproduction in the United States." *Archivum* 16 (1966): 127–50; *National Archives Accessions,* no. 60 (1967): 29–49.

microforms; National Archives

Leisinger lists and comments on the uses of microfilming as reference, space-saving or disposal, security, preservation, publication, acquisition, administration, and management. He then reports the results of a questionnaire on microfilming of archives and historical manuscripts in the various states and describes the microfilming program of the National Archives.

L25. LELAND, WALDO GIFFORD. "The Prehistory and Origins of the National Historical Publications Commission." *American Archivist* 27 (1964): 187–94. Reprinted in slightly revised form as "J. Franklin Jameson and the Origins of the National Historical Publications Commission," in *J. Franklin Jameson: A Tribute*, edited by Ruth Anne Fisher and William Lloyd Fox (Washington, D.C.: Catholic University of America Press, 1965).

Jameson, J. Franklin; NHPC

Leland describes the career of J. Franklin Jameson, emphasizing Jameson's role in the founding of the NHPC.

L26. LEMAY, J. A. LEO. "Franklin and the *Autobiography:* An Essay on Recent Scholarship." *Eighteenth-Century Studies* 1 (1967): 185–211. Reprinted, in part, in *CEAA Newsletter* 2 (July 1969): 6–8, as "The New Franklin Texts."

authentication; Franklin, Benjamin

While generally praising *The Papers of Benjamin Franklin*, LeMay criticizes the handling of texts whose authorship is in doubt. He also praises the APS-Yale edition of the *Autobiography*, noting, however, that the edition does not include all of Franklin's revisions and additions to the original manuscript. LeMay also discusses other current scholarship on Franklin, including biographies.

L27. LEMISCH, JESSE. "The American Revolution Bicentennial and the Papers of Great White Men: A Preliminary Critique of Current Documentary Publication Programs and Some Alternative Proposals." *American Historical Association Newsletter* 9 (November 1971): 7–21.

black history; editing, general; Native Americans; NHPC; social history; women's history

Lemisch discusses the projects of the NHPC and criticizes current documentary publication programs as too focused on "great white men." He also discusses the directions of the study of American history.

L28. LEMISCH, JESSE. "The Papers of a Few Great Black Men and a Few Great White Women." *Maryland Historian* 6 (1975): 60–65.

black history; editing, general; Native Americans; NHPRC; women's history

In an update of his 1971 article, Lemisch notes little progress toward publishing the papers of members of nonelite groups.

L29. LEOPOLD, RICHARD W. "The *Foreign Relations* Series: A Centennial Estimate." *Mississippi Valley Historical Review* 49 (1963): 595–612.

Foreign Relations series

Leopold describes the history of the *Foreign Relations* series, focusing on the problems of the series during the postwar era.

L30. LEOPOLD, RICHARD W. "The *Foreign Relations* Series Revisited: One Hundred Plus Ten." *Journal of American History* 59 (1973): 935–57.

Foreign Relations series

In this update of his 1963 review, Leopold describes the *Foreign Relations* series and appraises it. He also discusses some of the reasons for its lessening prestige.

L31. LEOPOLD, RICHARD W. "The Historian and the Federal Government." *Journal of American History* 64 (1977): 5–23.

access; Library of Congress; National Archives; NHPRC; presidential papers

Leopold discusses numerous aspects of the connection between historians and the government. Among the items discussed are the drive to make the National Archives an independent agency, the history of the NHPRC, the presidential library system, questions of access and declassification, and the role of the Library of Congress.

L32. LEVERE, TREVOR H., ED. *Editing Texts in the History of Science and Medicine: Papers Given at the Seventeenth Annual Conference on Editorial Problems, University of Toronto, 6–7 November 1981.* New York: Garland, 1982.

history of science

See articles by Cohen, I. Bernard; Drake, Stillman; Hall, Bert S.; and Voigts, Linda Ehrsam.

L33. LEVIN, HOWARD M., AND WENDY J. STROTHMAN. "Introducing Text/Fiche." *Scholarly Publishing* 7 (1975–76): 321–32.

microfiche; visual material

The authors describe a publication form that "combines pictorial microfiche, in full colour or black and white, with a printed text containing the conventional apparatus of the book along with . . . a caption list."

L34. LEVY, LEONARD W. Review of *The Papers of James Madison,* ed. William T. Hutchinson and William M. E. Rachal, vols. 4–7. *Journal of American History* 59 (1972): 115–17.

annotation; Madison, James; selection

Levy criticizes the volumes as overinclusive and overannotated.

L35. LEWIS, WILMARTH S. "Editing Familiar Letters." *Daedalus* 86 (1955): 71–77.

annotation; letters; search

Lewis discusses the problems of editing familiar letters, including location and annotation, and offers suggestions on appropriate writing style.

L36. LEWIS, WILMARTH S. "Editing Familiar Letters." In *Editing Correspondence*, edited by J. A. Dainard, 25–37.

annotation; control; letters; organization of editions; search; selection; transcription; Walpole, Horace

A general essay on editing correspondence, with examples from editing the Walpole correspondence.

L37. LINGELBACH, WILLIAM E. "Benjamin Franklin's Papers and the American Philosophical Society." *Proceedings of the American Philosophical Society* 94 (1955): 539–80.

American Philosophical Society; Franklin, Benjamin; funding

Lingelbach reviews APS support of the Franklin Papers project and describes the project itself.

L38. LINK, ARTHUR S. "Where We Stand Now and Where We Might Go." *Newsletter of the Association for Documentary Editing* 2 (February 1980): 1–4.

professional status; reviewing; training

Link discusses the state of the editorial profession. He is especially critical of the absence of common methodology, scholarly review, systematic training, and standards for selection and annotation. Link discusses the help that historical editors could get from editors in other fields.

L39. LINK, ARTHUR S., DAVID W. HIRST, JOHN WELLS DAVIDSON, AND JOHN E. LITTLE. Letter to the Editor. *Journal of American History* 70 (March 1984): 945–55.

annotation; objectivity; Wilson, Woodrow

A response to Juliette L. George, Michael F. Marmor, and Alexander L. George, "Research Note/Issues in Wilson Scholarship: References to Early 'Strokes.' " See also the subsequent letters of George, Marmor, and George.

L40. LINT, GREGG L. "Documentary Reviewing Reviewed: A Survey of the Book Review Policies of Selected Historical Journals." *Newsletter of the Association for Documentary Editing* 2 (September 1980): 1–2.

reviewing

Lint discusses the book review policy of the *American Historical Review* as it relates to documentary editions and the results of a survey of journals on their policies.

L41. LOEWENBERG, BERT JAMES. "Jared Sparks and the Records of the Republic." In his *American History in American Thought: Christopher Columbus to Henry Adams*, 221–238. New York: Simon and Schuster, 1972.

history of editing; Sparks, Jared

Loewenberg discusses the life and career of Jared Sparks, emphasizing Sparks's contribution to historical editing.

L42. LOEWENHEIM, FRANCIS L. "Guides to Microfilmed German Records: A Review." *American Archivist* 22 (1959): 445–49.

finding aids; Germany; microfilm

A review of the guides to German documents captured and microfilmed after World War II. See also articles by George D. Kent and Dagmar Horna Perman.

L43. LONG, E. B. "Southern Historical Society Papers Index." *Civil War History* 9 (1963): 280–82.

indexing; Southern Historical Society Papers

Long discusses the value of the Southern Historical Society Papers, the need for an index, and its preparation.

L44. LONG, WILLIAM B. "Stage-Directions: A Misinterpreted Factor in Determining Textual Provenance." *Text* 2 (1985): 121–37.

drama; seventeenth century; sixteenth century

Long argues that theatrical practice in the Elizabethan-Jacobean-Caroline era has been misunderstood and insufficiently studied, and that as a result editors have based decisions about provenance on inadequate or erroneous information.

L45. LUEY, BETH. *Handbook for Academic Authors.* New York: Cambridge University Press, 1987.

copyright; indexing; proofreading; publishing

A basic guide to finding and working with a publisher, including practical advice on copyright, proofreading, permissions, and indexing.

L46. LUSIGNAN, SERGE, AND JOHN NORTH, EDS. *Computing in the Humanities.* Waterloo, Ont.: University of Waterloo Press, 1977.

computers

This book contains twenty-eight papers from the Third International Conference on Computing in the Humanities, held in 1977.

M

M1. MACHLIS, PAUL. "Computer-Assisted Document Control For Editorial Projects." *Newsletter of the Association for Documentary Editing* 5 (September 1983): 6–11.

computers; control; Davis, Jefferson; Edison, Thomas; Henry, Joseph; Twain, Mark

Machlis focuses on the use of the computer catalog in editing projects. The use of computers at the Joseph Henry, Jefferson Davis, Mark Twain, and Thomas Edison projects is discussed in some detail.

M2. MACKENZIE, NORMAN H. "Hopkins, Robert Bridges and the Modern Editor." In *Editing British and American Literature, 1880–1920*, edited by Eric W. Domville, 9–30.

Bridges, Robert; dating; Hopkins, Gerard Manley

A description of the evolution of Hopkins manuscripts, with special attention to the use of infra-red imaging.

M3. MACLEAN, GERALD M. "What Is a Restoration Poem? Editing a Discourse, Not an Author." *Text* 3 (1987): 319–46.

Philips, Katherine; poetry; seventeenth century

MacLean explains the importance of literary history in editing poems on political events, discussing "a fully socialized and historicized editorial theory and practice." His examples are drawn from poems on the Restoration, particularly those of Katherine Philips.

M4. MADDEN, DAVID, AND RICHARD POWERS. *Writers' Revisions: An Annotated Bibliography of Articles and Books About Writers' Revisions and Their Comments on the Creative Process.* Metuchen, N.J.: Scarecrow Press, 1981.

authorial intention; bibliographies

After a brief description of revisions and an introduction to the methods and purposes of studying them, the authors provide an annotated bibliography of writings on the subject, arranged by the name of the author discussed. The second part of the bibliography covers books and articles in which writers discuss the creative process; this section is alphabetical by author or editor. Five indexes are provided.

M5. MAILLOUX, STEVEN. "Textual Scholarship and 'Author's Final Intention.'" In his *Interpretive Conventions: The Reader in the Study of American Fiction* (Ithaca: Cornell University Press, 1982), 93–125.

authorial intention; literary criticism

In this volume discussing the reader-response approach to literature, Mailloux devotes a chapter to textual scholarship. He argues that final intention should be determined aesthetically rather than chronologically.

M6. MALONE, DUMAS. "Tapping the Wisdom of the Founding Fathers." *New York Times Magazine,* 27 May 1956, p. 25.

editing, general; Founding Fathers projects

A general assessment of the Founding Fathers papers projects.

M7. MANNING, PETER J. "The Hone-ing of Byron's Corsair." In *Textual Criticism and Literary Interpretation,* edited by Jerome J. McGann, 107–26.

Byron, George Gordon, Lord; copyright

Manning discusses the significance of pirated editions.

M8. MARCUS, MAEVA, AND CHRISTINE JORDAN. "The Constitution and the Court." *Manuscripts* 39 (Fall 1987): 309–19.

Supreme Court

The authors describe the new light shed by documents collected for the Documentary History of the Supreme Court on such questions as federal jurisdiction and separation of powers.

M9. MARCUS, MAEVA, JAMES PERRY, JAMES BUCHANAN, CHRISTINE JORDAN, STEPHAN TULL, AND EMILY VAN TASSEL. "The Documentary History of the Supreme Court of the United States." *Prologue* 18 (Fall 1986): 181–88.

organization of editions; search; Supreme Court

The authors describe the purpose and focus of the project. They explain the search process and the organization of the volumes.

M10. MARX, LEO. "The American Scholar Today." *Commentary* 32 (1961): 48–53.

history of editing

Marx discusses a new phase in the study of American history, which he characterizes as "documentary, objective, professional, organized, or official." He offers as evidence the publication of a number of documentary projects and the Hamer *Guide.* He then discusses the relationship between "scientific" scholarly editing and humanistic scholarship.

M11. MATTHEWS, JOHN. "The Hunt for the Disraeli Letters." In *Editing Correspondence,* edited by J. A. Dainard, 81–92.

Disraeli, Benjamin; letters; search

Matthews explains the importance of a complete edition of Disraeli's correspondence and describes the difficulties and surprises of the search.

MI2. MAY, JAMES E. "Determining Final Authorial Intention in Revised Satires: The Case of Edward Young." *Studies in Bibliography* 38 (1985): 276–89.

authorial intention; Young, Edward

May discusses the application of the principles of final authorial intention to satirical writing "that is rhetorically conceived for a historical moment or that has a largely historical value to scholars."

MI3. MCADAM, E. L., JR. "The Textual Approach to Meaning." In *English Institute Essays, 1946,* 191–201. New York: Columbia University Press, 1947.

editing, general; textual criticism

A clear introduction to textual criticism, with well-chosen examples.

MI4. MCCLELLAND, JOHN. "Critical Editing in the Modern Languages." *Text* 1 (1984): 201–16.

apparatus; copy-text; France; Germany

McClelland compares the Anglo-American, French, and German attitudes toward and practices in selecting the copy-text, emending, and designing apparatus.

MI5. MCCLURE, JAMES P. "The Neglected Calendar." *Documentary Editing* 10 (September 1988): 18–21.

calendaring; search

McClure discusses the value of the calendar to researchers, as well as the different purposes served by the calendar and the documentary edition. He argues that the calendar should be given more attention as part of the documentary edition and that calendars should be produced "as editorial products in their own right."

MI6. McCOWN, ROBERT A. "Summary of the Proceedings of a Conference on the Publication of American Historical Manuscripts." In *The Publication of American Historical Manuscripts*, edited by Leslie W. Dunlap and Fred Shelley, 97–105.

editing, general

A summary of the meeting, including a paper on thematic approaches to documentary editing that does not appear in the volume.

MI7. McDONALD, FORREST. Review of *The Papers of Alexander Hamilton*, vols. 25 and 26. *William and Mary Quarterly* 37 (1980): 330–33.

annotation; Hamilton, Alexander; objectivity

McDonald criticizes the editors' attempts at objectivity which, he claims, led them to become "anti-Hamiltonian in their commentaries."

MI8. McELRATH, JOSEPH R., JR. "The ADE Guidelines for Reviewers of Editions." *Documentary Editing* 10 (December 1988): 22–23.

reviewing

These are the guidelines that the ADE approved for distribution. They recommend that reviews cover why the edition was published, how it was created, how well it was fashioned, and its probable impact.

MI9. McELRATH, JOSEPH R., JR. "The First Two Volumes of *The Writings of Henry D. Thoreau*: A Review Article." *Proof* 4 (1975): 215–35.

CEAA; copy-text; emendation; Thoreau, Henry David

McElrath praises *The Maine Woods* and is highly critical of *Walden*. He focuses on the choice of copy-text and decisions about emendation. He concludes with suggestions to improve the CEAA's vetting procedures.

M20. McELRATH, JOSEPH R., JR. "Practical Editions: Henry D. Thoreau's *Walden*." *Proof* 4 (1975): 175–82.

practical editions; Thoreau, Henry David

McElrath examined ten editions of *Walden* and found them generally corrupt.

M21. McELRATH, JOSEPH R., JR. "Tradition and Innovation: Recent Developments in Literary Editing." *Documentary Editing* 10 (December 1988): 5–10.

apparatus; authorial intention; CEAA; types of editing

McElrath discusses the debates between historical and literary editors, and among literary editors, focusing on the language of the debate, questions about apparatus, and authorial intention.

M22. McFEELY, WILLIAM S. "The Civility of Scholars." *College and Research Libraries* 35 (1974): 286–90.

access

McFeely presents the case for open access to editors' files for all legitimate scholars. See also John Y. Simon, "Editorial Projects as Derivative Archives."

M23. McGANN, JEROME J. *A Critique of Modern Textual Criticism.* Chicago: University of Chicago Press, 1983.

authorial intention; copy-text; history of editing

McGann sets out the central issues and controversies of textual criticism, discussing the theories of Bowers, Gaskell, and Tanselle. He urges broadening the critical focus to include an understanding of "the broadest cultural interests and relationships."

M24. McGANN, JEROME J. "The Monks and the Giants: Textual and Bibliographical Studies and the Interpretation of Literary Works." In his *Textual Criticism and Literary Interpretation*, 180–99.

editing, general; history of editing; literary criticism

Arguing that "textual criticism and bibliography are conceptually fundamental rather than preliminary to the study of literature," McGann reviews the history of the relationship and suggests a reconception of the field to make it more comprehensive. The reconception takes the form of a "program of historicist textual criticism."

M25. McGANN, JEROME J. "Shall These Bones Live?" *Text* 1 (1984): 21–40.

literary criticism

A discussion of the relationship between textual studies and several varieties of literary criticism.

M26. McGANN, JEROME J., ED. *Textual Criticism and Literary Interpretation*. Chicago: University of Chicago Press, 1985.

literary criticism; textual criticism

This collection of essays focuses on the relationship between textual criticism and literary interpretation, viewing textual studies as the "root and ground" of hermeneutics and interpretation as the "flower and the fruit." See articles by Gaskell, Philip ("*Night and Day*"); Honigmann, E. A. J. ("Date and Revision of *Troilus and Cressida*" and "Shakespeare as a Reviser"); Jack, Ian; Manning, Peter J.; McGann, Jerome J. ("The Monks and the Giants"); Patterson, Lee; Pearsall, Derek; Pizer, Donald ("Self-Censorship and Textual Editing"); and Warren, Michael J.

M27. McGirr, Newman F. "The Activities of Peter Force." *Records of the Columbia Historical Society* 42 (1942): 34–82.

American Archives; Force, Peter; history of editing; Library of Congress

An account of the professional life of Peter Force (1790–1868), printer, mayor of Washington, D.C., and compiler of the *American Archives*. The article also describes the volumes, which include fragments of original manuscripts.

M28. McHaney, Thomas L. "The Important Questions Are Seldom Raised." *Studies in the Novel* 7 (1975): 399–402.

CEAA

A response to John Freehafer's "Greg's Theory of Copy-Text and the Textual Criticism in the CEAA Editions." See also articles by Bruce Bebb and Hershel Parker, Vinton A. Dearing ("Textual Criticism Today"), Morse Peckham ("Notes on Freehafer"), and G. Thomas Tanselle ("Two Basic Distinctions"), all in the same issue.

M29. McHaney, Thomas L. Review of *The Works of Stephen Crane,* edited by Fredson Bowers, vols. 1, 5–7. *American Literary Realism* 4 (1971): 91–97; 391–94.

apparatus; Crane, Stephen

McHaney praises the introductory essays and discusses some of Bowers's textual emendations. He criticizes the organization and presentation of the apparatus in the volumes of short stories.

M30. McHANEY, THOMAS L. "The Textual Editions of Hawthorne and Melville." *Studies in the Literary Imagination* 2 (April 1969): 27–41.

accidentals; apparatus; copy-text; Hawthorne, Nathaniel; Melville, Herman

In this review of the first four volumes of the Centenary Edition of Hawthorne and the first two volumes of the Northwestern-Newberry Library Edition of Melville, McHaney summarizes the process of critical editing and compares the way the two editions have handled a variety of editorial problems.

M31. McKERROW, R. B. "The Treatment of Shakespeare's Text by His Earlier Editors, 1709–1768." *Proceedings of the British Academy* 19 (1933): 89–122.

eighteenth century; history of editing; Shakespeare, William

A history of the editing of Shakespeare in the eighteenth century.

M32. McKIVIGAN, JOHN R. "Capturing the Oral Event: Editing the Speeches of Frederick Douglass." *Documentary Editing* 10 (March 1988): 1–5.

authentication; Douglass, Frederick; oral materials; search; selection

McKivigan discusses the procedure for identifying, locating, and reconstructing Douglass's speeches, including the evaluation of variant stenographic reports. He also explains the procedures for choosing among various versions of the same speech delivered at different times.

M33. McLAVERTY, JAMES. "The Concept of Authorial Intention in Textual Criticism." *The Library*, 6th ser., 6 (1984): 121–38.

authorial intention

McLaverty seeks to "clarify the concept of intention and suggest what it should and should not be asked to do" by reviewing definitions and theories of intention, the ramifications of the concept for the editor, the relation between intention and error, the concept of final intention, and internal and external evidence.

M34. McLEOD, RANDALL. "Spellbound." In *Play-Texts in Old Spelling,* edited by G. B. Shand and Raymond C. Shady, 81–96.

compositorial studies; Renaissance; spelling

McLeod discusses the relationship beween typesetting and spelling, and the implications for editors.

M35. MEATS, STEPHEN E. "The Editing of Harold Frederic's Correspondence." *Review* 2 (1980): 31–39.

annotation; apparatus; CEAA; Frederic, Harold; indexing; letters

In this review of *The Correspondence of Harold Frederic,* edited by George E. Fortenberry, Stanton Gaines, and Robert H. Woodward, Meats praises the format, inclusion of letters to Frederic, and other editorial features. He considers the annotation excessive, the index uncomprehensive, and the system for numbering letters confusing. He also criticizes the editorial apparatus as wasteful. Finally, he questions the applicability of CEAA methods to personal documents.

M36. MEIER, AUGUST. Review of *The Frederick Douglass Papers,* ser. 1, vol. 1. *Journal of Southern History* 46 (1980): 433–35.

Douglass, Frederick; organization of editions; search

Meier is critical of the editors' decision to begin printing speeches while still obtaining correspondence, considering it "preferable to wait a few years and then present all the material in chronological order."

M37. MENDELSON, EDWARD. "The Fading Coal vs. the Gothic Cathedral or What to Do about an Author Both Forgetful and Deceased." *Text* 3 (1987): 409–16.

Auden, W. H.; authorial intention; copy-text

The coal and the cathedral represent two theories of authorship, and Mendelson discusses their implications for the editorial treatment of authorial revisions. He offers an extended example from W. H. Auden.

M38. MEREDITH, PETER. "Stage Directions and the Editing of Early English Drama." In *Editing Early English Drama*, edited by A. F. Johnston, 65–94.

drama; Middle Ages

Meredith discusses the nature, purpose, and origins of medieval stage directions. He then turns to their editorial treatment, urging that all such directions present in the original text (and only those) be included.

M39. MERIWETHER, JAMES B. "The Dashes in Hemingway's *A Farewell to Arms.*" *Papers of the Bibliographical Society of America* 58 (1964): 449–57.

censorship; Hemingway, Ernest

Meriwether describes the omission of words by Hemingway's American publisher for reasons of obscenity; Hemingway's subsequent restoration of those words when the novel was translated into French; and the effect of the omissions on the reading of the novel.

M40. MERIWETHER, JAMES B. "A Proposal for a CEAA Edition of William Faulkner." In *Editing Twentieth-Century Texts*, edited by Francess G. Halpenny, 12–27.

apparatus; CEAA; copyright; Faulkner, William

Meriwether describes both an ideal and a practicable edition of Faulkner. He sets out the difficulties of creating such an edition and offers the separation of apparatus from text as a solution.

M41. MERIWETHER, JAMES B. "Some Proofreading Precautions." *CEAA Newsletter* 2 (July 1969): 17–18.

proofreading

Meriwether recommends the use of the Hinman collator to catch printer's errors in lines reset without notice to the editors.

M42. MERRILEES, BRIAN. "Anglo-Norman." In *Editing Medieval Texts*, edited by A. G. Rigg, 86–106.

Anglo-Norman; history of editing; Middle Ages

A history of the editing of Anglo-Norman texts and recommendations for future editions.

M43. MESEROLE, HARRISON T. "Notes on Editing Seventeenth-Century American Poetry." *CEAA Newsletter* 2 (July 1969): 11–14.

poetry; seventeenth century

Meserole lists the main problems of editing seventeenth-century poetry as a dearth of original (or even early) texts; contradictory external information, and difficulty of attribution.

M44. METZ, G. HAROLD. "Disputed Shakespearean Texts and Stylometric Analysis." *Text* 2 (1985): 149–71.

authentication; computers; Shakespeare, William; statistical analysis

Metz describes a computer-assisted method of stylometric analysis and its application to texts attributed to Shakespeare.

M45. METZGER, BRUCE M. "History of Editing the Greek New Testament." In *Editing and Editors: A Retrospect,* edited by Richard Landon, 47–66.

Bible; history of editing

Metzger reviews editing of the Greek New Testament, beginning with editions prior to printing, through Erasmus and Beza, and on to scientific textual criticism beginning with Johann Jakob Griesbach in the late eighteenth century.

M46. MIDDLETON, ARTHUR PIERCE, AND DOUGLASS ADAIR. "The Mystery of the Horn Papers." *William and Mary Quarterly* 4 (1947): 409–45.

authentication; Horn papers; local history

The article reviews the history and subject of the Horn papers and the controversy over their authenticity. Middleton and Adair describe the procedures of the committee that debated the papers' authenticity and append the committee's official statement.

M47. MILLER, LEO. "Establishing the Text of Milton's State Papers." *Text* 2 (1985): 181–86.

Milton, John; search

Miller reviews the textual history of the state papers and the status of scholarship using them, and describes his efforts to unearth further texts.

M48. MILLER, LILLIAN B. Review of *The Correspondence and Miscellaneous Papers of Benjamin Henry Latrobe. Virginia Magazine of History and Biography* 94 (1986): 227–29.

annotation; history of science; Latrobe, Benjamin Henry; visual materials

This review demonstrates conflicting views on how the papers, drawings, and other effects of artists, engineers, architects, etc. should be edited, emphasizing differences in annotation.

M49. MILLGATE, JANE. "The Limits of Editing: The Problem of Scott's *The Siege of Malta.*" *Bulletin of Research in the Humanities* 82 (1979): 190–212.

Scott, Sir Walter; transcription

Millgate describes the circumstances under which *The Siege of Malta* was written, the nature of the manuscript, its physical condition, and "the editorial difficulties involved in confronting a document in which the mental and physical disabilities of the author enter at every point into the very texture of the work."

M50. MILLGATE, JANE, ED. *Editing Nineteenth-Century Fiction: Papers Given at the Thirteenth Annual Conference on Editorial Problems, University of Toronto, 4–5 November 1977.* New York: Garland, 1978.

fiction; nineteenth century

See articles by Millgate, Michael; Monod, Sylvère; Parker, Hershel ("Aesthetic Implications of Authorial Excisions"); Shillingsburg, Peter ("Textual Problems in Editing Thackeray"); and Thomson, Clive.

M51. MILLGATE, MICHAEL. "The Making and Unmaking of Hardy's Wessex Edition." In *Editing Nineteenth-Century Fiction,* edited by Jane Millgate, 61–82.

Hardy, Thomas

An account of the production of the Wessex edition of Hardy's work, as well as its limitations. Millgate explains the relationship between Hardy's revisions and contemporary publishing practice.

M52. MITCHELL, MEMORY F. "Editing the Papers of a Contemporary Governor." *American Archivist* 23 (1970): 11–18.

annotation; Sanford, Terry; selection; twentieth century

The author describes the problems that arise in editing the papers of a contemporary figure, emphasizing selection and annotation.

M53. MITCHELL, MEMORY F. "Publication of Documentary Volumes by the [North Carolina] Division of Archives and History." *Carolina Comments* 28 (November 1980): 164–71.

archives; North Carolina; state history

A condensation of a report assessing the documentary program of the North Carolina Division of Archives and History.

M54. MODERN LANGUAGE ASSOCIATION. *Professional Standards and American Editions: A Response to Edmund Wilson.* New York: MLA, 1969.

CEAA

This pamphlet, a response to Wilson's "The Fruits of the MLA," contains William M. Gibson's "The Center for Editions of American Authors"; John H. Fisher's "The MLA Editions of Major American Authors"; reprints of letters to the editor of the *New York Review of Books* by Ronald Gottesman, Paul Baender, Frederick Anderson, and Oscar Cargill; and a letter to Edmund Wilson from John C. Gerber.

M55. MODIANO, RAIMONDA. "Coleridge's Marginalia." *Text* 2 (1985): 257–68.

Coleridge, Samuel Taylor; marginalia

Modiano discusses the importance and difficulties of editing Coleridge's marginalia, emphasizing the decision about how much of the text upon which Coleridge was commenting to reprint and the problems of documenting the sources of Coleridge's ideas.

M56. MOGGRIDGE, D. E. "On Editing Keynes." In *Editing Modern Economists*, edited by D. E. Moggridge, 67–90.

authentication; economics; Keynes, John Maynard; organization of editions; selection

Moggridge reviews the history of Keynes's *Collected Writings* and discusses the project's generally "minimalist" approach toward annotation and apparatus. His main focus is on the selection of documents.

M57. MOGGRIDGE, D. E., ED. *Editing Modern Economists: Papers Given at the Twenty-Second Annual Conference on Editorial Problems, University of Toronto, 7–8 November 1989.* New York: AMS Press, 1988.

economics

See articles by Black, R. D.; Howson, Susan; Moggridge, D. E.; Rymes, T. K.; and Whitaker, John K.

M58. MONOD, SYLVÈRE. " 'Between Two Worlds': Editing Dickens." In *Editing Nineteenth-Century Fiction*, edited by Jane Millgate, 17–39.

annotation; audience; copy-text; Dickens, Charles; translation

A discussion of tailoring annotation policies to suit the reader, as well as a description of special textual difficulties presented by Dickens.

M59. MONROE, HASKELL M., JR. "The Grant Papers: A Review Article." *Journal of the Illinois State Historical Society* 61 (1968): 463–72.

Grant, Ulysses S.; project organization

Monroe describes the history of the Grant papers project, as well as Grant's life and career. He also discusses reviews of the first volume.

M60. MONROE, HASKELL M., JR. "The Papers of Jefferson Davis." *Manuscripts* 19 (1967): 28–32.

Davis, Jefferson

Monroe discusses the importance and history of the Jefferson Davis papers project, as well as the inadequacies of its predecessors.

M61. MONROE, HASKELL M., JR. "Some Thoughts for an Aspiring Historical Editor." *American Archivist* 32 (1969): 147–59.

editing, general; history of editing

Monroe provides a brief history of documentary editing in the United States; describes and evaluates the Jefferson, Adams, Franklin, Wilson, Madison, Clay, and Calhoun projects; and lists the desirable characteristics of an editor.

M62. MONTAGNES, IAN. "Microfiche and the Scholarly Publisher." *Scholarly Publishing* 7 (1975–76): 63–84.

microforms

An introduction to microfiche publishing, its benefits, and its limitations.

M63. MONTAGNES, IAN. "Perspectives on the New Technology." *Scholarly Publishing* 12 (April 1981): 219–29.

computers

This article discusses the revolutions in scholarly communications and suggests that the computer is neither the first nor the most important. Montagnes also discusses the computer's impact on various publishing functions.

M64. MONTGOMERY, WILLIAM. "Editing the Darwin Correspondence: A Quantitative Perspective." *British Journal for the History of Science* 20 (January 1987): 13–27.

computers; Darwin, Charles; letters; statistical studies

Montgomery discusses the value of quantitative analysis of documents, including estimating missing correspondence, determining what influenced the volume of correspondence, and the roles of various correspondents.

M65. MOORE, JOHN BASSETT. "The Diplomatic Correspondence of the American Revolution." *Political Science Quarterly* 8 (1893): 33–47.

history of editing; Sparks, Jared

Moore describes the defects in Jared Sparks's edition of the diplomatic correspondence of the American Revolution, including changing the style of the original, omission of undignified sections, suppression of passages that reveal the leaders of the Revolution to be less than perfect, and the elimination of material that might offend the British.

M66. MOORMAN, CHARLES. *Editing the Middle English Manuscript.* Jackson: University Press of Mississippi, 1975.

handbook; handwriting; Middle English

An introduction to "the palaeography, the language, and the textual tradition of the MSS" of Middle English, including exercises: a handbook for the beginning editor.

M67. MORGAN, EDMUND S. "John Adams and the Puritan Tradition." *New England Quarterly* 34 (1961): 518–29.

Adams papers

Morgan's article includes both a discussion of John Adams's personality and a review of Lyman Butterfield's edition of the Adams papers.

M68. MORGAN, WILLIAM JAMES. "Naval Documents of the American Revolution." In *Editing Naval Documents: An Historical Appreciation,* 19–25.

American Revolution; annotation; naval history; organization of editions; search; selection

Morgan describes the search, selection, organization, and annotation of documents for *Naval Documents of the American Revolution.*

M69. MORRIS, RICHARD B. "The Challenge of Historical Materials." *American Archivist* 4 (1941): 91–116.

archives; finding aids; microforms; preservation

Drawing on the experience of the destruction of European archives during World War II, Morris stresses the importance of decentralization and microfilming for the preservation of archival materials. He reviews then-current microfilming projects, describes the continuing role of letterpress editions, and cites the need for improved inventories and bibliographies. He also discusses business archives and special libraries.

M70. MORRIS, RICHARD B. "The Current Statesmen's Papers Publication Program: An Appraisal from the Point of View of the Legal Historian." *American Journal of Legal History* 11 (1967): 95–106.

Adams, John; Hamilton, Alexander; Jay, John; legal history

Morris discusses the importance of the papers of three prominent colonials—Adams, Hamilton, and Jay—to legal history.

M71. MORTON, RICHARD. "How Many Revenges in *The Revengers Tragedy?* Archaic Spellings and the Modern Annotator." In *Play-Texts in Old Spelling,* edited by G. B. Shand and Raymond C. Shady, 113–22.

annotation; spelling

Morton discusses "the glossing and annotation of individual archaic spellings."

M72. MOYLES, R. GORDON. "Iconoclast and Catalyst: Richard Bentley as Editor of *Paradise Lost.*" In *Editing Poetry from Spenser to Dryden,* edited by A. H. de Quehen, 77–98.

history of editing; Milton, John; poetry

Moyles assesses Bentley's editing of the epic, reviewing its textual history and the impact of Bentley's work.

M73. MUGRIDGE, DONALD. "The Adams Papers." *American Archivist* 25 (1962): 449–54.

Adams papers; Butterfield, Lyman H.

This article focuses on the papers of the Adams family and Lyman Butterfield's plans for the project. Mugridge also points out the ways in which this project is atypical.

M74. MUMFORD, LEWIS. "Emerson Behind Barbed Wire." *New York Review of Books,* 18 January 1968, pp. 3–5.

apparatus; audience; CEAA; Emerson, Ralph Waldo; journals; organization of editions

In this review of the Harvard edition of Emerson's journals and notebooks, Mumford praises the edition for its inclusiveness but criticizes its organization as disruptive and distracting, and its editorial apparatus as intrusive. This article was one of the opening shots in the extended debate over CEAA editions. See Edmund Wilson, "The Fruits of the MLA," as well as letters in the *New York Review,* 14 March and 19 December 1968. For further views, see articles indexed under CEAA.

M75. MUMFORD, LEWIS. Letter to the Editor. *New York Review of Books,* 14 March 1968, p. 36.

CEAA

Mumford's reply to letters by William M. Gibson and G. S. Rousseau in the same issue.

M76. MYERSON, JOEL. "Mrs. Dall Edits Miss Fuller: The Story of *Margaret and Her Friends.*" *Papers of the Bibliographical Society of America* 72 (1978): 187–200.

Fuller, Margaret; oral materials

Myerson discusses Caroline Healey Dall's edition of Fuller's "Conversations," discussions led by Fuller on Greek mythology. He compares the authorial fair copy manuscript with the 1895 printed version edited by Dall.

M77. MYERSON, JOEL. "Practical Editions: Ralph Waldo Emerson's 'The American Scholar.'" *Proof* 3 (1973): 379–94.

Emerson, Ralph Waldo; practical editions

Myerson examined twenty-seven reprintings of Emerson's oration, all of which he criticizes for carelessness and attempts at modernization. He also provides a brief textual history of the work.

M78. MYERSON, JOEL. Review of *The Autobiography of Benjamin Franklin: A Genetic Text,* ed. J. A. Leo Lemay and P. M. Zall. *Newsletter of the Association for Documentary Editing* 4 (May 1982): 9–10.

apparatus; Franklin, Benjamin; transcription

In this favorable review, Myerson sets out alternative methods of presenting manuscripts heavily revised by their authors.

N

N1. NEIMAN, STELLA DUFF, AND LESTER J. CAPPON. "Comprehensive Historical Indexing: The *Virginia Gazette* Index." *American Archivist* 14 (1951): 291–304.

indexing

The authors describe their indexing of a colonial newspaper, the *Virginia Gazette.* They list and discuss the four principal factors in compiling such an index: finances, personnel, general policies, and specific procedures.

N2. NELSON, RAYMOND. "Stalking Whitman with Shotgun and Bludgeon." *Virginia Quarterly Review* 55 (1979): 536–39.

annotation; selection; Whitman, Walt

In this review of *Walt Whitman: Daybooks and Notebooks,* Nelson criticizes the daybooks as trivial and the notebooks for inadequate annotation.

N3. NESBITT, BRUCE. "Lampmania: Alcyone and the Search for Merope." In *Editing Canadian Texts,* edited by Francess G. Halpenny, 33–48.

copy-text; Lampman, Archibald; poetry

A description of the state of the published and unpublished works of a major Canadian poet.

N4. NEW, MELVYN. "The Sterne Edition: The Text of *Tristram Shandy.*" In *Editing Eighteenth-Century Novels,* edited by G. E. Bentley, Jr., 67–89.

copy-text; Sterne, Laurence

A discussion of the problems of editing Sterne, especially the choice of a copy-text.

N5. NEW, WILLIAM H. "Some Comments on the Editing of Canadian Texts." In *Editing Canadian Texts*, edited by Francess G. Halpenny, 13–31.

annotation; Canada

Suggestions for research and publication in Canadian history and literature, along with a discussion of the problems of annotation.

N6. NEWCOMER, LEE NATHANIEL. "Manasseh Cutler's Writings: A Note on Editorial Practice." *Mississippi Valley Historical Review* 47 (1960): 88–101.

Cutler, Manasseh; history of editing

Newcomer relates the problems arising from the editorial practices used in the nineteenth-century publication of Manasseh Cutler's diary. He also discusses how an editor's interest in the subject can influence the project.

N7. NOGGLE, BURL. "A Note on Historical Editing: The Wilson Papers in Perspective." *Louisiana History* 8 (1967): 281–97.

funding; history of editing; Wilson, Woodrow

Noggle's article reviews the history of documentary editing and the state of funding for editorial projects. He also describes the history and criticisms of the Wilson project.

N8. NORDLOH, DAVID J. "On Crane Now Edited: The University of Virginia Edition of *The Works of Stephen Crane*." *Studies in the Novel* 10 (1978): 103–19.

authorial intention; copy-text; Crane, Stephen

In this highly critical review, Nordloh discusses the arrangement of items, completeness, the reliability and accuracy of the texts, the accessibility of the apparatus, and the subjugation of authorial intention to "rampant editorial ingenuity."

N9. NORDLOH, DAVID J. "The 'Perfect' Text: The Editor Speaks for the Author." *Newsletter of the Association for Documentary Editing* 2 (May 1980): 1–3.

annotation; authorial intention; transcription

Nordloh describes the characteristics of the perfect text, which should reproduce "what its author wanted." He also sets out principles for achieving such a text. See also Wayne Cutler, "The 'Authentic' Witness: The Editor Speaks for the Document."

N10. NORDLOH, DAVID J. "Socialization, Authority, and Evidence: Reflections on McGann's *A Critique of Modern Textual Criticism.*" *Analytical & Enumerative Bibliography*, n.s. 1 (1987): 3–12.

authorial intention

In this review, Nordloh argues that McGann misunderstands copy-text editing and that his proposal of a "socialized" concept of authorship renders textual editing impossible. See also Abbott, Craig S., "A Response."

N11. NORDLOH, DAVID J. "Substantives and Accidentals vs. New Evidence: Another Strike in the Game of Distinctions." *CEAA Newsletter* 3 (June 1970): 12–13.

accidentals; authorial intention

Nordloh offers examples of ways in which changes between manuscript and subsequent versions may be misinterpreted.

N12. NORDLOH, DAVID J. "Supplying What's Missing in Editions of Selected Letters." *Scholarly Publishing* 17 (1985–86): 37–47.

format; selection

Nordloh discusses how to decide what to publish and then gives basic principles on presenting text. The article also suggests what to do about information that is not included in the text.

N13. NORDLOH, DAVID J. "Theory, Funding, and Coincidence in the Editing of American Literature." In *Editing and Editors: A Retrospect*, edited by Richard Landon, 137–55.

CEAA; copy-text; funding; history of editing; NEH

Nordloh reviews the history of editing in the United States, emphasizing the relationships among NEH funding, CEAA guidelines, and the rigid application of copy-text theory.

N14. NORMAN, BUFORD. "Editing and Interpreting Fragmentary Texts: A Justification of Pascal's Text in MSL 527-Br 40." *Text* 2 (1985): 197–208.

fragments; Pascal, Blaise; philosophy

Norman emphasizes the need to keep in mind both the fragmentary nature of the *Pensées* and Pascal's style when editing the text.

N15. NORTON, DAVID L. "The Elders of Our Tribe." *The Nation*, 18 February 1961, 148–50.

funding; NHPC

This article discusses the projects of the NHPC, with a listing of the primary editing projects of major historical figures and information about their funding. Norton details problems with the papers of Franklin and Adams and discusses general editing problems. He also assesses the significance of NHPC projects.

N16. NOWELL-SMITH, SIMON. "Authors, Editors, and Publishers." In *Editor, Author, and Publisher,* edited by William J. Howard, 8–27. Toronto: University of Toronto Press, 1969.

letters; publishing; transcription

The author discusses the relationship between publisher and scholarly editor, urging cooperation and agreement on a "code" for the editing of correspondence.

O

O1. OAKMAN, ROBERT L. *Computer Methods for Literary Research.* Columbia: University of South Carolina Press, 1980.

computers

Oakman explains the fundamentals of literary computing and offers descriptions of several specific applications: concordances, historical dictionaries, scholarly bibliographies, textual editing, and stylistic analysis.

O2. OAKMAN, ROBERT L. "The Present State of Computerized Collation: A Review Article." *Proof* 2 (1972): 333–48.

collation; computers

Oakman discusses Project OCCULT and a computer collation procedure created by Margaret S. Cabaniss. He evaluates their practicality in data input, collation, algorithms, and data output.

O3. OBERG, BARBARA. "Articles for a Treaty of Peace: Make Room for the Library of America *Benjamin Franklin* Alongside *The*

Papers of Benjamin Franklin." *Documentary Editing* 10 (September 1988): 1–5.

Franklin, Benjamin; Library of America; selection

Oberg reviews the Library of America edition of Franklin's writings, edited by J. A. Leo Lemay, discussing selection, organization, transcription, and selection of texts. She also reviews Lemay's *The Canon of Benjamin Franklin, 1772–1776: New Attributions and Reconsiderations.*

04. OBERG, BARBARA. "Editing and the Teaching of History: Notes from the Gallatin Project." *AHA Perspectives* 23 (November 1985): 12–14.

training

Oberg describes a project in which undergraduates used methods and materials from the Albert Gallatin Papers project in a special course.

05. OBERG, BARBARA. "Interpretation in Editing: The Gallatin Papers." *Newsletter of the Association for Documentary Editing* 4 (May 1982): 7–9.

selection

A discussion of how interpretation occurs and the forces that influence it, focusing on Henry Adams's edition of the *Writings of Albert Gallatin* as an example.

06. OBERG, BARBARA. "Selection and Annotation: Deciding Alone." *Newsletter of the Association for Documentary Editing* 2 (February 1980): 6–9.

annotation; selection; solo editing

This article discusses the role of the solo editor within the profession and describes the problems and advantages of working alone.

07. OLSON, JAMES C. "The Scholar and Documentary Publication."
American Archivist 28 (1965): 187–93.

editing, general; form of publication

Olson details five principles agreed on by historians concerning documentary publication. He recommends increased development of cooperative enterprises, increased numbers of and better-managed documentary publication programs, and the publication of both letterpress and microfilm editions.

08. O'NEILL, JAMES E. "Copies of French Manuscripts for American History in the Library of Congress." *Journal of American History* 51 (March 1965): 674–91.

France; Library of Congress

O'Neill describes the Library of Congress's program of copying materials in French archives, which began in 1914, and provides a summary inventory of the collection.

09. ORAM, RICHARD W. "George Washington's Ledger Uncovered." *Documentary Editing* 8 (June 1986): 15–18.

authentication; ledgers; preservation; Washington, George

An account of the discovery, identification, and preservation of a Washington ledger.

010. ORTH, RALPH H. "An Edition of Emerson's Poetry Notebooks." *Documentary Editing* 6 (March 1984): 8–11.

annotation; Emerson, Ralph Waldo; notebooks; poetry; selection; transcription

Orth explains the selection and editorial procedures used in the publication of Emerson's poetry notebooks.

011. OTT, WILHELM. "Software Requirements for Computer-Aided Critical Editing." In *Editing, Publishing and Computer Tech-*

nology, edited by Sharon Butler and William P. Stoneman, 81–103. New York: AMS Press, 1988.

collation; computers; format; typesetting

Ott discusses the special features required in a typesetting program for critical editions, including the ability to set apparatus properly at the foot of the page, incorporate new characters, and generate tables of contents and indexes. He notes the ability to generate "work-in-progress" editions. Finally, he reviews the uses of computers for collation, indexing, generating concordances, and proofreading.

012. OTT, WILHELM. "A Text Processing System for the Preparation of Critical Editions." *Computers and the Humanities* 13 (January-April 1979): 29–35.

computers

Ott describes the advantages and uses of the composing program he selected.

013. OWEN, W. J. B. "Annotating Wordsworth." In *Editing Texts of the Romantic Period,* edited by John D. Baird, 47–71.

annotation; Wordsworth, William

A discussion of annotation as it "defines and defends the text."

014. OWSLEY, HARRIET CHAPPELL. "Discoveries Made in Editing the Papers of Andrew Jackson." *Manuscripts* 27 (1975): 275–79.

Jackson, Andrew; search

Written by the associate editor of the Andrew Jackson papers, this article concerns Jackson's early business dealings in Spanish-controlled Natchez. The discovery of the letters of a business associate, George Cochran, shed light on some of Jackson's early activities and prompted the author to call for a search of the Spanish archives to locate more Jackson records.

P

P1. PACEY, DESMOND. "On Editing the Letters of Philip Grove." In *Editing Canadian Texts*, edited by Francess G. Halpenny, 49–73.

Grove, Philip; letters; search; transcription

A description of the collection and editing of the letters of a noted Canadian novelist, along with extensive remarks about their significance.

P2. PALMER, M. "Archive Packs for Schools: Some Practical Suggestions." *Journal of the Society of Archivists* 6 (April 1979): 145–53.

archives; training

Palmer suggests a variety of ways that documents can be used in secondary school classrooms and provides guidelines for selecting appropriate documents and teaching aids.

P3. PAPENFUSE, EDWARD C. "Retreat from Standardization: A Comment on the Recent History of Finding Aids." *American Archivist* 36 (1973): 537–42.

finding aids; NUCMC

Papenfuse criticizes the lack of uniformity among guides and inventories of collections.

P4. PARKER, HERSHEL. "Aesthetic Implications of Authorial Excisions: Examples from Nathaniel Hawthorne, Mark Twain, and Stephen Crane." In *Editing Nineteenth-Century Fiction*, edited by Jane Millgate, 99–119.

authorial intention; Crane, Stephen; Hawthorne, Nathaniel; Twain, Mark

A discussion of the editorial implications of authorial excisions, with examples from Hawthorne, Twain, and Crane.

P5. PARKER, HERSHEL. "The Aesthetics of Editorial Apparatuses." *The Editorial Quarterly* 1 (1975): 4–8.

apparatus

Parker discusses the design, purpose, and usefulness of lists, emphasizing historical collations.

P6. PARKER, HERSHEL. "The First Nine Volumes of *A Selected Edition of W. D. Howells:* A Review Article." *Proof* 2 (1972): 319–32.

apparatus; funding; Howells, W. D.; project organization

Parker describes the funding and organization of the project and reviews the volumes. He praises the design and manufacture, and discusses the textual commentaries in detail.

P7. PARKER, HERSHEL. *Flawed Texts and Verbal Icons: Literary Authority in American Fiction.* Evanston, Ill.: Northwestern University Press, 1984.

authorial intention; copy-text; Crane, Stephen; James, Henry; literary criticism; Mailer, Norman; Twain, Mark

Parker discusses the choice of a copy-text that best embodies the author's intention, reviews textual theory and practice since the late 1950s, and promotes "a new biographico-textico-aesthetico 'movement.'" He focuses on the analysis of authorial revisions, with examples from Henry James, Mark Twain, Stephen Crane, and Norman Mailer. See also Cook, Don L., "Textual Ignorance," a review.

P8. PARKER, HERSHEL. "In Defense of Copy-Text Editing." *Bulletin of the New York Public Library* 75 (October 1971): 337–44.

annotation; CEAA; copy-text

After providing a summary of Greg's theory of copy-text, Parker offers a point-by-point response to Donald Pizer's "On the Editing of Modern American Texts." See also articles by John Freehafer ("How Not to Edit") and Norman S. Grabo, as well as Pizer's final response, in the same volume.

P9. PARKER, HERSHEL. "Melville and the Concept of 'Author's Final Intentions.'" *Proof* 1 (1971): 156–68.

authorial intention; copy-text; Melville, Herman

Parker discusses the applicability of Greg's theory of copy-text to the works of Melville.

P10. PARKER, HERSHEL. "The 'New Scholarship': Textual Evidence and Its Implications for Criticism, Literary Theory, and Aesthetics." *Studies in American Fiction* 9 (1981): 181–97.

textual criticism

Parker defines the "new scholarship" as "an approach to American fiction which employs bibliographical, biographical, textual, and historical research and which raises questions properly discussed by literary theorists and aestheticians." He describes the interests and work of such scholars, whom he contrasts with both the New Critics and CEAA editors.

P11. PARKER, HERSHEL. "Norman Mailer's Revision of the *Esquire* Version of *An American Dream* and the Aesthetic Problem of 'Built-in Intentionality.'" *Bulletin of Research in the Humanities* 84 (1981): 405–30.

authorial intention; Mailer, Norman; serialization

Parker traces the history of Mailer's revisions of the novel and the impact of the revisions. He argues that the novel as published in book form "is a classic case of an author's damaging his text by trying to alter a few patterns or parts of patterns," and that the revisions—despite Mailer's blessing—create a text without "full intentionality."

P12. PARKER, HERSHEL. "Practical Editions: Herman Melville's *Moby Dick.*" *Proof* 3 (1973): 371–78.

Melville, Herman; practical editions

Parker reviews the publishing history of *Moby Dick* and sets out a plan for an ideal practical edition.

P13. PARKER, HERSHEL. "Regularizing Accidentals: The Latest Form of Infidelity." *Proof* 3 (1973): 1–20.

accidentals

Parker argues against regularizing accidentals on the basis of too few examples, tracing this practice to a modern preference for tidiness that was not shared by authors before the twentieth century.

P14. PARKER, HERSHEL. Review of the Centenary Edition of the *Works of Nathaniel Hawthorne,* vols. 12 and 13. *Nineteenth-Century Fiction* 33 (1979): 489–92.

apparatus

Parker discusses the aesthetics of editorial apparatus and the problems of presenting both extensive information and a comprehensible text.

P15. PARKER, HERSHEL. " 'The Text Itself'—Whatever That Is." *Text* 3 (1987): 47–54.

authorial intention

Parker asserts the need to take into account the creative process when establishing a text.

P16. Parker, Hershel, with Bruce Bebb. "The CEAA: An Interim Assessment." *Papers of the Bibliographical Society of America* 68 (1974): 129–48.

accidentals; apparatus; CEAA; copy-text

Parker and Bebb review the history of the CEAA, the design of the editions, and the varying success of the editors' work in establishing a copy-text and handling accidentals. They also discuss the value of historical introductions. See also William M. Gibson and Edwin H. Cady, "Editions of American Writers, 1963."

P17. Parker, Hershel, and Brian Higgins. "Maggie's 'Last Night': Authorial Design and Editorial Patching." *Studies in the Novel* 10 (1978): 64–75.

authorial intention; Crane, Stephen

The authors describe the differences between chapter 17 of the 1893 *Maggie* and that of the Appleton edition. They are critical of Bowers's decision to base his edition of the novel on the Appleton edition and of his treatment of the text as arbitrary, highly subjective, and erratic.

P18. Parker, Wyman W. "How Can the Archivist Aid the Researcher?" *American Archivist* 16 (1953): 233–40.

archives

Parker enumerates the ways archivists can assist researchers through collection, preservation, duplication, evaluation, and dissemination.

P19. Parry, David. "A Margin of Error: The Problems of Marginalia in *The Castle of Perseverance*." In *Editing Early English Drama*, edited by A. F. Johnston, 33–64.

drama; Latin; marginalia; Middle Ages

Parry discusses whether Latin tags, some of which were written in the manuscript's margins, are integral to the text. He also discusses the differing responses to the play of readers and theatrical audiences and the contribution performance makes to scholarship.

P20. PARTON, JAMES. "Popularizing History and Documentary Sources." *American Archivist* 20 (1957): 99–109.

American Heritage; audience; popular history; public relations

Parton discusses the popularization of history and what makes documents of interest to the public.

P21. PASSMORE, JOHN. "A Philosopher of the Particulars." *Times Literary Supplement,* 24 June 1977, pp. 746–47.

annotation; apparatus; audience; James, William; philosophy; types of editing

In this review of three volumes of *The Works of William James,* Passmore evaluates the utility of the annotation and apparatus for the philosopher. See also Frederick Burkhardt's letter to the editor, 5 August 1977.

P22. PATTERSON, DAVID S. "The *American Foreign Policy* Series." *Documentary Editing* 8 (June 1986): 1–5.

American Foreign Policy series; annotation; computers; indexing; microfiche; search; selection

Patterson describes the series, its uses, and the preparation of each volume.

P23. PATTERSON, LEE. "The Logic of Textual Criticism and the Way of Genius: The Kane-Donaldson *Piers Plowman* in Historical Perspective." In *Textual Criticism and Literary Interpretation,* edited by Jerome J. McGann, 55–91.

history of editing; *Piers Plowman;* transmission of texts

Patterson explains and commends the editorial principles of the Kane-Donaldson edition and evaluates its significance to literary criticism. He discusses the distinction between internal ("lectional") and external ("documentary") evidence, and the criteria for judging such evidence.

P24. PEARSALL, DEREK. "Editing Medieval Texts: Some Developments and Some Problems." In *Textual Criticism and Literary Interpretation,* edited by Jerome J. McGann, 92–106.

Chaucer, Geoffrey; facsimiles; Middle Ages; *Piers Plowman*

Pearsall reviews the textual and editorial history of *The Canterbury Tales* and *Piers Plowman.* He then discusses the special problems presented by medieval works, including the inapplicability of the assumptions made by modern editors about the process of composition and publication. He also describes the advantages of working with facsimiles.

P25. PECKHAM, MORSE. "Notes on Freehafer and the CEAA." *Studies in the Novel* 7 (1975): 402–4.

CEAA

A response to John Freehafer's "Greg's Theory of Copy-Text and the Textual Criticism in the CEAA Editions." See also articles by Bruce Bebb and Hershel Parker, Vinton A. Dearing ("Textual Criticism Today"), Thomas L. McHaney ("The Important Questions"), and G. Thomas Tanselle ("Two Basic Distinctions"), all in the same issue.

P26. PECKHAM, MORSE. "Reflections on the Foundations of Modern Textual Editing." *Proof* 1 (1971): 122–55.

accidentals; editing, general; types of editing

Peckham argues for an "empirical language" for editing, developed from a clear understanding of what a textual editor does, rather than a set of principles evolved from a theory such as Greg's. He contrasts the work of textual editors with that of historians and concludes that a "definitive" version of a work and a single editorial method are both impossible.

P27. PERMAN, DAGMAR HORNA. "Microfilming of German Records in the National Archives." *American Archivist* 22 (1959): 433–43.

finding aids; Germany; microfilm

Perman describes the microfilming of German records captured during World War II, their organization, and the finding aids created. See also articles by George O. Kent and Francis L. Loewenheim.

P28. PETRY, MICHAEL J. "Editing Hegel's *Encyclopaedia*." In *Editing Polymaths: Erasmus to Russell*, edited by H. J. Jackson, 143–75.

annotation; Hegel, G. W. F.; philosophy; translation

Petry reviews the history of Hegel editions and explains the need for a critical English edition of the *Encyclopaedia*. He describes the annotation policy and problems of translation.

P29. PIZER, DONALD. "On the Editing of Modern American Texts." *Bulletin of the New York Public Library* 75 (March 1971): 147–53.

CEAA; copy-text

Pizer argues that "copy-text theory is unresponsive to the distinctive qualities of modern American texts." See also articles by John Freehafer ("How Not to Edit"), Norman S. Grabo, and Hershel Parker ("In Defense"), as well as Pizer's reply, in the same volume of the journal.

P30. PIZER, DONALD. "On the Editing of Modern American Texts: A Final Comment." *Bulletin of the New York Public Library* 75 (December 1971): 504–5.

CEAA; copy-text

Pizer's response to the criticisms of Norman S. Grabo and Hershel Parker in the same volume of the journal. See also John Freehafer's "How Not to Edit American Authors" and Pizer's original article, "On the Editing of Modern American Texts."

P31. PIZER, DONALD. "Self-Censorship and Textual Editing." In *Textual Criticism and Literary Interpretation*, edited by Jerome J. McGann, 144–61.

authorial intention; censorship; Crane, Stephen; Dreiser, Theodore; Norris, Frank

Pizer examines the ways of handling texts that have been censored by their authors, using as examples Crane's *Red Badge of Courage*, Dreiser's *Sister Carrie*, and Norris's *McTeague*. The issues he examines are external evidence, inferences about the author's intentions, differences in quality between the revised and unrevised works, and the existence of grounds for considering the first published version a "historical artifact that should continue to occupy the role of general reading text even if it has been subject to self-censorship."

P32. PIZER, DONALD. "Stephen Crane: A Review of Scholarship and Criticism Since 1969." *Studies in the Novel* 10 (1978): 120–45.

annotation; Crane, Stephen; organization of editions

On pages 123–27, Pizer discusses the Virginia edition, criticizing its organization, lack of historical annotation, and lack of critical context.

P33. POLLARD, A. W., GILBERT R. REDGRAVE, R. W. CHAPMAN, AND W. W. GREG, " 'Facsimile' Reprints of Old Books." *The Library*, 4th ser., 6 (1925–26): 305–28.

facsimiles; history of editing

The authors review the history of facsimile publication, photographic facsimiles, and typographic facsimiles.

P34. POLZER, CHARLES W., S.J. "The Documentary Relations of the Southwest." *Hispanic American Historical Review* 58 (August 1978): 460–65.

computers; finding aids; selection; Spanish

Polzer describes the collection, organization, and computerized indexing of documents of ethnohistorical character relating to the American Southwest.

P35. POLZER, CHARLES W., S.J. "The New World Archive." *Documentary Editing* 6 (June 1984): 8–12.

archives; New World Archive

Polzer gives reasons for establishing the New World Archive and provides information about the proposal for the archive and the details of its establishment and organization.

P36. POTTLE, FREDERICK A. *Pride and Negligence: The History of the Boswell Papers*. New York: McGraw-Hill, 1982.

Boswell, James; censorship; project organization; publishing; search

Pottle traces the history of Boswell's papers, including their physical location, censorship by family members, sale at various times, and the development of Boswell scholarship. He describes his own editing of the papers and their publication.

P37. POWER, EUGENE B. "The Manuscript Copying Program in England." *American Archivist* 7 (1944): 28–32.

England; microfilm

Power describes the microfilming of English records and manuscripts during World War II.

P38. PRITCHARD, ALLAN. "Editing from Manuscript: Cowley and the Cowper Papers." In *Editing Poetry from Spenser to Dryden*, edited by A. H. de Quehen, 46–76.

annotation; Cowley, Abraham; poetry

Pritchard relates the discovery and editorial problems of Cowley's *The Civil War.*

P39. PROUDFOOT, G. R. "Dramatic Manuscripts and the Editor." In *Editing Renaissance Dramatic Texts*, edited by Anne Lancashire, 9–38.

compositorial studies; copy-text; drama

A survey of editions of English Renaissance dramatic texts, the methods of establishing a text, and a warning against "excessive concentration on matters of sometimes fruitless speculation," bibliographic techniques of "limited practical utility," and "the attempt to codify into unduly rigid categories."

Q

Q1. QUEHEN, A. H. DE. "Editing Butler's Manuscripts." In *Editing Seventeenth-Century Prose*, edited by D. I. B. Smith, 71–93.

Butler, Samuel; dating; organization of editions

De Quehen describes the sources for Butler's posthumous works and the editing of two volumes of miscellaneous prose and verse. She discusses problems of ordering and dating the manuscripts and determining which folios might have been lost.

Q2. QUEHEN, A. H. DE, ED. *Editing Poetry from Spenser to Dryden: Papers Given at the Sixteenth Annual Conference on Editorial Problems, University of Toronto, 31 October-1 November 1980.* New York: Garland, 1981.

poetry

See articles by Frost, William; Hamilton, A. C.; Moyles, R. Gordon; Pritchard, Allan; and Roberts, Mark.

R

R1. RABEN, JOSEPH. "The Electronic Revolution and the World Just Around the Corner." *Scholarly Publishing* 10 (1979): 195–209.

computers

Raben discusses advances in technology and their uses in photocomposition. The article also deals with electronics in editing and in other phases of publishing.

R2. RAKOVE, JACK N. Review of *The Papers of Benjamin Franklin,* vols. 20–24. *William and Mary Quarterly* 42 (1985): 530–34.

Franklin, Benjamin; selection

Rakove discusses the problems of duplication of material that is printed in other editions and of dealing with a greatly expanded body of documents for a short period of time.

R3. RAPPORT, LEONARD. "Dumped from a Wharf into Casco Bay: The Historical Records Survey Revisited." *American Archivist* 37 (1974): 201–10.

finding aids; Historical Records Survey

Rapport reviews the history of the HRS and reports on what has become of the results.

R4. RAPPORT, LEONARD. "Fakes and Facsimiles: Problems of Identification." *American Archivist* 42 (1979): 13–58.

authentication

Rapport discusses the identification of reproductions and facsimiles of newspapers, manuscripts, and documents.

R5. RAPPORT, LEONARD. "Newspaper Printings of the Constitution: An Unresolved Mystery." *Manuscripts* 39 (Fall 1987): 327–36.

Constitution; newspapers

Rapport summarizes the contemporary newspaper printings of the Constitution.

R6. REAGOR, SIMONE. "Historical Editing: The Federal Role." *Newsletter of the Association for Documentary Editing* 4 (May 1982): 1–4.

funding; NEH; NHPRC

Reagor's article argues against continued federal funding of documentary editions under NHPRC guidelines. She discusses the original and current role of the commission in documentary editing, as well as duplication of programs between the NEH and the NHPRC. See also John Y. Simon, "In Response," in the same issue.

R7. REED, DANIEL J. "The Private Property Claim in Presidential Papers." In *The Publication of American Historical Manuscripts*, edited by Leslie W. Dunlap and Fred Shelley, 77–88.

access; Library of Congress; National Archives; Nixon, Richard M.; presidential papers; privacy

Reed reviews policy on the ownership of presidential papers and notes the questions raised during Watergate, pointing out the conflict between the doctrines of privacy and freedom of information.

R8. REEVES, THOMAS C. "The Search for the Chester Alan Arthur Papers." *Manuscripts* 25 (1973): 171–85. Reprinted from the *Wisconsin Magazine of History* 55 (Summer 1972), 310–19.

Arthur, Chester Alan; presidential papers; search

Reeves describes the search for the papers of a president who was secretive, who frequently destroyed papers, and whose career scholars neglected for many years.

R9. REICHENBERGER, ARNOLD G. "Editing Spanish *Comedias* of the XVIIth Century: History and Present-Day Practice." In *Editing Renaissance Dramatic Texts*, edited by Anne Lancashire, 69–96.

annotation; copy-text; drama; history of editing; seventeenth century; Spanish

A comprehensive review of the publication and editing of Spanish seventeenth-century drama from its origins to 1975. Reichenberger also discusses his own editorial practices in editions of Luis Vélez de Guevara and Lope Félix de Vega Carpio.

R10. REID, S. W. "Definitive Editions and Photocomposition." *Papers of the Bibliographical Society of America* 72 (1978): 321–26.

computers; proofreading

Reid details the difficulties of producing a definitive edition created by photocomposition, particularly those of proofreading.

R11. REID, WARREN R. "Public Papers of the Presidents." *American Archivist* 25 (1962): 435–39.

annotation; oral materials; presidential papers; selection; transcription

Reid recounts the history and progress of *Public Papers of the Presidents of the United States.*

R12. REIMAN, DONALD H. "Editing Shelley." In *Editing Texts of the Romantic Period,* edited by John D. Baird, 27–45. Reprinted, with a brief introduction, in Reiman's *Romantic Texts and Contexts,* 17–32.

dating; Shelley, Percy Bysshe; training

A description of the editing of *Shelley and His Circle,* a critical discussion of other editions of Shelley, and suggestions for future editions.

R13. REIMAN, DONALD H. "The Four Ages of Editing and the English Romantics." *Text* 1 (1984): 231–55. Reprinted, with a brief introduction, in his *Romantic Texts and Contexts,* 85–108.

history of editing; romanticism

Reiman reviews the editing of the Romantics by (1) heirs and disciples; (2) the "improvers" of the Victorian era; (3) the "scientific" editors represented by Harry Buxton Forman, Ronald B. McKerrow, Charlton Hinman, and Fredson Bowers; and (4) the historicist editors he endorses.

R14. REIMAN, DONALD H. "Gentlemen Authors and Professional Writers: Notes on the History of Editing Texts of the 18th and 19th Centuries." In *Editing and Editors: A Retrospect,* edited by Richard Landon, 99–136.

eighteenth century; history of editing; nineteenth century

Reiman discusses differences in attitudes between those who write for a living and "gentlemen authors"; the effects on authorship of technological change and changes in reading publics; and related developments in textual criticism and editing. He also examines the need for popular, clear-text editions.

R15. REIMAN, DONALD H. "Romantic Bards and Historical Editors." *Studies in Romanticism* 21 (1982): 477–96. Reprinted, with a brief introduction, in his *Romantic Texts and Contexts*, 109–29.

Erdman, David; history of editing; practical editions; romanticism

Reiman amplifies his study of the history of the editing of Romantic texts (see "The Four Ages of Editing"), reviews the career of David V. Erdman, discusses the danger that historical knowledge may interfere with editorial judgment, and points out increased attention by textbook publishers to textual integrity.

R16. REIMAN, DONALD H. *Romantic Texts and Contexts*. Columbia: University of Missouri Press, 1987.

history of editing; romanticism

In addition to the essays listed here ("Editing Shelley," "The Four Ages of Editing," "Romantic Bards and Historical Editors," and " 'Versioning' "), this collection includes reviews of Zillman's *Prometheus Unbound*, Rogers's Oxford Shelley, the Ohio Browning, the Bollingen Coleridge, the Cornell Wordsworth and the Norton *Prelude*, and the Oxford Byron, along with essays on noneditorial aspects of the Romantics.

R17. REIMAN, DONALD H. " 'Versioning': The Presentation of Multiple Texts." In his *Romantic Texts and Contexts*, 167–80.

editing, general; format

Reiman suggests making available, within one edition, "enough different *primary* textual documents and states of major texts . . . so that readers, teachers, and critics can compare for themselves two or more widely circulated basic versions of major texts." This publication of a variety of versions, rather than of a single "definitive" edition, would change the role of the editor.

R18. REINGOLD, NATHAN. "The Darwin Industry Encounters Tanselle and Bowers." *Documentary Editing* 10 (June 1988): 16–19.

annotation; calendaring; Darwin, Charles; history of science; letters; transcription

In this review of *A Calendar of the Correspondence of Charles Darwin, 1821–1882* and the first two volumes of *The Correspondence of Charles Darwin,* Reingold details the value of the *Calendar.* His discussion of the *Correspondence* focuses on the annotation, which he criticizes as addressing too narrow an audience, and the transcription, for its "rather uncritical application of concepts and techniques not wholly applicable to the materials involved and the uses they may receive." See also Frederick Burkhardt, "In Response."

R19. REINGOLD, NATHAN. "On Not Doing the Papers of Great Scientists." *British Journal for the History of Science* 20 (January 1987): 29–38.

history of science

Reingold discusses the purpose of editions of scientists' papers and argues for greater attention to institutions, movements, and communities, a trend that he believes is under way.

R20. REINGOLD, NATHAN. "The Papers of Joseph Henry." *Smithsonian Journal of History* 2 (1967): 69–71.

Henry, Joseph; history of science; microfilm

Reingold describes a comprehensive edition of the papers of Joseph Henry, supplemented by microfilm publication of all the Henry manuscripts.

R21. REINGOLD, NATHAN. "Reflections of an Unrepentant Editor." *American Archivist* 46 (1983): 14–21.

Boyd, Julian; Carter, Clarence; editing, general; history of editing; types of editing

Reingold reviews the history of documentary editing in the United States, focusing on the figures of Julian Boyd and Clarence Carter, and on the issues of transcription, annotation, subject matter, and form of publication.

R22. REINGOLD, NATHAN. "What Is a Federal Historian? A Historical Editor." *The Public Historian* 2 (1980): 89–91.

editing, general; federal historians

A brief description of the activities of an editor employed by the federal government.

R23. RICE, HOWARD C., JR. "Jefferson in Europe a Century and a Half Later: Notes of a Roving Researcher." *Princeton University Library Chronicle* 12 (1950): 19–35.

Jefferson, Thomas; search

Rice recounts his European search for the papers of Thomas Jefferson. He lists places he looked and explains why he looked there. Rice also discusses what he found and gives some information about Jefferson's life in Europe.

R24. RIGG, A. G., ED. *Editing Medieval Texts: English, French, and Latin Written in England: Papers Given at the Twelfth Annual Conference on Editorial Problems, University of Toronto, 5–6 November 1976.* New York: Garland, 1977.

Middle Ages

See articles by Godden, Malcolm; Hudson, Anne; Lancashire, Ian; Merrilees, Brian; and Rigg, George.

R25. RIGG, GEORGE. "Medieval Latin." In *Editing Medieval Texts*, edited by A. G. Rigg, 107–25.

copy-text; history of editing; Latin; Middle Ages; transcription

A review of the state of medieval Latin editions, and a discussion of problems in orthography and establishment of text.

R26. ROBBINS, J. ALBERT. "*American Literary Manuscripts:* Problems and Some Solutions." *The Editorial Quarterly* 1 (1975): 3–6.

finding aids; search

Robbins describes the uses and revision of *American Literary Manuscripts*.

R27. ROBERTS, MARK. "Problems in Editing Donne's *Songs and Sonets*." In *Editing Poetry from Spenser to Dryden*, edited by A. H. de Quehen, 15–45.

Donne, John; poetry

Roberts explains the difficulties raised by Grierson's 1912 edition and the importance of a theory of the text. He then sets out his own view of the textual situation and how his theory affects the editing of the poems.

R28. ROBSON, JOHN M. "A Mill for Editing." In *Editing the Victorians*, edited by N. John Hall, 1–13.

apparatus; copy-text; Mill, John Stuart; organization of editions

Robson describes the editing of the works of Mill, emphasizing the importance of a single textual editor, the thematic organization of the edition, the choice of copy-text, and the use of introductory essays and minimal annotation.

R29. ROBSON, JOHN M. "Practice, not Theory: Editing J. S. Mill's Newspaper Writings." *Studies in Bibliography* 41 (1988): 160–76.

journalism; Mill, John Stuart

Robson details the special problems arising from the inclusion of Mill's newspaper writings in his collected works. These arose in connection with selection, identification, organization, choice of copy-text, emendation, and apparatus.

R30. ROBSON, JOHN M. "Principles and Methods in the Collected Edition of John Stuart Mill." In *Editing Nineteenth-Century Texts*, edited by John M. Robson, 96–122.

apparatus; collation; copy-text; Mill, John Stuart; organization of editions; selection

A detailed description of the principles and practices adopted in Robson's edition of Mill.

R31. ROBSON, JOHN M., ED. *Editing Nineteenth-Century Texts: Papers Given at the Editorial Conference, University of Toronto, November 1966.* Toronto: University of Toronto Press, 1967.

nineteenth century

See articles by Barnes, Warner ("Nineteenth-Century Editorial Problems"); Bowers, Fredson (" 'Old Wine in New Bottles' "); Robson, John M. ("Principles and Methods"); Sanders, Charles Richard; and Weinberg, Bernard.

R32. ROGERS, GEORGE C., JR. "The Laurens Papers—Half-Way." *Proceedings of the South Carolina Historical Association* (1977): 37–48.

Laurens, Henry; search

Rogers reports progress and reviews the variety of research that the project has made possible.

R33. ROGERS, GEORGE C., JR. "The Sacred Text: An Improbable Dream." In *Literary & Historical Editing*, edited by George L. Vogt and John Bush Jones, 23–33.

annotation; apparatus; copy-text; history of editing; indexing; transcription; types of editing

A discussion of the development of editing and a comparison of the purposes and procedures of literary and historical editors.

R34. RONCAGLIA, AURELIO. "The Value of Interpretation in Textual Criticism." In *Medieval Manuscripts and Textual Criticism*, edited by Christopher Kleinhenz, 227–44. First published as "Valore e giuoco dell'interpretazione nella critica testuale," in *Studi e problemi di critica testuale*, edited by Raffaele Spongano (Bologna: Commissione per i Testi di Lingua, 1961), 45–62.

textual criticism

Roncaglia discusses the importance of context, sense, and style in textual criticism.

R35. ROSENBERG, ROBERT. "Technological Artifacts as Historical Documents." *Text* 3 (1987): 393–407.

artifacts; Edison, Thomas Alva; history of science

Rosenberg discusses the treatment of artifacts as documents, including their attribution, dating, selection, transcription, and annotation.

R36. ROSSINI, EGIDIO. "Introduction to the Edition of Medieval Vernacular Documents (XII and XIV Centuries)." In *Medieval*

Manuscripts and Textual Criticism, edited by Christopher Kleinhenz, 175–210.

editing, general; Middle Ages

Rossini discusses the basic problems and approaches to editing medieval nonliterary documents, especially legal documents.

R37. ROYSTER, CHARLES. Review of *The Papers of George Washington*, Colonial Series, vols. 1 and 2. *Journal of Southern History* 50 (1984): 108–10.

history of editing; Washington, George

Royster's review discusses the historical background of the papers and their importance as a national treasure and a source of scholarship. He also explains the scope and method of the project.

R38. RUBINSTEIN, E. "What Is the Text of a Film?" *Text* 3 (1987): 417–25.

authorial intention; film

Rubinstein raises such problems as defining the author of a film, dealing with the collaborative nature of films, postproduction alterations, and variant versions.

R39. RUDALL, B. H., AND T. N. CORNS. *Computers and Literature: A Practical Guide.* Cambridge, Mass.: Abacus Press, 1987.

computers

An introduction to the use of computers in literary research, including the preparation of concordances, databases, and bibliographies, and the identification of authors.

R40. RUNDELL, WALTER, JR. "Documentary Editing." In his *In Pursuit of American History: Research and Training in the*

United States, 260–83. Norman: University of Oklahoma Press, 1970.

history of editing; NHPC; professional status; training

Rundell details the evolution of U.S. documentary editing until the 1960s. He discusses graduate training in documentary editing, a survey on the acceptability of documentary editing as a dissertation, and the role of the NHPC in training editors.

R41. RUNGE, WILLIAM H. "The Madison Papers." *American Archivist* 20 (1957): 313–17.

Madison, James; project organization

Runge reviews the history of the Madison Papers and of their editing, and describes the project's editorial procedures.

R42. RUSSELL, MARVIN F. Letter to the Editor. *Journal of American History* 71 (June 1984): 216.

declassification; *Foreign Relations* series; National Archives

A response to Lorraine M. Lees and Sandra Gioia Treadway, "A Future for Our Diplomatic Past?"

R43. RUTLAND, ROBERT A. "Recycling Early National History Through the Papers of the Founding Fathers." *American Quarterly* 28 (1976): 250–61.

Founding Fathers; history of editing

Rutland examines the history of editing since World War II and assesses the impact of the Founding Fathers projects.

R44. RYMES, T. K. "Keynes's Lectures, 1932–35: Notes of a Representative Student. Problems in Construction of a Synthesis." In *Editing Modern Economists,* edited by D. E. Moggridge, 91–127.

economics; Keynes, John Maynard; oral materials

Rymes explains the purpose and problems of publishing a reconstruction of Keynes's lectures from student notes. The problems include evaluating the students' awareness of Keynes's purpose and underlying theories. Rymes also explains the procedures used in transcribing and synthesizing the notes.

S

S1. "THE SAGE OF MONTICELLO." *Times Literary Supplement*, 6 April 1951, pp. 205–7.

history of editing; Jefferson, Thomas; selection

This article discusses the selection policy and historical value of the first two volumes of the *Papers of Thomas Jefferson*. The author compares the editorial approaches of Paul Leicester Ford and Henry Cabot Lodge.

S2. SALADINO, GASPARE J. "Charmed Beginnings and Democratic Murmurings." *Documentary Editing* 6 (March 1984): 1–7.

annotation; indexing; Madison, James; transcription; Washington, George

This review essay covers volumes of the papers of Washington and Madison published in 1983. Saladino discusses the material contained in the editions, the editorial procedures, annotation policies, editorial notes, and indexes.

S3. SANDERS, CHARLES RICHARD. "Editing the Carlyle Letters: Problems and Opportunities." In *Editing Nineteenth-Century Texts*, edited by John M. Robson, 77–95.

annotation; authentication; Carlyle, Jane Welsh; Carlyle, Thomas; indexing; letters; search; selection; transcription

A thorough discussion of the problems and solutions found in editing the correspondence of Thomas and Jane Carlyle.

s4. SANDULESCU, C. GEORGE, AND CLIVE HART, EDS. *Assessing the 1984 "Ulysses."* Totowa, N.J.: Barnes & Noble, 1986.

Joyce, James

The proceedings of a conference evaluating the 1984 Garland edition of *Ulysses* that was edited by Hans Walter Gabler.

s5. SAVARD, PIERRE. "The Critical Edition of the *Oeuvres complètes* of François-Xavier Garneau." In *Editing Canadian Texts*, edited by Francess G. Halpenny, 75–80.

Canada; French; Garneau, François-Xavier

A description of a planned edition of the complete works of this historian and poet.

s6. SCHACHTERLE, LANCE. "Hardy Complete versus James Selected." *Documentary Editing* 8 (March 1986): 1–5.

annotation; Hardy, Thomas; James, Henry; letters; selection; transcription

A review of *The Collected Letters of Thomas Hardy*, vol. 4, edited by Richard Little Purdy and Michael Millgate, and *Henry James Letters*, vol. 4, edited by Leon Edel.

s7. SCHEIBE, SIEGFRIED. "Some Notes on Letter Editions: With Special Reference to German Writers." *Studies in Bibliography* 41 (1988): 136–48.

Germany; letters

Scheibe provides a definition of *letter* as a basis for selection decisions and discusses the distinctions among private, public, and polemic letters; the problems of lost letters; and the evidentiary value of letters.

s8. SCHOECK, R. J., ED. *Editing Sixteenth-Century Texts: Papers Given at the Editorial Conference, University of Toronto, 1965.* Toronto: University of Toronto Press, 1966.

sixteenth century

See articles by Graham, Victor E.; Kortepeter, Carl Max; Leech, Clifford ("A Note"); and Schoenbaum, S. ("Editing English Dramatic Texts").

s9. SCHOENBAUM, S. "Editing English Dramatic Texts." In *Editing Sixteenth-Century Texts*, edited by R. J. Schoeck, 12–24.

drama; sixteenth century; training; transcription

A report on the state of editions of sixteenth-century English drama expressing special concern about duplication of effort and the lack of anthologies. Schoenbaum also discusses modernization of spelling and the desirability of editing texts as dissertation projects. See also Clifford Leech's comments in the same volume.

s10. SCHOENBAUM, S. "Old-Spelling Editions: The State of the Art." In *Play-Texts in Old Spelling*, edited by G. B. Shand and Raymond C. Shady, 9–26.

annotation; drama

Schoenbaum reviews the status of ongoing editions of Elizabethan playwrights and comments on the value of annotation.

s11. SCHULZ, CONSTANCE B. "Essay Review: The Papers of Thomas Jefferson." *Pennsylvania Magazine of History and Biography* 109 (January 1985): 69–79.

annotation; Boyd, Julian; Jefferson, Thomas

Schulz reviews Boyd's editorial practices, describes his influence on the profession, and examines in detail the advantages and disadvantages of his method of annotation.

S12. SCHULZ, CONSTANCE B. " 'From Generation unto Generation': Transitions in Modern Documentary Historical Editing." *Reviews in American History* 16 (1988): 337–50.

First Federal Congress project; First Federal Elections project; history of editing; Jefferson, Thomas; Laurens, Henry; Ratification of the Constitution project

Schulz reviews twelve recent volumes of *The Papers of Thomas Jefferson, The Documentary History of the Ratification of the Constitution, The Documentary History of the First Federal Elections, Documentary History of the First Federal Congress,* and *The Papers of Henry Laurens.* She argues that all have participated in the "quiet revolution" of the 1970s yet demonstrate "a wide range of possible adaptations of editorial decision making in selection, organization, transcription, annotations, and indexing of documents."

S13. SCHULZ, CONSTANCE B. Review of *Papers of John Adams,* vol. 5. *Journal of Southern History* 51 (1985): 96–98.

Adams, John; selection; transcription

Schulz questions the editors' policy of omitting letters without a clear way of listing them and citing their location.

S14. SCHULZ, CONSTANCE B. Review of *The Revolution Remembered. Newsletter of the Association for Documentary Editing* 3 (May 1981): 6–8.

annotation; transcription

A review of *The Revolution Remembered: Eyewitness Accounts of the War for Independence*, ed. John C. Dann.

S15. SCHWEIK, ROBERT C., AND MICHAEL PRIET. "Editing Hardy." In *Editing the Victorians*, edited by N. John Hall, 15–41.

copy-text; Hardy, Thomas; letters; notebooks

After surveying the state of the editing of all Hardy's texts (notebooks, scrapbooks, letters, prose, and poetry), the authors discuss in detail the choice of copy-text for *Far from the Madding Crowd*.

S16. SCOTT, PATRICK. "Textual Criticism and Composition Research." *Newsletter of the Association for Documentary Editing* 5 (February 1983): 1–5.

copy-text

A discussion of the need for textual study of rhetoric texts.

S17. SELLERS, CHARLES G. Review of *The Papers of Henry Clay*, vol. 7. *Journal of Southern History* 49 (1983): 615–16.

access; Clay, Henry; Library of Congress; search

Sellers suggests that, because comprehensiveness has to be sacrificed in many documentary series owing to financial problems, a comprehensive collection of all documents collected at the various projects be kept at a central location such as the Library of Congress.

S18. SEYBOLD, CATHERINE. "The Lisle Letters at Chicago." *Scholarly Publishing* 13 (1981–82): 245–62.

annotation; letters; Lisle letters; publishing; visual material

An account of the project by the University of Chicago Press's manuscript editor, emphasizing the practical problems of copy-editing, design, and manufacture.

s19. SHAND, G. B., AND RAYMOND C. SHADY, EDS. *Play-Texts in Old Spelling: Papers from the Glendon Conference*. New York: AMS Press, 1984.

drama; old-spelling editions; Renaissance

See articles by Bevington, David ("Editorial Indications of Stage Business"); Edwards, Philip; Gaines, Barry; Gair, Reavley; Janzen, Henry D.; McLeod, Randall; Morton, Richard; Schoenbaum, S. ("Old-Spelling Editions"); Stallworthy, Jon; Turner, Robert Kean; Werstine, Paul; and Zitner, S. P.

s20. SHARP, RONALD. "Stillinger's Keats." *Review* 2 (1980): 127–36.

apparatus; copy-text; Keats, John

Sharp praises Jack Stillinger's *Poems of John Keats* for its clarity, useful apparatus, and careful selection and presentation of the text.

s21. SHAW, PETER. "The Adams Papers." *American Scholar* 35 (1966): 754–74.

Adams papers

Shaw reviews the history of the project and details how the papers were edited for the current publication.

s22. SHAW, PETER. "The American Heritage and Its Guardians." *American Scholar* 45 (1976): 733–51.

CEAA; types of editing

Shaw examines the editorial approaches of literary and historical editors and the criticisms leveled at both.

s23. SHAW, PETER. "A Dialogue: Peter Shaw and Robert J. Taylor on Editing the Adamses." *Newsletter of the Association for Documentary Editing* 2 (December 1980): 4–6.

Adams papers; annotation; selection

Shaw reviews Taylor's Adams edition, criticizing the lack of a table of contents and disagreeing with some of the selection and annotation procedures. See also Taylor's response, immediately following.

s24. SHELDON, RICHARD N. "Editing a Historical Manuscript: Jared Sparks, Douglas Southall Freeman, and the Battle of Brandywine." *William and Mary Quarterly* 36 (1979): 255–63.

Freeman, Douglas S.; Sparks, Jared; Washington, George

Sheldon compares Sparks's and Freeman's versions of a dispatch sent to George Washington during the battle of Brandywine and discusses the significance of the differences.

s25. SHELLEY, FRED. "The Choice of a Medium for Documentary Publication." *American Archivist* 32 (1969): 363–68.

form of publication

Shelley discusses the differences between selective and comprehensive editions and describes the characteristics of microfilm editions. He also lists guidelines for choosing which medium to use.

s26. SHELLEY, FRED. "Ebenezer Hazard: America's First Historical Editor." *William and Mary Quarterly* 12 (1955): 44–73.

Hazard, Ebenezer; history of editing

Shelley reviews the life of this country's first historical editor, emphasizing Hazard's publication of historical collections.

s27. SHELLEY, FRED. "The Interest of J. Franklin Jameson in the National Archives, 1908–1934." *American Archivist* 12 (1949): 99–130.

funding; Jameson, J. Franklin; National Archives

Shelley describes the political battles Jameson fought to get the Archives funded and to get a site for the building. The article ends with a short discussion of Jameson's role in setting up the administration of the National Archives.

s28. SHELLEY, FRED. "The Presidential Papers Program of the Library of Congress." *American Archivist* 25 (1962): 429–33.

microfilm; presidential papers

This article begins with a discussion of the congressional directive to collect presidential papers. Shelley then describes the preparation of complete microfilm editions of the papers and problems that arose.

s29. SHELLEY, FRED. "The Publication Program of the Maryland Historical Society." *American Archivist* 15 (1952): 309–20.

archives; local history; Maryland; state history

Shelley describes the Maryland Historical Society's publication program, which includes documents, records, books, pamphlets, leaflets, and a magazine.

s30. SHEPARD, WILLIAM P. "Recent Theories of Textual Criticism." *Modern Philology* 28 (1930): 129–41.

history of editing

Shepard reviews the early twentieth-century history of textual criticism, beginning with Lachmann and Bédier. He summarizes the methods of Dom Henri Quentin, chief of the papal commission on revision of the text of the Vulgate, and of W. W. Greg, and then presents the results of his own experiments with these two methods.

s31. SHEPPARD, WILLIAM F. "The Plight of 'Foreign Relations': A Plea for Action." *American Historical Association Newsletter* 9 (1971): 22–27.

Foreign Relations series; public relations

Sheppard reviews the history of the *Foreign Relations* series and calls for academic activism to help restore the series to its original state.

S32. SHERIDAN, EUGENE R. "Captain Smith Goes to Jamestown." *Documentary Editing* 10 (June 1988): 11–15.

annotation; Smith, John; transcription

In this review, Sheridan describes Philip L. Barbour's *The Complete Works of Captain John Smith* (1580–1631) as "magnificent" and "a model of editorial scholarship in its selection, presentation, and annotation."

S33. SHILLINGSBURG, MIRIAM J. "Computer Assistance to Scholarly Editing." *Bulletin of Research in the Humanities* 81 (1978): 448–63.

collation; computers

Shillingsburg discusses the use of computers in the Thackeray editions for collating texts and typesetting.

S34. SHILLINGSBURG, PETER L. "The Computer as Research Assistant in Scholarly Editing." *Literary Research Newsletter* 5 (1980): 31–45.

collation; computers

Shillingsburg evaluates the quality, efficiency, and economy of computerized collation and describes the computer system used by the Thackeray edition at Mississippi State University.

S35. SHILLINGSBURG, PETER L. "Critical Editing and the Center for Scholarly Editions." *Scholarly Publishing* 9 (1977–78): 31–40.

CSE; editing, general

A summary of the debates over the economics, definitiveness, copy-text theory, treatment of accidentals, and apparatus of scholarly editions, and the standards for CSE editions.

s36. SHILLINGSBURG, PETER L. "Editorial Problems Are Readers' Problems." In *Editing the Victorians,* edited by N. John Hall, 43–57.

apparatus; authorial intention

Shillingsburg discusses "the editorial problem of variant forms of intention and then the problem of presenting the record of variant intentions in scholarly editions." In resolving these problems, he suggests, the reader's needs should be paramount. Authors' intentions, he argues, change over time, and it is difficult both to determine intentions and to convey their complexity to the reader.

s37. SHILLINGSBURG, PETER L. "Key Issues in Editorial Theory." *Analytical & Enumerative Bibliography* 6 (1982): 3–16.

accidentals; apparatus; authorial intention

Shillingsburg defines terms relating to authorial intention and authority and then discusses the treatment of variants. See also G. Thomas Tanselle, "The Editorial Problem of Final Authorial Intention" and "Recent Editorial Discussion."

s38. SHILLINGSBURG, PETER L. *Scholarly Editing in the Computer Age: Theory and Practice.* Rev. ed. Athens: University of Georgia Press, 1986.

apparatus; authorial intention; computers; copy-text

In the "theory" section, Shillingsburg reviews concepts of textual authority, forms of presentation, authorial intention, and ideal texts, enumerating four different approaches to editing literary works. In the "practice" section, he discusses the practical implications of these theories. In "practicalities," he explains the use of computers to reduce costs, to collate texts, to set type, to build apparatus, and to compile indexes. He describes the CASE system (Computer Assistance to Scholarly Editing) in detail.

s39. SHILLINGSBURG, PETER L. "Textual Problems in Editing Thackeray." In *Editing Nineteenth-Century Fiction*, edited by Jane Millgate, 41–59.

authorial intention; copy-text; illustrations; Thackeray, William Makepeace

A discussion of the problems of editing Thackeray, emphasizing the determination of authorial intention and the variety of texts.

s40. SHOWMAN, RICHARD K., AND CHARLENE BANGS BICKFORD. "Documenting a Consummate Politician: The Papers of George Washington." *Documentary Editing* 10 (September 1988): 11–15.

annotation; Washington, George

In this review of the first two volumes of the Revolutionary War and the Presidential series of *The Papers of George Washington*, the authors focus on annotation, beginning with a discussion of Daniel Feller's " 'What Good Are They Anyway?' "

s41. SIDNELL, MICHAEL. "Yeats in the Light of Day: The Text and Some Editions." In *Editing British and American Literature, 1880–1920*, edited by Eric W. Domville, 49–63.

Yeats, William Butler

A review of existing Yeats editions.

s42. SIFTON, PAUL G. "The Provenance of the Thomas Jefferson Papers." *American Archivist* 40 (1977): 17–30.

authentication; Jefferson, Thomas

Sifton reviews the history of Jefferson's papers from Jefferson's time to the beginning of the Boyd edition.

s43. SIMON, JOHN Y. "The Canons of Selection." *Documentary Editing* 6 (December 1984): 8–12.

selection

Simon discusses the scope of documentary editing projects and selection procedures. He first details the contributions of Clarence Carter and then lists his own standards.

s44. SIMON, JOHN Y. "The Collected Writings of Ulysses S. Grant." *Civil War History* 9 (1963): 277–79.

Grant, Ulysses S.; project organization; search

Simon discusses the reasons for establishing the Grant project and lists the major figures involved. He also describes the methods used in preparing the edition and collecting the material.

s45. SIMON, JOHN Y. "Editorial Projects as Derivative Archives." *College and Research Libraries* 35 (1974): 291–94.

access; photocopying

Simon begins with a discussion of the influence of the Xerox age on the study of history and emphasizes the problems faced by the keepers of documents. He describes the policy of the U. S. Grant Association concerning requests for using its collections.

s46. SIMON, JOHN Y. "Editors and Critics." *Newsletter of the Association for Documentary Editing* 3 (December 1981): 1–4.

history of editing; NHPRC

Simon discusses the criticism of historical editing. He starts with the twenty-year "honeymoon" in which praise was almost universal and then moves on to the next ten years, when the critics took over. The criticism surrounded the subjects chosen for editorial projects (see, for example, articles by Jesse Lemisch), funding for editing projects (e.g., Simone Reagor, "Historical Editing: The Federal Role"), and the issues raised by G. Thomas Tanselle ("The Editing of Historical Documents").

s47. SIMON, JOHN Y. "In Response." *Newsletter of the Association for Documentary Editing* 4 (May 1982): 5–6.

federal historians; funding; NHPRC

Simon's article responds to Simone Reagor's "Historical Editing: The Federal Role." Simon argues that some classic documentary editions violate Reagor's standards and notes the existence of a corps of federal historians.

s48. SIMON, JOHN Y. "In Search of Margaret Johnson Erwin: A Research Note." *Journal of American History* 69 (March 1983): 932–41.

authenticity; Civil War; dating; Erwin, Margaret Johnson; letters

Simon notes extensive inaccuracies in John Seymour Erwin's *Like Some Green Laurel: Letters of Margaret Johnson Erwin.* See also Erwin's and Beverly Jarrett's subsequent letters and Simon's letter to the editor in response.

s49. SIMON, JOHN Y. Letter to the Editor. *Journal of American History* 70 (June 1983): 225–26.

authenticity; Erwin, Margaret Johnson; letters

A response to the letters of John Seymour Erwin and Beverly Jarrett.

s50. SIMPSON, BROOKS D. "Blacks in Blue and the Fight for Freedom." *Documentary Editing* 7 (September 1985): 6–10.

annotation; black history; *Freedom;* military history; organization of editions

Simpson reviews series II of *Freedom: A Documentary History of Emancipation, 1861–1867,* with special attention to organization, annotation, and coverage of the subject.

s51. SIMPSON, CLAUDE M., JR. "The Practice of Textual Criticism." In James Thorpe and Claude M. Simpson, Jr., *The Task of the Editor,* 33–52. Los Angeles: University of California, Los Angeles, William Andrews Clark Memorial Library, 1969.

Hawthorne, Nathaniel; notebooks; transmission of texts

Simpson describes the difficulties of determining the original text of Hawthorne's notebooks and discusses the significance of the evidence produced by bibliographical analysis.

s52. SIMPSON, CLAUDE M., JR., WILLIAM H. GOETZMANN, AND MATTHEW J. BRUCCOLI. "The Interdependence of Rare Books and Manuscripts: The Scholar's View." *Serif* 9 (Spring 1972): 3–22.

archives; manuscript collectors

The authors discuss and illustrate the literary and historical scholar's dependence on archivists, rare books librarians, and collectors, and the uses of manuscripts and other research materials.

s53. SIRACUSA, JOSEPH. "Reply to Professor Etzold." *Newsletter of the Society for Historians of American Foreign Relations* 8 (June 1976): 14–15.

professional status

Siracusa advances the argument that documentary editing is scholarly and that it is important to the profession. See also

Thomas H. Etzold, "The Great Documents Deluge," and Frank G. Burke, "Rebuttal."

s54. SLANY, WILLIAM Z. "Historians in the Department of State." *Newsletter of the Society for Historians of American Foreign Relations*, March 1979, pp. 18–22.

federal historians; *Foreign Relations* series; training

Slany describes the activities and training of historians employed by the Department of State, including those who edit the *Foreign Relations* series.

s55. SLANY, WILLIAM Z. "History of the *Foreign Relations* Series." *Newsletter of the Society for Historians of American Foreign Relations*, March 1981, pp. 10–19.

Foreign Relations series; history of editing

Slany reviews the history of the series from the end of World War II until 1980 and discusses its future prospects.

s56. SMITH, D. I. B. "Editing Marvell's Prose." In *Editing Seventeenth-Century Prose*, edited by D. I. B. Smith, 51–69.

censorship; copy-text; Marvell, Andrew

A discussion of the special difficulties of establishing a text in the case of works that have been censored and printed surreptitiously.

s57. SMITH, D. I. B., ED. *Editing Eighteenth-Century Texts: Papers Given at the Editorial Conference, University of Toronto, October 1967.* Toronto: University of Toronto Press, 1968.

eighteenth century

See articles by Bentley, G. E., Jr. ("William Blake's Protean Text"); Besterman, Theodore; Brack, O M, Jr. ("The Ledgers of William Strahan"); Greene, Donald; Hemlow, Joyce; and Howard, William J.

s58. SMITH, D. I. B., ED. *Editing Seventeenth-Century Prose: Papers Given at the Conference on Editorial Problems, University of Toronto, November 1970.* Toronto: Hakkert, 1972.

seventeenth century

See articles by Holmes, D. M., and H. D. Janzen; Kelley, Maurice; Quehen, A. H. de; Smith, D. I. B. ("Editing Marvell's Prose"); Story, G. M.; and Zimansky, Curt A.

s59. SMOCK, RAYMOND W. "A Bicentennial Legacy Honorable to the Nation." *Manuscripts* 39 (Fall 1987): 277–84.

funding; preservation

A progress report on the Documentary Heritage Trust, and a plea for support.

s60. SMOCK, RAYMOND W. "Technology and the Future of Documentary Editing." *Documentary Editing* 6 (December 1984): 1–7.

archives; computers

Smock lists the editors and editions that pioneered the use of computers. He then discusses the possible future role of computers in editing and the changing roles of the historian and archivist.

s61. SOMERSET, J. A. B. " 'this hawthorn-brake our tiring-house': Records of Early English Drama and Modern Play-texts." In *Editing Early English Drama,* edited by A. F. Johnston, 95–119.

drama; history of editing; Middle Ages; public records; Shakespeare, William

Somerset briefly discusses problems in existing editions of medieval drama and then describes the editing of local records and their usefulness in editing plays.

s62. SOWARDS, J. K. "On Editing Erasmus." In *Editing Polymaths: Erasmus to Russell,* edited by H. J. Jackson, 77–97.

Erasmus, Desiderius; translation

Sowards describes the *Collected Works of Erasmus,* its history, management, editorial guidelines, translation procedures, annotation, and commentary.

s63. SPEER, MARY B. "On Editing Old French Texts." *Newsletter of the Association for Documentary Editing* 5 (September 1983): 1–3.

editing, general; handbook; Old French

Speer discusses the reasons for publishing a manual on editing Old French texts, the audience to which it is directed, the contents of the manual, and its reception. She also summarizes the conflict between Bédierists and neo-Lachmannians that has divided editors of Old French.

s64. SPENCE, MARY LEE. "The Use of a Wife's Papers: Jessie Benton Frémont." *Documentary Editing* 8 (December 1986): 6–10.

Frémont, Jessie Benton; selection; women's history

Spence reviews Jessie Benton Frémont's role in the career of her husband, John C., and discusses the importance of including the papers of wives in editions of their husbands' papers.

s65. SPEVACK, MARVIN. "The Editor as Philologist." *Text* 3 (1987): 91–106.

annotation; editing, general

Spevack discusses the importance of philological sophistication in editing, particularly in collation and annotation.

s66. SPIKER, SINA. *Indexing Your Book: A Practical Guide for Authors.* Rev. ed. Madison: University of Wisconsin Press, 1987.

indexing

A basic guide to the theory and mechanics of indexing that plays down the role of computers in indexing.

s67. SPILLER, ROBERT E. "The Impossible Dream: Adventures in Editing American Literary Texts." *The Library Chronicle* 42, 2 (1978): 83–97.

CEAA; copy-text; CSE; history of editing; types of editing

In reviewing his fifty-year editorial career and relevant events in the profession, Spiller concludes: "There are many kinds of texts that serve many different uses and the editor alone has the right to choose the kind that he will produce, just so he announces his procedure in a preface and then sticks with thorough scholarly integrity to his own rules."

s68. SPRINGER, HASKELL. "Practical Editions: Washington Irving's *The Sketch Book.*" *Proof* 4 (1975): 167–74.

Irving, Washington; practical editions

Springer reviews the textual history of *The Sketch Book* and evaluates its reprinting in two complete texts and six anthologized excerpts.

s69. STACHEL, JOHN. " 'A Man of my Type'—Editing the Einstein Papers." *British Journal for the History of Science* 20 (January 1987): 57–66.

Einstein, Albert

Stachel describes the shaping features of the Einstein edition: comprehensiveness, chronological organization, literal transcription, and "annotation as an aid to interpretation." He then discusses the appropriateness of this approach, its uses, and expected results.

s70. STALLWORTHY, JON. "Old-Spelling Editions: The State of the Business in 1978." In *Play-Texts in Old Spelling,* edited by G. B. Shand and Raymond C. Shady, 141–51.

publishing

Stallworthy discusses finding a publisher and the costs of publication, and offers some alternative methods of publication.

s71. STEVENS, MICHAEL E. "Documentary Editing in the Southeastern State Archives." *Documentary Editing* 7 (June 1985): 8–13.

archives; funding

Stevens discusses the role of public and private state organizations, with a focus on groups active in Virginia, North Carolina, and South Carolina. Each organization's history and current status is given as is general information about their editorial policies and differences from the NHPRC.

s72. STEWART, JAMES BREWER. "Garrison Again, and Again, and Again, and Again. . . ." *Reviews in American History* 4 (1976): 539–45.

Garrison, William Lloyd; letters; selection

In his review of volumes 3 and 4 of *The Letters of William Lloyd Garrison,* Stewart discusses the effect of excluding letters to Garrison. See also Aileen S. Kraditor, "Editing the Abolitionists."

s73. STEWART, KATE. "James Madison as an Archivist." *American Archivist* 21 (1958): 243–57.

Madison, James

Stewart describes Madison's processing of his papers.

s74. STORY, G. M. "The Text of Lancelot Andrewes's Sermons." In *Editing Seventeenth-Century Prose,* edited by D. I. B. Smith, 11–23.

Andrewes, Lancelot; annotation; sermons; transmission of texts

An evaluation of the 1629 edition of Andrewes's sermons by Bishops Laud and Buckeridge.

s75. STRAWHORN, JOHN M. "Word Processing and Publishing." *Scholarly Publishing* 12 (1980–81): 109–21.

computers

Strawhorn's article provides an introduction to word processing and its uses in publishing.

s76. STUBER, FLORIAN. "On Original and Final Intentions, or Can There Be an Authoritative *Clarissa?*" *Text* 2 (1985): 229–44.

authorial intention; copy-text; Richardson, Samuel

Stuber discusses the selection of a copy-text for *Clarissa,* reviewing the novel's printing history and recommending the third edition as copy-text. He also discusses the validity of restoring original authorial intention as an editorial goal.

s77. SULLIVAN, ERNEST W., II. "The Problem of Text in Familiar Letters." *Papers of the Bibliographical Society of America* 75 (1981): 115–26.

Donne, John; letters

Sullivan discusses the problems of editing familiar letters when the only available texts are those transmitted by earlier editors.

s78. SWERDLOW, N. M. "Translating Copernicus." *Isis* 72 (1981): 73–82.

Copernicus, Nicholas; history of science; translation

Swerdlow reviews three English editions of *De revolutionibus*, the most recent being the 1978 Johns Hopkins University Press edition, edited by Jerzy Dobrzycki, translated by Edward Rosen. He finds fault with the quality of the underlying text, the translation, and the annotation.

s79. SYRETT, HAROLD C. "Alexander Hamilton Collected." *Columbia University Forum* 5 (1962): 24–28.

Hamilton, Alexander; search

This article describes the problems that arose in collecting Hamilton's papers. Syrett also provides background information about other editing projects.

s80. SYRETT, HAROLD C., AND JACOB E. COOKE. "The Papers of Alexander Hamilton." *The Historian* 19 (1957): 168–81.

Hamilton, Alexander; search; selection

The authors detail problems in editing the papers of Hamilton, including the difficulties in collecting papers ranging from destruction by his widow to refusals by individuals to permit copying. Syrett and Cooke also discuss editorial and publication procedures and selection guidelines.

T

T1. TANSELLE, G. THOMAS. "Bibliographical Problems in Melville." *Studies in American Fiction* 2 (1974): 57–74.

accidentals; Melville, Herman

Tanselle comments on "the inseparability of descriptive bibliography and editing," explains the usefulness of publishers' records, and describes some of the special problems arising in Melville's work.

T2. TANSELLE, G. THOMAS. "The Case Western Reserve Edition of Sherwood Anderson: A Review Article." *Proof* 4 (1975): 183–209.

Anderson, Sherwood

Tanselle is highly critical of the edition's editorial plan and its execution, and he finds the edition inaccurate and unreliable.

T3. TANSELLE, G. THOMAS. "Classical, Biblical, and Medieval Textual Criticism and Modern Editing." *Studies in Bibliography* 36 (1983): 21–68.

editing, types of; history of editing

Tanselle discusses "the relations between textual work on early or medieval manuscripts and that on later printed texts," arguing that the editors working in both areas have much to learn from one another.

T4. TANSELLE, G. THOMAS. "The Editing of Historical Documents." *Studies in Bibliography* 31 (1978): 1–56. Reprinted in his *Selected Studies in Bibliography*, 451–506.

editing, general; history of editing; transcription

A survey of historical editing after World War II that criticizes the field for vague and often self-contradictory statements of editorial method and for overuse of expanded transcription. This article launched a continuing debate; see, for example, Don L. Cook, "The Short Happy Thesis"; John Y. Simon, "Editors and Critics"; Robert J. Taylor, "Editorial Practices"; and Gordon S. Wood, "Historians and Documentary Editing."

T5. TANSELLE, G. THOMAS. "Editorial Apparatus for Radiating Texts." *The Library* 29 (1974): 330–37.

apparatus

Tanselle describes the appropriate apparatus for a text derived from a process of combining a variety of radiating texts.

T6. TANSELLE, G. THOMAS. "The Editorial Problem of Final Authorial Intention." *Studies in Bibliography* 29 (1976): 167–211. Reprinted in his *Selected Studies in Bibliography,* 309–53.

authorial intention

Tanselle defines "intention" and its critical implications and then discusses the difficulties of distinguishing authorial from nonauthorial alterations and of deciding which alterations indicate the author's "final intention."

T7. TANSELLE, G. THOMAS. "External Fact as an Editorial Problem." *Studies in Bibliography* 32 (1979): 1–47. Reprinted in his *Selected Studies in Bibliography,* 355–401.

authorial intention; transcription; types of editing

Tanselle discusses how editors should handle textual references to external facts. His examples are drawn from both fiction and historical documents.

T8. TANSELLE, G. THOMAS. "Greg's Theory of Copy-text and the Editing of American Literature." *Studies in Bibliography* 28 (1975): 167–229. Reprinted in his *Selected Studies in Bibliography,* 245–307, and *Textual Criticism Since Greg,* 1–63.

accidentals; apparatus; CEAA; copy-text

Tanselle reviews Greg's theory of copy-text and Bowers's amplification and application of that theory. He explains the CEAA's adoption of Greg's theory as well as its requirements for apparatus. Tanselle then responds to criticisms of CEAA editions by Edmund Wilson ("The Fruits of the MLA"); Paul Baender ("The Meaning of Copy-Text"); Donald Pizer ("On the Editing of Modern American Texts"); John Freehafer ("How Not to Edit American Authors"); Morse Peckham

("Reflections on the Foundations of Modern Textual Editing"); James Thorpe (*Principles of Textual Criticism*); and Philip Gaskell (*A New Introduction to Bibliography*).

T9. TANSELLE, G. THOMAS. "Historicism and Critical Editing." *Studies in Bibliography* 39 (1986): 1–46. Reprinted in his *Textual Criticism Since Greg*, 109–54.

types of editing

This article examines literary editorial theory of the late 1970s and the first half of the '80s. Tanselle considers the views expressed during this time to be representative of an unsophisticated attitude toward historicism. He also discusses the extreme views of the debate on literary editing.

T10. TANSELLE, G. THOMAS. "Literary Editing." In *Literary & Historical Editing*, edited by George L. Vogt and John Bush Jones, 35–56.

apparatus; copy-text; journals; letters; transcription; types of editing

Tanselle argues that, rather than distinguishing between "literary" and other kinds of editing, we should distinguish between writings intended for publication and those not. He then discusses the implications of this distinction for such issues as transcription, apparatus, and choice of copy-text.

T11. TANSELLE, G. THOMAS. "The Meaning of Copy-Text: A Further Note." *Studies in Bibliography* 23 (1970): 191–96.

copy-text

In this response to Paul Baender's "The Meaning of Copy-Text," Tanselle argues that the term remains relevant and unambiguous.

T12. TANSELLE, G. THOMAS. "The New Editions of Hawthorne and Crane." *The Book Collector* 23 (Summer 1974): 214–29.

CEAA; copy-text; Crane, Stephen; Hawthorne, Nathaniel; history of editing

Tanselle surveys the aims and accomplishments of the centenary edition of Hawthorne and the Virginia edition of Crane. He also reviews the history and criticism of the CEAA editions.

T13. TANSELLE, G. THOMAS. "Presidential Address." *Text* 1 (1984): 1–9.

history of editing; Society for Textual Scholarship

In this address, delivered at the first meeting of the Society in 1981, Tanselle reviews the history of textual scholarship and discusses the difficulties and issues confronting the field.

T14. TANSELLE, G. THOMAS. "Problems and Accomplishments in the Editing of the Novel." *Studies in the Novel* 7 (1975): 323–60.

accidentals; CEAA; copy-text; novels; practical editions

Tanselle reviews the special problems of editing novels (as opposed to shorter works), surveys current editions of novels in the United States (including CEAA editions) and England, and discusses the state of practical editions.

T15. TANSELLE, G. THOMAS. "Recent Editorial Discussion and the Central Questions of Editing." *Studies in Bibliography* 34 (1981): 23–65. Reprinted in his *Textual Criticism Since Greg*, 65–107.

audience; CEAA; editing, general

Tanselle surveys the editorial literature that grew up around the Center for Editions of American Authors in the second half of the 1970s. He then considers what he believes to be the central questions of editing, focusing on audience, authorial intention, and "indifferent" variants.

T16. TANSELLE, G. THOMAS. *Selected Studies in Bibliography.* Charlottesville: University Press of Virginia, 1979.

A collection of essays that first appeared in *Studies in Bibliography.* See Tanselle's "The Editing of Historical Documents," "The Editorial Problem of Final Authorial Intention," "External Fact as an Editorial Problem," "Greg's Theory of Copy-Text and the Editing of American Literature," and "Some Principles for Editorial Apparatus."

T17. TANSELLE, G. THOMAS. "Some Principles for Editorial Apparatus." *Studies in Bibliography* 25 (1972): 41–88. Reprinted in his *Selected Studies in Bibliography,* 403–50.

apparatus; audience

Tanselle argues that decisions about apparatus should be based on the volume's expected audience. He then discusses the arrangement of the apparatus, symbols and abbreviations, and the possibilities for treating textual notes, emendations, line-end hyphenation, and historical collation.

T18. TANSELLE, G. THOMAS. *Textual Criticism Since Greg: A Chronicle, 1950–1985.* Charlottesville: University Press of Virginia, 1987.

See his "Greg's Theory of Copy-Text and the Editing of American Literature"; "Historicism and Critical Editing"; and "Recent Editorial Discussion and the Central Questions of Editing." See also Boydston, Jo Ann, "A Critical Chronicle."

T19. TANSELLE, G. THOMAS. "Textual Scholarship." In *Introduction to Scholarship in Modern Languages and Literatures,* edited by Joseph Gibaldi, 29–52. New York: MLA, 1981.

apparatus; authorial intention; copy-text; editing, general

An introduction to textual editing, with definitions of basic terms, statements of basic issues, and explanations of editorial processes.

T20. TANSELLE, G. THOMAS. "Textual Study and Literary Judgment." *Papers of the Bibliographical Society of America* 65 (1971): 109–22.

editing, general; literary criticism

Tanselle discusses the "importance of critical powers in editorial procedure—of the way in which a critical *edition* is, in itself and of necessity, also a critical *study*."

T21. TANSELLE, G. THOMAS. "Two Basic Distinctions: Theory and Practice, Text and Apparatus." *Studies in the Novel* 7 (1975): 404–6.

CEAA

A response to John Freehafer's "Greg's Theory of Copy-Text and the Textual Criticism in the CEAA Editions." See also articles by Bruce Bebb and Hershel Parker, Vinton A. Dearing ("Textual Criticism Today"), Thomas L. McHaney ("The Important Questions"), and Morse Peckham ("Notes on Freehafer"), all in the same issue.

T22. TAYLOR, GARY. "Revising Shakespeare." *Text* 3 (1987): 285–304.

editing, general; Shakespeare, William

Taylor argues that Shakespeare did revise his own plays, basing his conclusion on historical and bibliographical evidence rather than on critical interpretation.

T23. TAYLOR, ROBERT J. "A Dialogue: Peter Shaw and Robert J. Taylor on Editing the Adamses." *Newsletter of the Association for Documentary Editing* 2 (December 1980): 6–9.

Adams papers; annotation; selection

Taylor responds to Peter Shaw's review of the Adams papers (immediately preceding) by explaining his selection and annotation procedures.

T24. TAYLOR, ROBERT J. "Editorial Practices—An Historian's View." *Newsletter of the Association for Documentary Editing* 3 (February 1981): 4–8.

apparatus; editing, general; types of editing

Taylor concedes Tanselle's criticism ("The Editing of Historical Documents") that documentary editors fail to follow their own statements of method. However, he argues for editorial discretion and readable, uncluttered texts. He also insists on the need to treat printed documentary sources differently than literary works.

T25. TAYLOR, ROBERT J. "One Historian's Education." *William and Mary Quarterly* 41 (1984): 478–86.

professional status; reviewing

Taylor reviews his career as a historian and editor with comments about the place of editing within the profession of history. He includes suggestions about reviewing documentary editions.

T26. TEUTE, FREDRIKA J. "Views in Review: A Historiographical Perspective on Historical Editing." *American Archivist* 43 (1980): 43–56.

annotation; editing, general; form of publication; NHPRC; objectivity

Teute criticizes the prominence that documentary editing gives to elites, excessive annotation, and claims of objectivity.

She urges the use of microfilm editions rather than comprehensive letterpress editions.

T27. THOMSON, CLIVE. "On Editing Zola's Fiction." In *Editing Nineteenth-Century Fiction*, edited by Jane Millgate, 83–98.

copy-text; Zola, Emile

Thomson enumerates the available texts of Zola's work, discusses modern editions, and sets out the textual problems raised by the works. He closes with suggestions for future editors of Zola.

T28. THORP, WILLARD. "Exodus: Four Decades of American Literary Scholarship." *Modern Language Quarterly* 26 (1965): 40–61.

history of editing

Thorp reviews the history of American literary scholarship from the beginning of the twentieth century and then examines recent trends, including bibliographical research.

T29. THORPE, JAMES. "The Aesthetics of Textual Criticism." *PMLA* 80 (1965): 465–82. Revised and reprinted in Thorpe's *Principles of Textual Criticism*, 3–49.

authorial intention; copy-text

Thorpe discusses the problems of determining authorial intention and establishing a copy-text in view of editorial intervention, proofreading errors, changes introduced in dramatic productions, and authorial revision (in proof and printed versions). He concludes: "The basic goal of textual criticism is . . . the verification or recovery of the words which the author intended to constitute the literary work. . . . The work of art is . . . always tending toward a collaborative status, and the task of the textual critic is always to recover and preserve its integrity at that point where the authorial intentions seem to have been fulfilled."

T30. THORPE, JAMES. "The Establishment of the Text." In his *Principles of Textual Criticism*, 171–202.

apparatus; authorial intention; copy-text; editing, general

Thorpe examines some of the reasons that editions prove not to be "definitive," including the discovery of additional texts, the use of corrupt texts, new standards, and new methods. He then discusses the principles and procedures of establishing a text, listing five major steps: collecting the texts, analyzing them, selecting the copy-text, perfecting it, and explaining the perfected text.

T31. THORPE, JAMES. "The Ideal of Textual Criticism." In James Thorpe and Claude M. Simpson, Jr., *The Task of the Editor*, 1–32. Los Angeles: University of California, Los Angeles, William Andrews Clark Memorial Library, 1969. Revised and reprinted in Thorpe, *Principles of Textual Criticism*, 50–79.

authorial intention; history of editing; transmission of texts

Thorpe discusses the ideal of textual criticism, its claims to be scientific, and its limitations.

T32. THORPE, JAMES. "Literary and Historical Editing: The Values and Limits of Diversity." In *Literary & Historical Editing*, edited by George L. Vogt and John Bush Jones, 13–22.

annotation; copy-text; Hamilton, Alexander; Hawthorne, Nathaniel; Jefferson, Thomas; Milton, John; types of editing

A review of the practices of several modern American editions and a comparison of the concerns of literary and historical editors.

T33. THORPE, JAMES. *Principles of Textual Criticism*. San Marino, Calif.: Huntington Library, 1972.

See Thorpe, James, "The Aesthetics of Textual Criticism," "The Ideal of Textual Criticism," "The Province of Textual Criticism," "Textual Analysis," "The Treatment of Accidentals," and "The Establishment of the Text."

T34. THORPE, JAMES. "The Province of Textual Criticism." In his *Principles of Textual Criticism*, 80–104.

bibliography; editing, general; history of editing

An attempt to delineate the roles of bibliography and textual editing, and an argument for the editor's use of methods beyond those of bibliography.

T35. THORPE, JAMES. "Textual Analysis." In his *Principles of Textual Criticism*, 105–30.

editing, general; history of editing; textual criticism

Thorpe discusses the role, hypothesis, main forms, limitations, and usefulness of textual analysis, that part of textual criticism whose "specific purpose . . . is to try to establish the relationship among the various texts of a literary work in order to achieve the general purpose" of determining which text "most nearly fulfills the author's intentions."

T36. THORPE, JAMES. "The Treatment of Accidentals." In his *Principles of Textual Criticism*, 131–70. An expanded version of Thorpe's *Watching the Ps & Qs*.

accidentals; authorial intention; compositorial studies; transcription

Thorpe discusses the effects of altering accidentals, authors' general lack of interest in such details, printers' practices, and arguments for and against modernization.

T37. THORPE, JAMES. *The Use of Manuscripts in Literary Research: Problems of Access and Literary Property Rights.* New York: MLA, 1979.

access; archives; copyright; search

In this guide to manuscript research, Thorpe offers advice on background research, finding aids, conducting a search, and dealing with archives and private collectors. He then reviews the copyright law as it relates to manuscripts and other unpublished material in the United States and abroad.

T38. THORPE, JAMES. *Watching the Ps & Qs: Editorial Treatment of Accidentals.* Lawrence: University of Kansas Libraries, 1971. Expanded in Thorpe's "The Treatment of Accidentals."

accidentals; authorial intention; compositorial studies; transcription; transmission of texts

Thorpe argues that authorial intention should determine editorial treatment of accidentals and, through a review of authors' and printers' practices, suggests that punctuation and spelling were generally of little concern to authors.

T39. TODD, WILLIAM B. "On the Use of Advertisements in Bibliographical Studies." *The Library*, 5th ser., 8 (1953): 174–87.

bibliography; dating

Todd discusses the value of newspaper advertisements for books in dating publication and providing other information.

T40. TODD, WILLIAM B. "Problems in Editing Mark Twain." *Books at Iowa* 1 (April 1965): 3–8.

apparatus; copy-text; Twain, Mark

Todd notes the problems of establishing a text and the sigla for the various issues of Twain's works.

T41. TODD, WILLIAM B. *Procedures for Collating Twain's Minor Works.* Iowa City: University of Iowa, 1965.

collation

A method of sight-collating by teams of readers, issued as an appendix to Baender and Todd, *Rules and Procedures*.

T42. TOMPKINS, E. BERKELEY. "The NHPRC in Perspective." In *The Publication of American Historical Manuscripts*, edited by Leslie W. Dunlap and Fred Shelley, 89–96.

NHPRC

The director of the National Historical Publications and Records Commission discusses various aspects of the NHPRC, beginning with its history. The membership and major publications of the commission are detailed as are its services, awards, and records program. Tompkins also describes the Commission's funding sources.

T43. TRASK, DAVID F., AND WILLIAM Z. SLANY. "What Lies Ahead for the *Foreign Relations* Series." *Newsletter of the Society for Historians of American Foreign Relations*, March 1978, pp. 26–29.

Foreign Relations series

Trask and Slany discuss future plans for the series that are designed to include material from other agencies, expand annotation, speed up publication, make more documents available on microfilm, and reduce costs and prices.

T44. TUCKER, EDWARD L. "The Longfellow Letters." *Newsletter of the Association for Documentary Editing* 5 (September 1983): 3–6.

Longfellow, Henry Wadsworth; transcription

A review of *The Letters of Henry Wadsworth Longfellow*, vols. 5 and 6, edited by Andrew Hilen.

T45. TURNER, ROBERT KEAN. "Accidental Evils." In *Play-Texts in Old Spelling*, edited by G. B. Shand and Raymond C. Shady, 27–33.

accidentals; Massinger, Philip; old-spelling editions

Turner discusses the treatment of accidentals in old-spelling editions, drawing his examples from *The Plays and Poems of Philip Massinger.*

U

U1. UNITED STATES. COMMITTEE ON DEPARTMENT METHODS. *Documentary Historical Publications of the United States Government: Report to the President.* Washington, D.C., 1909.

federal government; history of editing

This report reviews the government's programs of historical publication from the colonial period through 1908 both chronologically and topically; surveys the field of U.S. history, indicating gaps in the published documentary record; reviews the publication programs of other governments; and provides the draft of a bill to create a Commission on National Historical Publications. The report includes the costs of government historical publication programs from 1890 to 1909.

U2. UNITED STATES. NATIONAL HISTORICAL PUBLICATIONS AND RECORDS COMMISSION. *Report to the President.* Washington, D.C., 1978.

NHPRC

The 1978 report describes the Commission's history and activities. It includes two appendices: a progress report on the publications and records programs and a "Statement of National Needs and Preferred Approaches for Historical Records in the United States."

U3. UNITED STATES. NATIONAL HISTORICAL PUBLICATIONS COMMISSION. *The National Historical Publications Commission,*

1934–1950: A Report to the Commission. Washington, D.C., 1951.

NHPC

This NHPC report discusses the background of the commission and the changes it has undergone.

U4. UNITED STATES. NATIONAL HISTORICAL PUBLICATIONS COMMISSION. *A National Program for the Publication of Historical Documents: A Report to the President.* Washington, D.C.: Government Printing Office, 1954.

Library of Congress; NHPC

The 1954 report outlined a program for the publication of historical documents, including the names of five people whose complete papers should be published. The NHPC also planned documentary histories of the ratification of both the Constitution and the Bill of Rights and of the first Federal Congress. The report also recommends establishing a national register of archival and manuscript collections as part of the Library of Congress catalogue.

U5. UNITED STATES. NATIONAL HISTORICAL PUBLICATIONS COMMISSION. *A National Program for the Publication of the Papers of American Leaders: A Preliminary Report to the President of the United States.* Washington, D.C.: National Historical Publications Commission, 1951.

NHPC

This report contains the results of a survey of scholars concerning documentary editing. The role of the commission is discussed, as are its suggestions for national programs.

U6. UNITED STATES. NATIONAL HISTORICAL PUBLICATIONS COMMISSION. *A Report to the President Containing a Proposal to Meet Existing and Anticipated Needs Over the Next Ten*

*Years Under a National Program for the Collection, Pres-
ervation, and Publication, or Dissemination by Other Means,
of the Documentary Sources of American History.* Washington, D.C., 1963.

funding; NHPC

The 1963 Report is divided into four parts: the value of history;
the responsibilities of the commission; an appraisal of current
problems; and recommendations.

V

V1. VAN BURKLEO, SANDRA F. "Denaturing Count Fosco's Croc-
odile: The Limits of 'Critical' Documentary Editions." *Documentary Editing* 9 (September 1987): 11–15.

organization of editions; transcription

In this review of vols. 4–6 of the *Documentary History of the
First Federal Congress of the United States of America,* Van
Burkleo focuses on the nonchronological arrangement of the
materials. She comments as well on the occasional use of "perfected" texts.

V2. VANDIVER, FRANK E. "The Jefferson Davis Papers." *Civil War
History* 9 (1963): 279–80.

Davis, Jefferson; project organization

Jefferson Davis's role in American history is discussed as are
the inadequacies of previous editions of his papers. Vandiver
also gives some specific information about the newest edition
of Davis's papers.

V3. VAN DUSEN, ALBERT E. "In Quest of that 'Arch Rebel' Jonathan
Trumbull, Sr." In *The Publication of American Historical*

Manuscripts, edited by Leslie W. Dunlap and Fred Shelley, 31–46. Iowa City: University of Iowa Libraries, 1976.

funding; search; selection; Trumbull, Jonathan, Sr.

This article details the problems and methods of the author's search for the Trumbull papers. Van Dusen also discusses the selection process and financing.

v4. VAN EE, DAUN. "Kimball's Churchill-Roosevelt Correspondence: The Best of Both Worlds." *Documentary Editing* 8 (June 1986): 6–9.

annotation; Churchill, Winston; illustrations; organization of editions; Roosevelt, Franklin D.; transcription

A review of *Churchill and Roosevelt: The Complete Correspondence,* vols. 1–3, edited by Warren F. Kimball.

v5. VINAVER, EUGÈNE. "Principles of Textual Emendation." In *Medieval Manuscripts and Textual Criticism,* edited by Christopher Kleinhenz, 139–66. Part 1 reprinted from *Studies in French Language and Medieval Literature Presented to Professor Mildred K. Pope* (Manchester: Manchester University Press, 1939), 351–69; part 2 reprinted from *Mélanges pour Jean Fourquet,* edited by Paul Valentin and Georges Zink (Paris: Klincksiecke, 1969), 355–66.

Middle Ages; textual criticism

Vinaver analyzes the sources of scribal error and discusses the implications of his analysis for textual emendation and the aims of textual criticism.

v6. VOGT, GEORGE L. "Introduction: The Historical Editor's View." In *Literary & Historical Editing,* edited by George L. Vogt and John Bush Jones, 1–5.

computers; funding; history of editing; microforms; professional status; social history; types of editing

A review of changes in the field from the 1960s to the 1980s.

v7. VOGT, GEORGE L., AND JOHN BUSH JONES, EDS. *Literary and
Historical Editing.* Lawrence: University of Kansas Libraries,
1981.

types of editing

See articles by Battestin, Martin C. ("A Rationale of Literary
Annotation"); Cullen, Charles T. ("Principles of Annota-
tion"); Jones, John Bush ("Introduction"); Rogers, George C.,
Jr. ("The Sacred Text"); Tanselle, G. Thomas ("Literary Ed-
iting"); Thorpe, James ("Literary and Historical Editing"); and
Vogt, George L.

v8. VOIGTS, LINDA EHRSAM. "Editing Middle English Texts: Needs
and Issues." In *Editing Texts in the History of Science and
Medicine,* edited by Trevor H. Levere, 39–68.

history of medicine; Middle English; translation

Voigts reviews the scope and classification of Middle English
medical manuscripts and discusses the need for and problems
of editing the Middle English versions of academic medical
texts.

v9. VON FRANK, ALBERT J. "Genetic Versus Clear Texts: Reading
and Writing Emerson." *Documentary Editing* 9 (December
1987): 5–9.

apparatus; audience; computers; Emerson, Ralph Waldo; journals; sermons

Von Frank discusses the choice between genetic and clear text,
using examples from Emerson's journals and sermons. He argues that a genetic text offers more information, whereas a

clear text is more accessible to a general audience and, if properly annotated, can provide the same information. He also describes a computerized method of producing both sorts of text.

W

WI. WALKER, ALICE. "Principles of Annotation: Some Suggestions for Editors of Shakespeare." *Studies in Bibliography* 9 (1957): 95–105.

annotation; Shakespeare, William

Walker discusses the usefulness of the *Oxford English Dictionary* in editing Shakespeare, particularly the possibility of reducing annotation of ordinary vocabulary.

W2. WALKER, JOHN A. "Editing Zola's Correspondence: When Is a Letter Not a Letter?" In *Editing Correspondence*, edited by J. A. Dainard, 93–116.

letters; Zola, Emile

A discussion of what constitutes a letter, with a survey of the editions of letters of five nineteenth-century French authors.

W3. WARREN, MICHAEL J. "Textual Problems, Editorial Assertions in Editions of Shakespeare." In *Textual Criticism and Literary Interpretation*, edited by Jerome J. McGann, 23–37.

drama; facsimiles; Shakespeare, William

Warren proposes a new edition of Shakespeare "which would involve the encounter with the earliest versions in photographic reproduction with their original confusions and corruptions unobscured by the interferences of later sophistication," because "the early text or texts as printed object have to become the basic focus of study."

w4. WEINBERG, BERNARD. "Editing Balzac: A Problem in Infinite Variation." In *Editing Nineteenth-Century Texts*, edited by John M. Robson, 60–76.

Balzac, Honoré de

Weinberg questions the applicability of traditional philological techniques to the works of Balzac.

w5. WEITENKAMPF, FRANK. "What Is a Facsimile?" *Papers of the Bibliographical Society of America* 37 (1943): 114–30.

facsimiles; illustrations

Emphasizing the technology of printing, Weitenkampf reviews the history of facsimile editions of text and illustrations before and after the advent of the camera, which "marks a revolution in facsimile making."

w6. WEITZMANN, KURT. "The Relation Between Text Criticism and Picture Criticism." In his *Illustrations in Roll and Codex*, 182–92. Princeton: Princeton University Press, 1947, 1970.

visual material

Weitzmann compares the criticism of text and picture, discussing the different views taken of changes and errors by copyists, evidence, dating, and development of stemmata.

w7. WELLS, STANLEY. *Re-Editing Shakespeare for the Modern Reader.* Oxford: Clarendon Press, 1984.

drama; emendation; Shakespeare, William; spelling

The general editor of the Oxford Shakespeare offers four lectures on modernization of spelling and punctuation, traditional emendations, and the treatment of stage directions, as well as a justification of a new Shakespeare edition.

w8. WELLS, STANLEY. "Revision in Shakespeare's Plays." In *Editing and Editors: A Retrospect*, edited by Richard Landon, 67–97.

authorial intention; censorship; drama; Shakespeare, William

Wells discusses the question of whether Shakespeare revised his own plays, the problems raised by such revision, and possible solutions. The causes for revision include censorship and a desire to improve the text, sometimes during rehearsal.

w9. WERSTINE, PAUL. "The Editorial Usefulness of Printing House and Compositor Studies." In *Play-Texts in Old Spelling*, edited by G. B. Shand and Raymond C. Shady, 35–64 (35–42 first appeared in *Analytical & Enumerative Bibliography* 2 [1978]: 153–65).

compositorial studies; Shakespeare, William

Werstine discusses the value of studying the printing houses and compositors who produced texts. His examples are drawn from *Love's Labour's Lost*.

w10. WEST, JAMES L. W., III. "The SCADE *Gatsby*: A Review Article." *Proof* 5 (1977): 237–56.

copy-text; facsimiles; Fitzgerald, F. Scott

West reviews Matthew Bruccoli's facsimile edition of the composite holograph draft of *The Great Gatsby* and its companion volume of apparatus. He is critical of the introduction and the choice of copy-text which, he contends, renders the apparatus "nearly valueless."

w11. WHALLEY, GEORGE. "On Editing Coleridge's Marginalia." In *Editing Texts of the Romantic Period*, edited by John D. Baird, 89–118.

annotation; Coleridge, Samuel Taylor; dating; format; marginalia; search

A description of the process of locating, editing, and presenting Coleridge's marginal notes.

W12. WHITAKER, JOHN K. "Editing Alfred Marshall." In *Editing Modern Economists,* edited by D. E. Moggridge, 43–66.

computers; copyright; economics; letters; Marshall, Alfred; search; selection

Whitaker discusses his editing of Marshall's correspondence, unpublished manuscript material, and published works. He also discusses possible innovative uses of computers for storage and display of texts.

W13. WHITEHILL, WALTER M., ED. "Publishing the Papers of Great Men." *Daedalus* 86 (1955): 47–79.

Founding Fathers projects

See articles by Boyd, Julian P. ("Some Animadversions"); Butterfield, Lyman H. ("The Adams Papers"); Labaree, Leonard W. ("The Papers of Benjamin Franklin"); and Lewis, Wilmarth S.

W14. WIBERLEY, STEPHEN E., JR. "Editing Maps: A Method for Historical Cartography." *Journal of Interdisciplinary History* 10 (Winter 1980): 499–510.

maps; visual materials

Wiberley discusses the editing of old maps and describes the procedures of the staff of the *Atlas of Early American History.*

W15. WIGGINS, HENRY H. "Publisher to Alexr. Hamilton, Esqr." *Scholarly Publishing* 9 (1977–78): 195–206, 347–60.

funding; Hamilton, Alexander; publishing

A history of Columbia University Press's publication of *The Papers of Alexander Hamilton*, emphasizing the financial, administrative, and publishing aspects.

W16. WILLCOX, WILLIAM B. "Reviewing the Reviewers." *Newsletter of the Association for Documentary Editing* 1 (March 1979): 5–6.

reviewing

Willcox claims that the current standards of reviewing documentary editions are low and suggests that they might be improved by inviting graduate students and recent Ph.D.'s to become reviewers.

W17. WILLIAMS, PHILIP, JR. "New Approaches to Textual Problems in Shakespeare." *Studies in Bibliography* 8 (1956): 3–14.

compositorial studies; Shakespeare, William

Williams explains the uses and deficiencies of compositor analysis in editing Shakespeare.

W18. WILLIAMS, T. HARRY. "Abraham Lincoln—Principle and Pragmatism in Politics: A Review Article." *Mississippi Valley Historical Review* 40 (1953): 89–106.

annotation; Lincoln, Abraham; selection

Williams's article provides a description of *The Collected Works of Abraham Lincoln* and a comparison with earlier Lincoln collections. Included in the article are the editorial procedures used and a section on Lincoln's principles and economic thought focusing on his beliefs and actions concerning slavery.

W19. WILSON, CLYDE N. Review of *The Papers of Andrew Jackson*, vol. 1. *Virginia Magazine of History and Biography* 89 (1981): 210–11.

Jackson, Andrew; reviewing

Wilson lists seven criteria for evaluating documentary publications based on collection, identification and verification, selection, editorial methodology, annotation, index, and format.

w20. WILSON, DOUGLAS EMORY. "Joyce's Masterpiece Rescued from Its Textual Corruption." *Documentary Editing* 7 (September 1985): 1–5.

annotation; Joyce, James; transcription

In this review of *Ulysses/A Critical and Synoptic Edition*, Wilson examines the problems and errors in earlier editions. He then discusses and explains changes made in the edition under review. The editorial and annotation policy of the edition are also described.

w21. WILSON, DOUGLAS EMORY. Letter to the Editor. *Documentary Editing* 10 (September 1988): 24.

Joyce, James

Wilson expresses some reservations about his earlier review of Hans Walter Gabler's edition of *Ulysses* ("Joyce's Masterpiece Rescued").

w22. WILSON, EDMUND. "The Fruits of the MLA." *New York Review of Books*, 26 September 1968, pp. 10ff. Reprinted, and expanded, in Wilson's *The Devils and Canon Barham: Ten Essays on Poets, Novelists and Monsters* (New York: Farrar, Straus and Giroux, 1973), 154–202.

apparatus; audience; CEAA; Howells, William Dean; Twain, Mark

In this essay—the most notorious of the criticisms of the CEAA editions—Wilson focuses on the editions of Howells and Twain. See also Lewis Mumford's "Emerson Behind

Barbed Wire," to which Wilson refers, the MLA's booklet, *Professional Standards and American Editions: A Response to Edmund Wilson*, and the continuing debate over the issues Wilson raised, indexed under CEAA.

w23. WILSON, EDMUND. Letter to the Editor. *New York Review of Books*, 14 March 1968, p. 35.

CEAA

A response to Lewis Mumford's "Emerson Behind Barbed Wire."

w24. WILSON, JOHN F. "Jonathan Edwards' *A History of the Work of Redemption.*" *Newsletter of the Association for Documentary Editing* 5 (May 1983): 1–3.

audience; Edwards, Jonathan; history of religion; sermons; transcription

Wilson explains the problems presented by a text that was originally delivered as a sermon and subsequently edited and published by someone other than the author. He lists a variety of ways the text might be treated and his reasons for suggesting a microfilm-facsimile and a "reading version" to meet the needs of both students and scholars.

w25. WOLF, EDWIN, 2ND. "Evidence Indicating the Need for Some Bibliographical Analysis of American-Printed Historical Works." *Papers of the Bibliographical Society of America* 63 (1969): 261–77.

editing, general; types of editing

Wolf provides examples of variants found in presumptive duplicates of revolutionary era historical publications, in support of the argument that historical as well as literary materials require bibliographical analysis.

w26. WOLF, EDWIN, 2ND. "Historical Grist for the Bibliographical Mill." *Studies in Bibliography* 25 (1972): 29–40.

editing, general; types of editing

Wolf urges that the techniques of bibliographical analysis be applied to historical materials.

w27. WOOD, GORDON S. "Historians and Documentary Editing." *Journal of American History* 67 (March 1981): 871–77.

Adams papers; copy-text; selection

In this review of *The Papers of John Adams,* Wood discusses the historian's concerns in choosing a text and selecting which documents are to be published. He suggests that documents available in other modern editions not be reprinted and that complete calendars be provided for material not printed.

w28. WOODRING, CARL. "Recording from Coleridge's Voice." *Text* 3 (1987): 367–76.

Coleridge, Samuel Taylor; oral material

In this discussion of editing Coleridge's lectures, Woodring describes the sources, previous editions, and his own work.

w29. WOODS, MARJORIE CURRY. "Editing Medieval Commentaries: Problems and a Proposed Solution." *Text* 1 (1981): 133–45.

commentaries; Middle Ages

Woods describes medieval commentaries on texts in various subjects and offers suggestions for their editing.

w30. WOODSON, THOMAS. "The Title and Text of Thoreau's 'Civil Disobedience.'" *Bulletin of Research in the Humanities* 81 (1978): 103–12.

authorial intention; copy-text; Thoreau, Henry David

Woodson disagrees with the decision of Wendell Glick, editor of volume 3 of *The Writings of Henry D. Thoreau*, on his choice of copy-text and his choice of "Resistance to Civil Government" over "Civil Disobedience" as its title.

w31. WOODWARD, C. VANN. "History from Slave Sources." *American Historical Review* 79 (April 1974): 470–81.

black history; oral materials

In this review essay, Woodward discusses historians' neglect of compilations of interviews with ex-slaves, and describes and evaluates the Federal Writers Project narratives.

w32. WRIGHT, ESMOND. "Making History." *The Listener and BBC Television Review*, 15 November 1962, pp. 803–4.

editing, general; funding; selection

Wright discusses U.S. editing projects and how they were financed. He also lists the problems such projects present for historians and emphasizes the importance of the selection of documents.

w33. WRIGHT, ESMOND. "The Papers of Great Men." *History Today* 12 (1962): 197.

Adams papers; editing, general; NHPC

In this review of *The Diary and Autobiography of John Adams*, Wright argues for the importance of documentary editing, claiming that it is transforming the methodology and character of U.S. history.

Y

Y1. YEANDLE, LAETITIA. "The Evolution of Handwriting in the English-Speaking Colonies of America." *American Archivist* 43 (1980): 294–311.

authentication; dating; handwriting; transcription

Yeandle analyzes samples of handwriting from the seventeenth and eighteenth centuries with a view to helping the archivist or editor transcribe, identify, and date manuscripts.

Z

Z1. ZALL, P. M. "The Manuscript and Early Texts of Franklin's *Autobiography*." *Huntington Library Quarterly* 39 (1976): 375–84,

Franklin, Benjamin

Zall reviews the history of Benjamin Franklin's autobiography, from manuscript through its original and subsequent publications.

Z2. ZELLER, HANS. "A New Approach to the Critical Constitution of Literary Texts." *Studies in Bibliography* 28 (1975): 231–64.

authorial intention; copy-text; emendation; German

Zeller compares the state of German critical editing with that of British and American editing. He focuses on the development of an eclectic text from multiple authority, the issue of authorial intention, and the conditions under which emendation is permissible.

23. ZIMANSKY, CURT A. "Editing Restoration Comedy: Vanbrugh and Others." In *Editing Seventeenth-Century Prose*, edited by D. I. B. Smith, 95–122.

drama; Fielding, Henry; practical editions; transcription; Vanbrugh, Sir John

A treatment of the editorial and literary problems that crop up in preparing a popular edition of Restoration comedy.

24. ZITNER, S. P. "Excessive Annotation, or Piling Pelion on Parnassus." In *Play-Texts in Old Spelling*, edited by G. B. Shand and Raymond C. Shady, 131–39.

annotation

Zitner describes as excessive any annotation that leads the reader "to consider questions not immediately relevant to an understanding of the text itself" and offers five categories into which excessive annotation may fall.

Editorial
Mysteries

A NUMBER OF GOOD MYSTERY NOVELS feature historical and literary documents as motives, red herrings, or weapons. The editors of these documents are themselves detectives or victims, though not in my experience villains.

The following list makes no claim to include every novel in which a manuscript or editor figures. I have included only those that I have read with some pleasure and am willing to recommend to friends. It does seem, however, that mystery writers have included scholarly editors in a surprising number of their works. In a brief survey, for example, I discovered only two bird-watching murders and three operatic ones. Surely there are more birdwatchers and opera buffs than there are scholarly editors. Or does our field disproportionately invite mayhem?

Barnard, Robert. *The Case of the Missing Brontë.* New York: Scribner, 1983. Reprint. New York: Dell, 1984.

An elderly Englishwoman has discovered what may be the manuscript of an unknown Brontë novel. Whether or not it is genuine, someone wants it badly enough to kill.

Barnard, Robert. *Death of a Literary Widow.* (Originally published as *Posthumous Papers.*) London: Collins, 1979. New York: Scribner, 1980. Reprint. New York: Dell, 1981.

An American scholar is editing the papers of an English working-class novelist, which are housed in the attic of the home shared by the writer's ex-wife and his widow, when fire breaks out. What secrets did the papers contain—and who set the fire?

Blake, Nicholas [C. Day Lewis]. *End of Chapter.* New York: Harper, 1957. Reprint. New York: Harper & Row Perennial Library, 1977.

The mysterious reappearance of passages deleted from the galleys of a general's autobiography (particularly mysterious since the book antedates computer typesetting) leads to charges of libel—and murder.

Cross, Amanda [Carolyn Heilbrun]. *The James Joyce Murder.* New York: Macmillan, 1967. Reprint. New York: Ballantine, 1982.

Murder interrupts two professors of English who are sorting through the papers of Sam Lingerwell, the American publisher of James Joyce. Is the clue—or something more—buried in the correspondence? Or is Bloom's kidney a red herring?

Daly, Elizabeth. *The Book of the Crime.* New York: Holt, Rinehart & Winston, 1951. Reprint. New York: Bantam, 1983.

Henry Gamadge, a consultant on books, autographs, and inks, moonlights as a detective in numerous Daly novels. In this one, the discovery of an old book sets off one mysterious chain of events and reveals another.

Daly, Elizabeth. *The Book of the Lion.* New York: Holt, Rinehart & Winston, 1951. Reprint. New York: Bantam, 1985.

This time, Henry Gamadge is invited to appraise the papers left by a contemporary poet, which appear to include a rare Chaucer manuscript.

Eco, Umberto. *The Name of the Rose.* 1980. Translated from the Italian by William Weaver. New York: Harcourt Brace Jovanovich, 1983. Reprint. New York: Warner, 1984.

The key to the murders of several fourteenth-century monks seems to lie in the monastery library's manuscript collection. I can say no more.

Goodrum, Charles. *The Best Cellar.* New York: St. Martin's Press, 1987.

The rivalry between two doctoral candidates leads to discoveries about Thomas Jefferson, the First Families of Virginia, and the Congress that in turn lead to murder. Manuscripts in the Library of Congress, along with the work of a variety of academic and public historians, provide vital clues for the historian-sleuths.

Hare, Cyril [Alfred Alexander Gordon Clark]. *An English Murder.* Boston: Little, Brown, 1951. Reprint. New York: Harper & Row Perennial Library, 1978.

A German historian doing research in the family papers at an English country house solves a baffling mystery by using his knowledge of English constitutional law.

Hopkins, Kenneth. *Body Blow.* New York: Holt, Rinehart & Winston, 1962. Reprint. New York: Harper & Row Perennial Library, 1985. *Dead Against My Principles.* New York: Holt, Rinehart, & Winston, 1960. Reprint. New York: Harper & Row Perennial Library, 1984. *She Died Because....* New York: Holt, Rinehart & Winston, 1957. Reprint. New York: Harper & Row Perennial Library, 1984.

In the course of these mystery novels, William Blow, editor of the complete works of Abraham Cowley and the complete works of Samuel Butler (which goes to the publisher when the editor is in his eighties), moves on to the works of Robert Southey. (At one point, feeling a bit overwhelmed, he contemplates an edition of the Poetical Works of David Hume; Hume wrote only one poem.) Since his mind strays to his editorial work to the detriment of his detection, he is not always the first to solve the crime, but he has a great deal of fun anyway.

Innes, Michael [J. I. M. Stewart]. *The Ampersand Papers.* New York: Dodd, Mead, 1979. Reprint. New York: Penguin, 1980.

Dr. Sutch, an archivist hired to unearth treasures from the disordered papers at Lord Ampersand's castle, is found dead at the foot of a cliff. Was he pushed? And what had he found?

Innes, Michael [J. I. M. Stewart]. *From London Far.* London: Gollancz, 1946. Reprint. New York: Penguin, 1962.

Professor Meredith, taking a break from the collation of a manuscript owned by the Duke of Nesfield, happens on a distinctly unacademic adventure.

Innes, Michael [J. I. M. Stewart]. *The Long Farewell.* New York: Dodd, Mead, 1958. Reprint. New York: Harper & Row Perennial Library, 1982.

Had Lewis Packford truly discovered some priceless Shakespeare marginalia? And was his discovery the cause of his death?

Langton, Jane. *The Minuteman Murder.* (Originally published as *The Transcendental Murder.*) New York: Harper & Row, 1964. Reprint. New York: Dell, 1980.

A meeting of Concord's Alcott Association explodes at the announcement that a cache of hitherto unknown—and sexually suggestive—letters among the Transcendalists has been uncovered. But consequences far more serious than controversy soon follow.

Parker, Robert B. *The Godwulf Manuscript.* Boston: Houghton Mifflin, 1974. Reprint. New York: Berkley, 1975.

A fourteenth-century illuminated manuscript has been stolen from a Boston university and is being held for ransom. Is it the captive of the Student Committee Against Capitalist Exploitation? Or some more sinister force?

Taylor, Andrew. *Caroline Minuscule.* London: Gollancz, 1982. Reprint. New York: Penguin, 1984.

When an expert on the medieval script Caroline Minuscule is found dead, one of his graduate students agrees to complete the editorial work of his mentor. Murder and more ensue in this engrossing but thoroughly nasty novel.

Williams, David. *Unholy Writ*. New York: St. Martin's Press, 1976. Reprint. New York: Mysterious Press, 1984.

Mark Treasure, investment banker and amateur detective, works with a young Shakespeare scholar to unravel a mystery of real estate, manuscripts, and murder.

Index

A

access, B116, B131, H17, H28, J2, J15, L31, M22, R7, S17, S45, T37

accidentals, B55, B69, B70, B80, B107, C34, F23, G11, G39, J33, L14, M30, N11, P13, P16, P26, S37, T1, T8, T14, T36, T38, T45. *See also* substantives; transcription

Adams, Herbert Baxter, B96

Adams, John, M70, S13

Adams papers, A5, B7, B30, B123, B130, B144, B145, B148, B151, B154, B155, F18, J20, M67, M73, S21, S23, T23, W27, W33

ADE, B45, B51

administration, J2, K25. *See also* organization of projects

American Archives, M27

American Foreign Policy series, P22

American Heritage, P20

American Philosophical Society, L37

American Revolution, M68

American State Papers, C29

Anderson, Sherwood, T2

Andrewes, Lancelot, S74

Anglo-Norman, M42

annotation, A15, B6, B16, B33, B41, B55, B85, B93, B115, B124, B128, B140, B141, B152, C1, C13, C15, C30, C34, C36, C39, C50, C55, D3, D17, D21, D24, E3, F6, F7, F10, F11, F23, F28, G5, G7, G9, G13, G15, G27, G33, G34, G37, H6, H10, H15, H20, H24, H28, H30, H33, H44, H57, H63, H69, J17, J27, K2, K14, L4, L12, L13, L19, L20, L23, L34–36, L39, M17, M35, M48, M52, M58, M68, M71, N2, N5, N9, O6, O10, O13, P8, P21, P22, P28, P32, P38, R9, R11, R18, R33, S2, S3, S6, S10, S11, S14, S18, S23, S32, S40, S50, S65, S74, T23, T26, T32, V4, W1, W11, W18, W20, Z4

anthologies, B43, J1

Anthony, Susan B., H50

apparatus, A7, A11, A14, B24, B65, B74, B78, B80–83, B87, B89, B115, B143, B152, C1, C52, G4, G23, G33, H1, H7, H23, H24, H45, K9, K17, L13, M14, M21, M29, M30, M35, M40, M74, M78, P5, P6, P14, P16, P21, R28,

D

About the Author

BETH LUEY is Senior Lecturer and founding director of the Historical Editing and Publishing Program at Arizona State University, as well as editor of *Book Research Quarterly* and a consulting editor of *The Historian*. She is the author of *Handbook for Academic Authors* (Cambridge University Press, 1987) and of numerous articles on the history and practice of publishing, which are drawn from her years of experience as an editor. Luey is Chair of the Information Committee of the Association for Documentary Editing, and she is a member of the Board of Directors of the National Council on Public History as well as the chair of its Publications Committee. She holds an A.M. from Harvard and a B.A. from Radcliffe; her current research is on the financing of scholarly publishing.